ROTH FAMILY FOUNDATION

Music in America Imprint

Michael P. Roth

and Sukey Garcetti

have endowed this

imprint to honor the

memory of their parents,

Julia and Harry Roth,

whose deep love of music

they wish to share

with others.

The publisher gratefully acknowledges the generous support of the Music in America Endowment Fund of the University of California Press Foundation, which was established by a major gift from Sukey and Gil Garcetti, Michael P. Roth, and the Roth Family Foundation.

SOUNDING RACE IN RAP SONGS

Sounding Race in Rap Songs

LOREN KAJIKAWA

UNIVERSITY OF CALIFORNIA PRESS

University of California Press, one of the most distinguished university presses in the United States, enriches lives around the world by advancing scholarship in the humanities, social sciences, and natural sciences. Its activities are supported by the UC Press Foundation and by philanthropic contributions from individuals and institutions. For more information, visit www.ucpress.edu.

University of California Press
Oakland, California

Library of Congress Cataloging-in-Publication Data

Kajikawa, Loren, 1975– author.
    Sounding race in rap songs / Loren Kajikawa.
      pages cm
    Includes bibliographical references, discography, filmography, and index.
      ISBN 978-0-520-28398-5 (cloth : alk. paper) — ISBN 978-0-520-28399-2 (pbk. : alk. paper) — ISBN 978-0-520-95966-8 (ebook)
      1. Rap (Music)—Social aspects—United States.   2. Music and race.   3. Race awareness—United States.   4. Racism in popular culture—United States.   I. Title.
      ML3918.R37K35   2015
      782.421649—dc23

                                                        2014044822

Manufactured in the United States of America

24   23   22   21   20   19   18   17   16   15
10   9   8   7   6   5   4   3   2   1

In keeping with a commitment to support environmentally responsible and sustainable printing practices, UC Press has printed this book on Natures Natural, a fiber that contains 30% post-consumer waste and meets the minimum requirements of ANSI/NISO Z39.48-1992 (R 1997) (Permanence of Paper).

In memory of Anne Dhu McLucas

Contents

Acknowledgments

First, I'm grateful to Mary Francis and her incredible team at UC Press. They shepherded this book from initial draft to final manuscript with great care and efficiency.

Chapters 1 and 2 were drafted during a fellowship in residency at the Oregon Humanities Center. The OHC also provided a subvention for permissions and indexing, and I am grateful to Julia Heydon and the OHC staff for their support.

Chapters 3 and 4 began as dissertation chapters. Special thanks to my committee members Robert Fink, George Lipsitz, Susan McClary, and my advisor Robert Walser. Much of chapter 4 also appears in an article of the same name published in the *Journal of the Society for American Music* 3, no. 3 (Fall 2009): 341–64.

A shout out to all who went above and beyond to offer their time and expertise. Thank you to the members of the Kosher Five (Steve Gordon, Bill Heller, and Richard Taninbaum) for their memories and sense of humor. Big ups to Michael Holman and Will Fulton for their respective insights about the old and new schools. Much respect to Ann Schafer for her sound advice, and to Bobby Chastain, Amy Lese, Bodie Pfost, Wesley Price, and Susanne Scheiblhofer for their able research assistance. Peace to Oliver Wang and Daniel Martinez HoSang for their constant support. Blessings to Felicia Miyakawa and Joseph Schloss for their feedback and encouragement. And everlasting gratitude to Charles Hiroshi Garrett, who generously responded to multiple drafts of the manuscript.

Colleagues, students, and staff in the University of Oregon's School of Music and Dance have provided continuous support and inspiration. I'm grateful to Brad Foley, Habib Iddrisu, Toby Koenigsberg, Phyllis Paul, Jeff

Stolet, Chet Udell, and Ed Wolf for helping to make research and teaching about popular music a more central part of the school's mission. I've also learned much from working with talented graduate and undergraduate students, especially Kai Finlayson, Eliot Grasso, Lauren Joiner, Aaron Manela, Nathan Moore, Marissa Ochsner, Brandon Parry, Sean Peterson, and Mark Samples. Special thanks to Lori Kruckenberg, Mark Levy, Anne Dhu McLucas, Marian Smith, and Marc Vanscheeuwijck for protecting the writing time of their junior colleague. I only wish I could share a copy of this book with Anne, who left us way too soon.

I've also been kept afloat by the intellectual energy of colleagues across the University of Oregon campus. In particular, I have benefited from my associations with both the Ethnic Studies Department and the Folklore Program. I'm indebted to Lynn Fujiwara for organizing a work-in-progress talk on behalf of this project, and to Joe Lowndes and Larry Wayte for serving as respondents. I also want to thank Kirby Brown, Mai-Lin Chang, Charise Cheney, Thea Chroman, John Fenn, Lisa Gilman, Ocean Howell, Brian Klopotek, Sharon Luk, Norma Martinez HoSang, Steve Morozumi, Priscilla Ovalle, Daniel Rosenberg, Ben Saunders, Carol Silverman, Will Terry, and Priscilla Yamin for their friendship and support.

Over the years, many others also have given freely of their time by answering queries and providing useful suggestions. They include Bill Adler, Phil Bedel, Jeff Chang, Dale Chapman, Shannon Dudley, Kevin Fellezs, Phillip Gentry, Suzie Gibbons, Daniel Goldmark, Roger Grant, Edwin Hill, Hua Hsu, Travis Jackson, Mark Katz, Eric Leeds, Brian McWhorter, Charlton Payne, Ben Piekut, Stephen Rodgers, Chris Shaw, Cecilia Sun, Justin Williams, Deborah Wong, Griffin Woodworth, and Christina Zanfagna. (I know I have forgotten more than a few names that deserve to be on this list. Please accept my humblest apologies if you are one of them.)

Thank you to my parents, Lloyd Kajikawa and Ronna Del Valle, and to my sister, Alisa Kajikawa, for their unconditional love and support. Thanks also to my extended family in the many clans branching out from the Kajikawa, Kurasaki, Mason, and Berry lines. I'm also thankful for my "found" relations in the Del Valle, Rubinstein, Oshima, and Tanner families.

I'm grateful for my children, Maya and Kenzo. Their silliness and lack of patience have helped to keep my priorities in line. I want to make it clear to them that the songs discussed in this book are historically important, but not necessarily my personal favorites. I much prefer hearing them reciting rhymes on the way to school, and I look forward to continuing their indoctrination in the music of Rakim, De La Soul, and many others. Finally, and most importantly, my wife Mika Tanner is not only the best live-in reader a scholar could ask for but also an inspiration to me as a writer, parent, and partner. She brightens my life with love and laughter, and I must have done something noble in a previous life to deserve her. Without her love and support there is no way this book could have been written.

Introduction

Sounding Race in Rap Songs

Do the Right Thing, director Spike Lee's controversial 1989 film exploring simmering racial tensions in a Brooklyn neighborhood on the hottest day of the year, opens with actress Rosie Perez dancing to Public Enemy's song "Fight the Power." Framed by a series of urban backdrops representing the film's Bedford-Stuyvesant setting, Perez performs a set of hip hop–inspired dances as the credits play. Appearing in multiple costumes, including boxing trunks and gloves, she moves with an intensity that embodies the song's seriousness and righteous anger. Her "kinetic narrative" gives life to the words of the song, connecting her bodily gestures to rapper Chuck D's lyrics and political sentiments.[1] This body–music connection established in the opening sequence carries over to one of the film's main characters, Radio Raheem, who, as his name suggests, always appears carrying a large boombox that plays nothing other than "Fight the Power." Often filming Radio Raheem (played by actor Bill Nunn) from below and using wide angles to emphasize his large size, Lee portrays the young, muscular black man as a towering figure, and Public Enemy's song becomes an audible manifestation of his imposing presence.

Although associated primarily with Radio Raheem, "Fight the Power" comes to represent more than a single character's personal soundtrack. The song appears nine times in *Do the Right Thing* and performs a central role in the narrative. The film's plot turns on a conflict that arises between Sal, the Italian American owner of a neighborhood pizzeria, and Buggin' Out, a black political provocateur who demands that Sal (played by actor Danny Aiello) add pictures of African American heroes to the pizzeria's Wall of Fame. In the film's climactic scene, Radio Raheem and Buggin' Out enter the pizzeria and attempt to force Sal to acquiesce to their demands. The men trade obscenities while "Fight the Power" plays loudly on Raheem's boom-box. As the confrontation escalates to a fever pitch, Sal grabs his baseball bat from under the shop's counter and bashes Raheem's radio until the music stops. The thirty seconds of silence that follows is the film's dramatic apex, leading to a race riot that releases the tensions that have been mounting steadily throughout the film.

Spike Lee's prominent use of "Fight the Power" in *Do the Right Thing* underscores an important fact: rap artists produce (and listeners interpret) musical meanings at the level of the song. Although this fact is sometimes overlooked in writing that treats hip hop and rap music holistically as a genre or culture, songs are what artists work hard at crafting and what listeners encounter in their daily lives.[2] Lee, for example, personally commissioned "Fight the Power" for use as the film's title track, explaining his choice just after the film's release as follows: "I wanted it to be defiant, I wanted it to be angry, I wanted it to be very rhythmic. I thought right away of Public Enemy."[3] To give Lee the level of intensity he required, the group's production team (the aptly named Bomb Squad) used sampling and sequencing technology to loop drum, bass, and guitar parts from two different James Brown tracks.[4] Over these parts, they layered numerous other samples to create a dense, polyrhythmic groove, whose audible force supported and amplified Chuck D's lyrics.[5]

As *Time* magazine observed soon after the film's release, "Fight the Power" drew its potency from a combination of "combustive rhythms and rebellious rhymes."[6] The *New York Times* offered that Public Enemy's music was "the sound of urban alienation, where silence doesn't exist and sensory stimulation is oppressive and predatory."[7] Both of these quotes from mainstream publications exemplify how descriptive language about sound can trade in racialized imagery. Although the *New York Times* review was mostly favorable, the author's characterization of "Fight the Power" as the sound of "urban alienation" (read as black anger) conjures an image that the paper's largely white, middle-class readership would interpret as dangerous and hostile. *Time* uses fiery language ("combustive") to describe the sounds that support the group's message of defiance. In the context of Lee's film, which ends with the burning of Sal's Pizzeria, such evocative language might be understandable. However, citing the racial paranoia of movie executives and film critics who worried that *Do the Right Thing* might lead to actual rioting by black audiences (a fear that never materialized), Lee has rejected words such as "incendiary" to describe the film.[8] Although Lee admits that he hoped the film would be provocative, the constant repetition of volatile language in media depictions of *Do the Right Thing* unfairly associates the film with actual burning and looting. In similar fashion, music reviewers, even when being complementary, often characterized Public Enemy's music as "incendiary" and "brutal."[9] *New York Times* journalist Stephen Holden once described the group's music as contemplating "a violent response to the white establishment."[10] Like Lee's movie, Public Enemy's songs and public statements were dogged by intense scrutiny and censure for the way they invoked and evoked race.[11]

The point here is not to suggest that these statements are simply wrong or racist. Rather, these reviews illustrate how often descriptions of rap music and other related art forms rely on racial code words to convey their meanings. Countless journalistic descriptions of "Fight the Power" recycle the same fiery imagery, suggesting that the song reflects racial anger and violent tendencies. Such language testifies to the role that Public Enemy's music played in constructing an image of blackness symbolizing social conflict, an effect described in this book as *sounding race*.

In fact, we do not even see Public Enemy perform in the film; nor do we need to see them to recognize the blackness of "Fight the Power." The song's resonance in *Do the Right Thing* depends in part on the "affiliating identifications" it inspires, the way Spike Lee capitalizes on the meaning of Public Enemy's music outside the film.[12] By the time they recorded "Fight the Power," the group had codified an approach to songwriting that fans and critics interpreted as radical blackness (the subject of this book's second chapter). As the group's popularity spread through live tours, music videos, and album and merchandise sales, they became symbols of a black authenticity rooted in defiance and confrontation. Thus, "Fight the Power" represented not only Radio Raheem, but also, as Spike Lee put it, "the theme of young black America."[13] When Sal smashes the boom box, he does more than destroy a treasured possession. He threatens to silence the community itself.[14]

How did rap music gain the ability to make race audible in these ways? By Spike Lee's own admission, there was something already in the sound of Public Enemy's music that attracted him to the group.[15] Charging them with delivering *Do the Right Thing*'s anthem, he capitalized on rap music's aesthetic codes to help present his views about how blackness was being experienced at a particular moment in 1989. One of this book's main goals is to describe how such codes—the aesthetic features that give rise to musical meaning—came into existence and how they have been manipulated to project a variety of identities. As Spike Lee's use of "Fight the Power" suggests, the *sound* of a song can carry quite a bit of content along with it, and this information includes ideas about race. However, given that race is not a biological essence (something one is born with) but rather a changeable, context-dependent social construct, how have rap's projections of racial identity varied over time and from artist to artist?

For years, scholars have emphasized the need to account more fully for the effects of rap music aesthetics, or what music theorist Adam Krims has called hip hop's "poetics of identity."[16] Yet, the formal dimensions of individual rap songs have largely escaped the scrutiny of scholars. By historicizing the sounds, lyrics, and imagery of some of rap music's biggest hits, including the Sugarhill Gang's "Rapper's Delight" (1979), Public Enemy's "Rebel Without a Pause" (1987), Dr. Dre's "Nuthin' But a 'G' Thang" (1992), and Eminem's "My Name Is" (1999), this book explores the production of racial meaning across rap's first two decades as a commercial genre. Combining formal analysis with historical contextualization, each chapter explores how rap musicians voice concerns, reach audiences, and articulate the attitudes and cultural sensibilities of what historian Jeff Chang and others have called the hip hop generation.

HIP HOP, RAP, AND RACE

In discussing rap music's relationship to something as complicated and fraught as race, it is important for me to explain clearly my use of the terms *hip hop* and *rap*, which are often conflated in contemporary discourse. I use *hip hop* to designate the culture and practices of live performance from which the genre of commercial music called *rap* developed. Although the culture of hip hop is essential to rap music, the primary goal of this study is not to make claims about hip hop as a culture but to explore the ideological dimensions of rap as popular music. In other words, rather than ground my analysis in a particular community of hip hop practitioners, I seek a greater understanding of the way rap songs circulate as mass-mediated "texts." Although it is impossible to neatly separate hip hop culture from the rap music industry, making this distinction has a practical purpose when it comes to understanding race as a category of analysis.

In some instances, race can prove a problematic, even unproductive, category for analysis in hip hop–related research. For example, in his ethnography of hip hop producers, Joseph Schloss argues that race and ethnicity rarely, if ever, factor in to how producers evaluate the quality of their own work or the work of their peers. He therefore chooses to avoid discussing the racial or ethnic identities of his informants because (he says) they never once cited it as important or relevant to their musical activities.[17] Schloss concludes that for beat makers "the rules of hip-hop are African American, but one need not be African American to understand or follow them."[18]

Indeed, from its earliest days in New York, hip hop's ranks included a number of Latino (mainly Puerto Rican) members, and the music and dance styles themselves drew on a blend of African American, Jamaican, Puerto Rican, and other cultural influences. Since then, hip hop and rap music have grown to include performers and audiences from communities across the nation and globe. In the 1990s, for example, Filipino Americans hailing from the San Francisco Bay Area came to dominate hip hop DJing (also known as turntablism).[19] By the turn of the century, b-boying (also known as breakdancing) competitions routinely featured finalists representing France, South Korea, and Japan.[20] For many, the perceived "color-blindness" of hip hop—that it often seems open to anyone who can demonstrate significant mastery of its formal elements—is one of its most attractive qualities. It would be a gross misrepresentation of hip hop culture to deny its diverse body of practitioners and fans hailing from a variety of racial and ethnic backgrounds. Recent research on localized underground hip hop scenes even suggests that the culture is transforming the way race is lived by encouraging its practitioners to abandon fixed, essentialist notions of identity and embrace a more fluid, "situational" model.[21]

Yet, despite hip hop's undeniable diversity, one can get very different ideas about race when turning toward rap as a genre of popular music. Like rock and roll before it, rap music emerged from the margins of U.S. society to redefine its center and amplify many of its contradictions. However, unlike rock and roll, rap never became "white." As one of the most influential music genres of the last three decades, rap has cultivated a mainstream audience and become a multi-million-dollar industry by promoting highly visible (and often controversial) representations of black masculine identity. Although all kinds of people make and listen to rap music, the industry that produces it has tended to focus almost exclusively on cultivating and promoting black male artists. Unlike the worlds of DJing and b-boying, where hip hop's ethnic diversity is reflected at the highest level of competition, rap moguls have consistently put their money on black (with an important exception to be discussed in the book's fourth chapter). Thus, to call attention to the way that rap has remained "black" is to do more than acknowledge the skin color of its most popular and best-known practitioners. By competing for hegemony in the marketplace, the musicians discussed in this book have helped construct varying notions of racial authenticity— what it means to be "real." From the frequently used phrase "keeping it real," which describes the practice of staying true to one's culture and values, to numerous song titles, such as Jay-Z's "Real Niggaz," Erik Sermon's "Stay Real," or Common's "Real People," rap musicians and fans ascribe great value to authentic expression.

This commitment to realness does not mean that one finds homogeneous portrayals of racial identity in rap songs. As a genre, rap music projects multiple, even contradictory, ideas about race and reality. The same era that witnessed Public Enemy's rise to fame also included gangsta rappers N.W.A., popular bohemian groups De La Soul and A Tribe Called Quest, and pop-oriented acts such as DJ Jazzy Jeff & the Fresh Prince. Yet it is fair to say that without being considered "real" in some way or another, rappers have no hope for commercial success. And virtually without fail throughout the 1980s and 1990s, this realness was connected to blackness. As sociologists of cultural production remind us, such authenticity (racial or otherwise) is a quality that musicians seek to inhabit but that listeners ultimately ascribe; it is not a quality inherent in cultural objects themselves.[22] Rap authenticity is, like racial meaning, socially constructed. Moreover, just because rap's projections of race are constructed does not mean that they can simply be unmasked as false and, therefore, inconsequential. Fortunes are made and unmade, and careers are launched or come to a crashing halt all based on evaluations of authenticity. Outside the music industry, the stakes are higher. Race might be a fiction, but it is a fiction that continues to shape life in the United States.

SOUNDING RACIAL FORMATION

As an ideology of difference with roots in scientific discourse, definitions of race typically appeal to differences in skin color, body types, or other traits assumed to be biologically inborn. Social scientists Michael Omi and Howard Winant define race as "an unstable and 'de-centered' complex of social meanings" constantly being transformed through a political process they term "racial formation."[23] Although primarily defined by state institutions, racial meanings are subjected to confirmation, contestation, and transformation through a variety of social activities.[24] For example, the twentieth century witnessed a number of political movements geared toward addressing the profound inequities caused by racial discrimination. Culminating in the political movements of the 1960s, numerous political actors and events have transformed how race is discussed today.

Beginning with Franz Boas's work in the early twentieth century, cultural anthropology reimagined racial difference as a social construct, not a biological fact. If human differences thought to be natural and biological turned out to be cultural, then, Boas and his supporters (including W. E. B. Du Bois) argued, racial inequality could be overcome. Seeking a way to counter biological racism in the aftermath of World War II, cultural anthropologists and other social scientists promoted the term "ethnicity." This genealogy has relevance to contemporary interpretations of difference described as either "racial" or "ethnic"—the former suggesting a difference that is *immutable* and grounded in nature, the latter describing a difference that is changeable and grounded in culture.

Although it might be tempting to replace all instances of the term *race* with the term *ethnicity*, the continued salience of biologically rooted notions of human difference, such as those related to the legacy of chattel slavery and racialized immigration law—institutions in which biological inheritance (i.e., skin color and body type) determined life chances—still render the concept of race crucial. Moreover, the differences ascribed to race versus those ascribed to ethnicity often reflect experiences and histories unique to the United States, including contemporary understandings of American musical life. For example, because of the legacy of popular music genres that were developed in concert with the system of Jim Crow segregation, much African American music—from jazz and R&B to soul and rap—is generally regarded as "black music" rather than "ethnic music."[25] Black music has long served as a dividing line in the music industry and also as a focal point for writers grappling with the depths of the African American experience. The writings of Fredrick Douglas and W. E. B. Du Bois, for example, both ascribe great social significance to the emotional power of slave singing.[26] But it is probably the groundbreaking book *Blues People* by Imamu Amiri Baraka (Leroi Jones) that has been most influential on late-twentieth-century writing about black music in U.S. society.[27]

Published in the midst of the civil rights movement, Baraka's work rejected the notion that black musical talent springs forth from some mystical, natural place inside African Americans. Instead, he argued, black music developed over time as enslaved Africans and their descendants responded to life in the United States and engaged actively in the struggle for freedom. His work represented a long-overdue "insider's" perspective on the meaning of black music, raising the critical stakes for studies of black culture. Not only did his project push the boundaries in terms of what scholars could learn from listening to popular music, it also called into question the work of "outsiders," mainly white music critics, who discussed black music on aesthetic grounds without any attempt to relate stylistic changes to the social forces that motivated them. Baraka's eventual conception of black music as a "changing same" provided a model for musical aesthetics concretely grounded in African

American culture but flexible enough to be creatively reimagined across time and space.[28] In Baraka's wake, numerous others, including Olly Wilson, Samuel Floyd, Jr., Paul Gilroy, Rickey Vincent, Cheryl Keyes, Tricia Rose, Guthrie Ramsey, Jr., Mark Anthony Neal, and Ronald Radano, to name only a few, have offered studies that probe the social, cultural, political, and artistic dimensions of black musical history.

The importance of social and political context to discussions of musical production has not been lost on hip hop scholars. Rap music's first two decades as a commercial genre (the 1980s and 1990s) coincided with a post–civil rights atmosphere fraught with ongoing racial divisions. Despite the many politicians and pundits promoting "color-blind" social policies, the closing decades of the twentieth century witnessed ongoing racial inequality. The hip hop generation confronted massive shifts in the labor market, a result of a fundamental restructuring in the U.S. economy. In the 1970s, as millions of well-paying blue-collar jobs were lost, "white flight" and suburbanization furthered residential segregation and widened the income gap between white and black Americans. Between 1978 and 1986, for example, the bottom 20 percent of income earners—a category in which blacks and Latinos were overrepresented—experienced the greatest decline in real wages.[29] These changes were accompanied by funding crises and reductions in vital social services, such as public education, and black and Hispanic inhabitants of New York City and other major metropolitan areas were some of the hardest hit. The 1980s and 1990s also witnessed unprecedented growth in both state-owned and privately operated prisons. Fueled in part by fears related to gang violence and the crack cocaine "epidemic," the U.S. criminal justice system grew increasingly punitive, imprisoning nonviolent drug offenders for longer and longer periods of time. By the turn of the century, the United States had the world's largest prison population, and through the relative ease of policing street-level dealers and buyers in inner-city neighborhoods, the rates of arrest, conviction, and incarceration of blacks remained many times more than that for whites and other racial groups.[30]

As George Lipsitz argues, these patterns of inequality are underwritten by a "possessive investment in whiteness," a system of racial stratification founded upon the historically segregated housing market.[31] White suburban youth live an existence vastly different from their African American counterparts in the urban ghettos of the United States. Yet, through rap music, generations of young people have been raised with an incredibly vivid, albeit technologically mediated, relationship with blackness. Rap music continues to cross lines of race, class, and nation, and millions of people care about it deeply. Like professional sports, rap is a cultural arena in which the most prominent actors are black even though the majority of its spectators are not. The genre's symbolic investment in blackness deserves closer scrutiny, especially because its projections of identity sometimes highlight and sometimes obscure the impact of such ongoing racial inequality.

My reason for analyzing individual hit songs is not, therefore, to prove that they are somehow better than others. Rather, it is to explain how each song produces particular ideas about race and genre. Such analyses are less about proving a singular meaning than they are about providing an understanding of the aesthetic grounds from which rap's projections of race emerge. In other words, this book seeks to demonstrate how specific songs enable listeners to make arguments about race. In the 1980s and 1990s, influential artists including the Sugarhill Gang, Grandmaster Flash and the Furious Five, Run-D.M.C., Public Enemy, N.W.A., Dr. Dre, and Eminem all worked in a commercial genre understood as "black," but they provided listeners with varying interpretations of what race could sound like.

By interpreting popular singles as successful claims about racial authenticity, each chapter analyzes how rap music participates in the construction of race. Regardless of how much any individual listener cares for the songs discussed in this book, those artists and songs deemed popular, successful, and authentic at any given point in history promise to tell us something about common understandings of race in U.S. culture.[32] If Public Enemy's "Fight the Power" inspired fear in some and pride in others, then these reactions are intimately tied, not only to the subject position of the group's listeners, but also to how their music sounded in the context of contemporary popular music.

This book argues that, as a paradigm for identity, rap music allows us not only to see but also to *hear* how mass-mediated culture engenders new understandings of race. Although it might seem counterintuitive, race is not simply an effect of sight (i.e., a recognition of differences in skin color and body type). The way we see race is also mediated by our other senses.[33] For example, although blind people acquire their knowledge about the social world through non-sight-based pathways—learning to hear, feel, smell, and taste race—they continue to "visualize" race, describing people as black or white, despite never having observed the physical differences most people assume to be fundamental to racial distinction.[34]

One can immediately appreciate the applicability of these ideas to the study of race and music. Fans, critics, and musicians in the United States, for example, employ visual metaphors every time they speak about "black

music." In fact, one might imagine some *sounds* as blacker than others, leading to questions that might seem absurd if taken literally: Whose music is
blacker, Will Smith's or Public Enemy's? Or better yet, whose music is
blacker, Vanilla Ice's or Eminem's? Although we need not assume these
questions to be productive ones, that we can even imagine an answer to a
question about the relative blackness of two Caucasian rappers suggests that
musical content is actually more important to racial representation than the
skin color of particular performers. To claim that Eminem is blacker than
Vanilla Ice or that Public Enemy is blacker than Will Smith would not be a
quantitative statement about skin tone as much as it would represent a qualitative estimation of the artists' respective musical identities. Such evaluations are made in the shadow of racially based standards of authenticity that
vary according to time and place. In 1989, for example, Public Enemy
sounded blacker to those convinced that real blackness (i.e., hip hop authenticity) personifies defiance, rebelliousness, and political engagement.

In fact, very little content is conveyed by racial categories themselves,
except for the fact that they are mutually exclusive (e.g., black is not white,
and white is not black).[35] Rather, racial categories, such as those applied to
music, acquire their meaning through various social practices. At the "micro
level" where musicians produce and fans listen to rap songs, race becomes
meaningful (and audible) when particular aesthetic approaches become
associated with certain ideas about social reality. To paraphrase Ingrid
Monson's thoughts on the study of race in jazz music, instead of attempting to assign various music examples to "essentialized" categories of black
or white, we should ask: In what ways do rap musicians and fans draw upon
a wide range of cultural and musical knowledge to articulate particular aesthetics and ideological positions through music?[36]

Indeed, there is no straightforward or "intrinsic" connection between
the racial identity of artists (or fans) and the meaning of musical texts.[37]
Songs do not simply "reflect" or "express" the lives of listeners or musicians. Rather, a sense of identity is created from the encounters that people
have with music.[38] If language provides a frame for interpreting the sounds
that listeners experience (think of the way the critics discussed earlier
described Public Enemy's music as "combustive" or "incendiary"), then
these ideas can become attached to particular sounds that musicians choose
to employ. When musicians work within the norms of a particular genre or
subgenre, their manipulation of sound mobilizes the concepts and ideas
attached to particular musical conventions. In this exchange between sound
and discourse about sound, musicians help to shape the meaning of what
we hear.[39]

MAKING MEANING IN RAP MUSIC

At times, the meaning of particular songs might appear to be self-evident. Eric B. & Rakim's "Microphone Fiend" is about Rakim's love of MCing; Run-D.M.C.'s "It's Like That" is about the difficult social realities confronting young people; Public Enemy's "Fight the Power" is about—well, you know. But the words an MC chooses only reveal a part of what makes rap songs compelling. A rapper's delivery and flow can actually de-emphasize a word's literal meaning by emphasizing its sound. As music journalist and critic Kelefa Sanneh explains, "Rhyme [in rap music], like other phonetic techniques, is a way to turn a spoken phrase into a musical phrase—a 'rhythmic argument,' as Jay-Z put it. *Bap bap bapbap*. Rapping is the art of addressing listeners and distracting them at the same time."[40] Taking this musical nature of MCing seriously, the work of some recent scholars has turned away from analyzing content entirely, concentrating instead on a more thorough investigation of MCs' rhythmic flow, rhyme scheme, and wordplay.[41]

In some ways, the tendency to privilege words and imagery over sound is an understandable outcome related to rap music's birth as a commercial genre. Rap music's first big hit, "Rapper's Delight" (the subject of this book's first chapter), highlighted the MC or rapper at the expense of the DJ. By bringing the MC to center stage, rap music reversed the hierarchy of hip hop's early years, in which DJs were the main attraction and de facto group leaders, and MCs have been overshadowing their DJs and producers ever since. Yet, instrumental tracks, colloquially known as beats, are essential to rap music. Had "Rapper's Delight" featured the rhythmic chanting of three unaccompanied voices, the recording might have sold a few thousand copies. With its backing beat, based on an interpolation of Chic's "Good Times," it sold more than a few million.

Beats enliven a rapper's flow by sounding a steady counter-rhythm that helps structure and complement the vocal performance.[42] This "dual rhythmic relationship" is at the heart of the pleasure that fans and artists find in the music, and it is for this reason that rap music is sometimes referred to as the art of beats and rhymes.[43] However, beats do more than provide rhythmic accompaniment. Whether played by a live band, programmed into a drum machine, or sampled from pre-existing recordings, beats convey a remarkable variety of sounds and textures. As in other genres of music, from German *Lieder* to heavy metal, the sounds that producers choose when crafting rap songs reflect their expressive goals. Music critics and journalists who write about rap have long relied on an abundance of colorful language to describe its sonic character. Writing in 1988 for the *Village Voice*, for example, Robert Christgau described Public Enemy's beats as "abrading and exploding."[44] In doing so, he sought to explain how the group's sonic aesthetic amplified Chuck D's lyrics, making the group sound as militant and defiant as they claimed to be. Yet, more often than not, debates about rap's political implications become mired in considerations of lyrics and video imagery alone.

In no way does this book argue that meaning (racial or otherwise) resides exclusively, or even primarily, within rap music's beats. Rather, I seek to explain how the choices rap producers make—selecting one sound and not another one—amplify and in some cases transform the information that listeners receive from a song's lyrics or music video. Proceeding from the assumption that the tools of notation and analysis developed for the study of Western classical music should not be applied uncritically to rap music, I have developed my own set of methodologies, grounded in concepts emerging from recent ethnographic work on the history, culture, and aesthetics of rap producers and hip hop DJs.[45] Understanding rap as the result of specific musical decisions rooted in hip hop traditions, my methods of music analysis revolve around the study of how producers manipulate breakbeats, also commonly known as "breaks."

Initially understood as short, percussion-heavy, polyrhthmic passages that appear in many songs recorded in the 1960s and 1970s, breaks have been central to hip hop from the music's earliest days in the Bronx. In fact, it is fair to say that hip hop music itself was born in 1973 when DJ Kool Herc began isolating and featuring breakbeats to the delight of dancers at his parties in the South Bronx. As rap music developed into a commercial genre and as new technologies became available, breaks continued to provide producers not only raw sonic material, but also aesthetic concepts that guide how they structure sound. Producers also tried out new approaches to working with breakbeats: hiring studio musicians to re-record them; programming drum machines to imitate them; and using sampling-sequencing technology to capture and rearrange them. Turning my attention toward the sonic qualities of these individual breaks as well as the manner in which they have been manipulated, I seek to interpret how beats play an important role in constituting musical meaning.

Ascribing significance to the musical choices that producers make when working with breaks is no straightforward matter. Although oral history and ethnographic work on hip hop DJs and rap music producers confirms the break as a central organizing category worthy of analysis, there is no generally accepted hermeneutic framework in hip hop studies for moving from specific musical choices to statements about their meaning.[46] What is more, producers do not generally choose samples in order to comment upon their original meaning. In fact, any meanings that might be attached to a given sample, or to the cultural context from which it emerged, are usually of little importance to producers.[47] Rather, producers choose to work with samples because they sound—for lack of a better term—*good*. What matters is the skill that producers demonstrate in selecting and manipulating breaks, not the original context from which they come. One can also presume that the same holds true for most listeners, especially because hip hop producers often go out of their way to sample obscure sources. Although we can imagine scenarios where most listeners are aware of a sample's origin (e.g., Puff Daddy's tribute to the Notorious B.I.G. based on the Police's "Every Breath You Take"), it is safest to assume that the majority of listeners enjoy rap music without giving much consideration to the samples from which it is built.

Where can one look, then, to ground a claim about the meaning or significance of the musical choices that producers make in working with breaks? Schloss's ethnography of hip hop producers suggests one possibility. Although the origins of a given break do not usually matter, Schloss explains that a producer's choices are guided by an overriding concern with *sound*: whether or not a particular sample matches the "vibe" of the song they are helping construct. Vibe strikes me as an appropriately flexible category for encompassing the effect of particular breaks at the level of the song. *Pace* Schloss, however, by expanding the possibilities for what rap could sound like, rap producers have accomplished more than making compelling music. By feeding what Tricia Rose has called "America's post–civil rights appetite for racially stereotyped entertainment," rap producers also have proven that breaks can function as a powerful force in the shaping of racial perceptions.[48]

Focusing on musical style, the following chapters seek to complement and extend previous work on rap's musical aesthetics and politics by calling attention to producers' artistic decisions and the role that they play in constituting song-level meaning. Although previous scholarship has helped contextualize rap and hip hop music as a culture bound together by common histories, politics, and aesthetic predilections, it is important to remember that rap musicians also make distinct creative decisions that give rise to a rich diversity of sounds and identities. By understanding rap music as an expression of cultural continuity *and* stylistic change, each chapter asks a different set of questions about racial representation for which attention to the music's formal dimensions helps provide answers. For example, how did Sugar Hill Records's translation of live DJ performance into recording-studio songs enable rap music to begin sounding race to a national audience? What developments in music production helped lead to Public Enemy's much-celebrated "too black, too strong" musical style? How did changes in Dr. Dre's approach to beat making help construct two very different understandings of Los Angeles's urban geography and gangsta identity? How did white rapper Eminem's debut single parody rap's musical conventions to help him negotiate racially based standards of authenticity? And finally, what do the answers to all of these questions tell us about the significance of race in rap music at the dawn of the twenty-first century?

Answering these questions will require shifting the conversation about rap's political dimensions to include more attention to song-level detail and stylistic difference. To emphasize this point, each chapter takes its title from a well-known and commercially successful single by one of rap's best-known artists, and the song becomes a lens through which to examine the genre's various constructions of identity, from the birth of rap music in 1979 to the rise of the genre's first white superstar in 1999. However, basing each chapter around a single song does not mean focusing exclusively on one recording at a time. Historicizing each song with respect to its musical and social context, *Sounding Race* seeks a fuller picture of rap's role as an artistic practice and sonic force.

In examining individual recordings—all of which can be heard easily with a quick search of the Internet—my methods depart somewhat from those of past scholars.[49] Rather than attempt to transcribe every pitch and rhythm in a given track, I often choose to forgo such specificity in order to ground my analysis more squarely in terms directly related to rap music's production.[50] By paying more attention to the musical process behind rap recordings, I hope not only to give greater credit where credit is due to rap's producers, but also to examine how rap's musical conventions are—like race—socially constructed. Genres, such as gangsta rap (the subject of chapter 3), do not exist apart from the sociohistorical processes that create and transform them. Like race, rap's musical norms are constantly contested and in flux. Combining new approaches to formal analysis with historical contextualization, the following four chapters of this book explore the relationship between stylistic evolution and racial formation in rap music's first two decades as a commercial genre, roughly 1979–1999. This journey begins with a deceptively simple question: What is a rap song?

Chapter 1, "'Rapper's Delight': From Genre-less to New Genre," examines the shift from the live-performance practices of Bronx DJs to rap's first commercial singles, a transition that gave birth to the rap song as an entity and a popular-music phenomenon. Today we take for granted the existence of the rap song. Prior to 1979, however, hip hop music existed in a very different form. Early hip hop DJs built their sets from dozens of pre-existing recordings whose breakbeats they could isolate and rearrange spontaneously in performance. Analyzing bootleg recordings of live sets by Grandmaster Flash that took place in 1978, prior to rap's first seminal hit, I demonstrate how rap's mainstream debut was more than a change in economic scale; it was also a profound shift in form. Replacing the DJ with studio musicians performing an arrangement of a groove interpolated from Chic's "Good Times," Sylvia Robinson was the first rap producer to translate the way DJs worked with breaks into a new form of songwriting. Tied closely to disco, which at the time was experiencing a racialized backlash, rap's first musical conventions were immediately interpreted as "black music," laying the foundation upon which new racial meanings would emerge.

Chapter 2, "'Rebel Without a Pause': Public Enemy Revolutionizes the Break," builds on the previous chapter's insights and traces developments in rap music production leading to the recording of Public Enemy's 1987 single, "Rebel Without a Pause." Surveying changes in rap music production, including the introduction of drum machines, turntables, and eventually sampling-sequencing technology, I historicize Public Enemy's iconic style and explain how it exemplifies the relationship between new racial meanings and new musical practices. I argue that to understand how Public Enemy came to sound "like a fist in the air"—as one critic put it—we need a better sense of the musical developments feeding into their approach.

Chapter 3, "'Let Me Ride': Gangsta Rap's Drive into the Popular Mainstream," explores stylistic change in the music's most infamous subgenre, so-called gangsta rap. By situating the advent of "G-funk" (gangsta funk) in the mid-1990s neoliberal reconquest of urban space, this chapter traces a connection between rap music's expression of race and its increasing access to mainstream commercial markets. In particular, I explore how Dr. Dre, the producer behind Snoop Doggy Dogg's debut album, *Doggystyle* (1993), and his own solo album *The Chronic* (1992), created a new style of rap music befitting the cultural climate of post-riot Los Angeles. By evoking the quintessential Southern Californian experience of automobility, *The Chronic*'s hit singles moved away from representations of race as confrontation and toward a new understanding of blackness in hip hop as transcendence and autonomy.

Chapter 4, "'My Name Is': Signifying Whiteness, Rearticulating Race," discusses the artistic strategy behind white rapper Eminem's 1999 mainstream debut. Comparing his first promotional LP, *Infinite* (1996), with the Dr. Dre–produced single that brought him to fame, I argue that Eminem's success hinged on the way his music deftly negotiated rap's racially based standards of authenticity. Surveying critical response to Eminem's popularity, I contextualize this musical strategy with respect to the neoliberal politics of "color-blindness." Exploring the use of parody in "My Name Is," I argue that rather than denying the importance of race, the music and video of the song poked fun at various representations of whiteness in order to carve out a niche for the white rapper. By making whiteness audible, Eminem's debut effort recast whiteness as a racialized minority identity, a proposition that neatly encapsulated both hopes and fears regarding race's significance at the close of the twentieth century.

Although popular music does not often adopt a straightforward historiographical position, we can still learn much about history by paying attention to it. As George Lipsitz explains, "popular music can mark the present as history, helping us understand where we have been and where we are going."[51] The chapters that follow attempt to show some of the directions that rap music has pointed, arguing against the stereotypical, homogeneous characterizations of the genre that too often appear in public discourse. These are not the only stories that can or should be told about rap music's past. Others can trace different but equally important paths through the same time period, and I sincerely hope that they do.

The songs I have selected open a window onto highly influential notions of rap authenticity (and thus racial identity) at important moments in the genre's first two decades. This is in large part why I have chosen them. By highlighting the central role that musical style plays in racial representation, *Sounding Race* seeks a richer understanding of rap music as a site of conflict and contestation, as a genre whose history is rife with dynamic transformations leading to a variety of identities, and most of all as an art form where sound plays a key role in these processes.

PART I

Stylistic Change and Racial Formation in Rap's First Decade

1 "Rapper's Delight"

From Genre-less to New Genre

I was approached in '77. A gentleman walked up to me and said, "We can put what you're doing on a record." I would have to admit that I was blind. I didn't think that somebody else would want to hear a record re-recorded onto another record with talking on it. I didn't think it would reach the masses like that. I didn't see it. I knew of all the crews that had any sort of juice and power, or that was drawing crowds. So here it is two years later and I hear, "To the hip-hop, to the bang to the boogie," and it's not Bam, Herc, Breakout, AJ. Who is this?[1]

DJ Grandmaster Flash

I did not think it was conceivable that there would be such thing as a hip-hop record. I could not see it. I'm like, record? Fuck, how you gon' put hip-hop onto a record? 'Cause it was a whole gig, you know? How you gon' put three hours on a record? Bam! They made "Rapper's Delight." And the ironic twist is not how long that record was, but how short it was. I'm thinking, "Man, they cut that shit down to fifteen minutes?" It was a miracle.[2]

MC Chuck D

["Rapper's Delight"] is a disco record with rapping on it. So we could do that. We were trying to make a buck.[3]

Richard Taninbaum (percussion)

As early as May of 1979, *Billboard* magazine noted the growing popularity of "rapping DJs" performing live for clubgoers at New York City's black discos.[4] But it was not until September of the same year that the trend garnered widespread attention, with the release of the Sugarhill Gang's "Rapper's Delight," a fifteen-minute track powered by humorous party rhymes and a relentlessly funky bass line that took the country by storm and introduced a national audience to rap. Although rap was written about as "black music" from its first mention in *Billboard*, the first rap song to call attention to racial and ethnic difference was not recorded by an African American artist. This honor belongs to "Take My Rap . . . Please," a song released about one month after "Rapper's Delight" as various producers and independent labels attempted to cash in on the new craze for "rapping deejay records."[5] The only recording ever made by Steve Gordon and the Kosher Five, this now forgotten but historically significant recording represents the first song by a white rapper as well as the first recorded rap parody.[6]

"Take My Rap" was written by Gordon, a part-time radio deejay, and his friends, including Richard Taninbaum and Bill Heller. Taninbaum (percussion) and Heller (bass) were studio musicians who often worked for Reflection Records, an upstart disco label that had scored a minor hit with "Struck By Boogie Lightning."[7] Thinking back on the making of the record, the three men—all Caucasian Jews with Yiddish-speaking parents—remember that since rap was a "black thing," they thought it would be funny to write a song based on the question: "What would a Jew do with a rap song?"[8]

Although the song began as a joke between friends, the musicians were able to convince Reflection Records owner Jack Levy to record and release the single commercially. Figure 1 shows the twelve-inch cover, with the song title printed in faux Hebraic script. Dressed in beach attire, Gordon sits reclining between two women: a young blonde in short shorts and tank top and an elderly, gray-haired woman wearing a dress and fur coat.[9] The odd pairing of sexy lady and Jewish grandma make the group's humorous intent clear, and the song itself offers up a number of ironic juxtapositions. The lyrics tell the unlikely story of a Jewish salesman who becomes a rap star after his date drags him to a club with music that is "too loud" and a DJ that is "talking to the crowd." Delivered in a thick Yiddish accent, Gordon's performance makes use of a variety of Jewish cultural references. He mentions chopped liver and Maalox, and describes rap as "just a simple spiel." Replacing the smooth rapping style and urban slang of black MCs with a stiff flow made more awkward by the insertion of various Yiddish idioms (e.g., "Oy vey!"), the song highlights Gordon's ethnic identity for laughs.

Although the main target of their humor was their parents' generation of Yiddish-speaking Jews, the Kosher Five's foray into rap also reveals a number of assumptions about the emergent genre. Most obviously, the song's humor depends on the incongruity of a Jewish man rapping, a style of music presumed to be the domain of African American performers. "Take My Rap" thus illustrates how rap music, from its very beginning as a commercial genre, could make identity audible. By subverting genre-specific expectations, Steven Gordon and the Kosher Five made a spectacle of their Jewishness.

Figure 1. Cover, Steve Gordon and the Kosher Five, "Take My Rap . . . Please,"
Reflection Records MOM 667, 1979.

Although the lyrical clichés and Yiddish accent are indispensible, "Take My Rap" also draws upon its musical track—coded as dance music—to reinforce this ironic juxtaposition. As Taninbaum recalls in the epigraph to this chapter, he easily understood the formula behind the Sugarhill Gang's "Rapper's Delight" as "a disco record with rapping on it."[10] In the studio, Gordon performed his schtick over a funky disco arrangement—four-on-the-floor kick drum, syncopated guitar riffs, and bass ostinato—that was the standard accompaniment for the first rap singles released in 1979 and 1980. In fact, the beat used to record "Take My Rap" was also recycled to provide the backing track for *four* other rap songs released by Reflection Records.[11]

On the one hand, the use of the same disco beat to create five different singles reflects the entrepreneurial spirit of rap's first years, a period when cash-strapped independent producers sought to maximize the return on their investments. On the other hand, the fact that the Kosher Five's beat could be used as the foundation for songs by African American performers—both male and female—suggests something else: in 1979, rap style might have been understood immediately as "black," but rap beats had not yet begun sounding particular identities.

From where, then, did the stylistic norms of rap's first beats come? And what did it mean in the closing months of 1979 for rap to be understood as a "black thing"? In other words, what underlying forces allowed for the rise of this new entity, the rap song? To answer these questions, this chapter returns to a pivotal moment in hip hop and rap music history when DJs' and MCs' practices of live performance were being translated into studio-produced songs. The most important of these recordings was the Sugarhill Gang's "Rapper's Delight," which spawned dozens of imitators and helped establish rap music as a new commercial genre. Although it was not the first commercially released song to feature rapping, "Rapper's Delight" shot up *Billboard's* Disco and Hot 100 charts to introduce millions of listeners to the new style.[12] Yet, rapping, one of the core elements associated with hip hop culture, dates back to the early 1970s. Its spread, like that of DJing, dancing, and graffiti, predated "Rapper's Delight" by more than five years. In fact, hip hop's key musical elements—rapping and DJing—were part of a thriving local subculture long before rap music captivated the national imagination. Within New York's club scene, the Sugarhill Gang, which included MCs Big Bank Hank, Wonder Mike, and Master Gee, were virtually unknown. The sudden success of their song "Rapper's Delight" shocked local figures who rightly considered themselves true pioneers of the style.[13]

In numerous ways "Rapper's Delight" represented a departure from what was occurring in New York's clubs. I will use the term *hip hop* to designate the culture and practices of live performance from which *rap* the genre of commercial music developed. A main difference between the two, as Joseph Schloss explains in his study of the relationship between dancers and DJs in hip hop's early years in New York, is that hip hop was not originally centered around the production of discrete songs. Instead, as I will discuss in detail, early disc jockeys or DJs laid down a nonstop flow of music for partygoers and dancers while rappers or MCs maintained a party atmosphere with lyrical routines and call-and-response chants. The advent of rap music recordings forever altered this dynamic and led to the creation of the rap song, tipping the balance of power away from the DJ and toward the MC.

The music industry's incursion meant that "hip hop as activity" became "hip hop as musical form," and the transformation of hip hop music into a recorded commodity produced important changes that distinguish commercially recorded songs from the live performances that inspired them.[14] The recording session for "Rapper's Delight," for example, took place in two distinct stages. First, Sugar Hill Records co-owner and producer Sylvia Robinson worked with studio musicians to record the song's musical track. But, having trouble convincing a legitimate crew to record for her, Robinson decided to form her own group. Big Bank Hank was discovered during his shift at a pizza parlor. Some days later, after the group had been assembled, MCs Big Bank Hank, Wonder Mike, and Master Gee entered the studio to rap over the prerecorded track. Many of the lyrics that they recited were drawn from the routines of other, more established live performers. For example, weeks before the release of "Rapper's Delight," Grandmaster Caz of the Cold Crush Brothers remembers loaning Big Bank Hank a book of his lyrics. For the recording of "Rapper's Delight," Hank rapped lyrics from Caz's book, even reciting rhymes that include Caz's stage name: Casanova Fly.[15] As one of the music's most notorious examples of "biting" (stealing another's style and attempting to pass it off as one's own), "Rapper's Delight" has become a paradigmatic symbol of hip hop's commercial exploitation.

The Sugarhill Gang's blatant inauthenticity, however, tends to overshadow a profound formal shift that accompanied live hip hop's translation into commercial rap music. A key difference between live hip hop and recorded rap involves the role of the DJ in producing the musical beat that MCs rap over. For "Rapper's Delight," studio musicians—not a DJ—created the beat. Once the main attraction at live events, DJs suddenly found themselves relegated to a marginal role in the recording studios of rap's first years. In fact, it is even possible that the lack of a DJ was key to the success of "Rapper's Delight." The DJ was at the center of the club scene, and the MCs (or rappers) "were on stage at the discretion of the DJ, the king of the party, and at the mercy of his subjects, the audience."[16] But the Sugarhill Gang, not beholden to a DJ, were free to create rhymes focusing more on the "funny stories" and "hookish slang" that appealed to a wider audience experiencing the music, not through live performances, but through the radio, as songs.[17] The use of studio musicians to craft the beats for these songs remained the dominant approach to production in rap's first few years.

Comparing recordings of pre-1979 hip hop events to rap music's first hit single, "Rapper's Delight," we can see how the musical dimensions of rap songs differed from live DJ performances. Although producers like Robinson replaced the DJ with studio musicians, they did not wholly abandon the concepts or aesthetic predilections that DJs had cultivated prior to the advent of rap. In particular, rap's first producers inherited from DJs a commitment to breakbeats: the relatively brief, polyrhythmic instrumental passages that appear on numerous recordings released in the 1960s and 1970s. This "break-centered" approach provided a foundation for numerous future developments in musical production. As rap musicians developed new ways of making beats—the musical tracks that supported a rapper's lyrics—they laid the groundwork for new ways of sounding race. Not surprisingly, news outlets that began to take notice of the rap phenomenon discussed its musical features in familiar terms, drawing upon and recycling long-standing notions about black sound. Revisiting the world of hip hop music before the advent of rap songs, we gain a greater appreciation for the musical innovations of hip hop's first artists, as well as a better understanding of the formal elements, musical concepts, and cultural meanings that would be manipulated for years to come by rap's producers.

HIP HOP BEFORE HIP HOP

Regarded as a key pioneer in hip hop's musical evolution, DJ Kool Herc (b. Clive Campbell) cultivated an approach to playing records that continues to inform contemporary hip hop and rap production. In the summer of 1973, Herc and his sister Cindy began throwing dance parties in the recreation room of their apartment building at 1520 Sedgwick Avenue in the South Bronx. The positive response to these parties encouraged Herc to expand into larger venues, leading him to become one of the most famous DJs in the Bronx. He is regarded today as a founding father of hip hop, and his success depended in part on the musical techniques he pioneered at these parties. Herc's musical innovations, which laid the foundation for rap music, resulted from a dynamic interaction between the DJ and the dancers at his parties. Noticing that the dancers (hip hop's first "b-boys") were responding to certain kinds of records—and certain parts of those records that featured energetic polyrhythmic grooves—Kool Herc became the first Bronx DJ to develop a method for isolating and repeating breakbeats, or "breaks" as they also became known.[18]

Herc called his innovation, which involved using two turntables to shuttle back and forth between the break sections that he had identified on his records, the "merry-go-round." When one break was near ending, Herc could transition into a new one or repeat the one just played, providing partygoers with the juiciest parts of each song. As Herc explains, "On most records people have to wait through a lot of strings and singing to get to the good part of the record. But I give it to them all up front."[19] By playing the crisp, handclapping break from James Brown's "Give It Up or Turn It Loose," transitioning into the rapid-fire percussion of Michael Viner's Incredible Bongo Band's "Bongo Rock," and then fading into the chugging, anthem-like groove of Babe Ruth's "The Mexican," Herc created something new from previously existing materials.[20] Extending relatively brief moments of funk into something of greater length and significance, Herc and his followers recognized the power of what he had discovered, and Herc began reserving the merry-go-round for the climactic moments at his parties, ramping up the energy and inspiring the dancers at his parties late into the morning.[21]

The records that Kool Herc played were not hip hop as most people think of it today. Before there were commercially recorded and released rap singles, hip hop music did not exist independently of events held at clubs, parks, community centers, and other venues.[22] In other words, although something conceptually distinct (if not always labeled "hip hop") existed for years prior to "Rapper's Delight," rap *songs* did not. Hip hop music began as the playing of recordings from soul, funk, R&B, rock, and other genres—recordings whose origins were often far removed from the Bronx.[23] To be a successful DJ, one had to amass and master a vast record collection, and a veritable cottage industry developed in New York to satisfy the demand for breakbeat records.[24] Knowledge about which records to buy and the location of breaks on these records became trade secrets.

As Kool Herc's approach to DJing garnered increasing attention, other aspiring Bronx DJs attempted to emulate and even improve on his style. In May of 1974, sixteen-year-old Joseph Saddler attended one of Herc's parties. Although inspired by what he witnessed, Saddler remembers having mixed feelings about Herc's technique. Despite his "monumental" insight about zeroing in on the breaks, Herc had not—at least to Saddler's ears—satisfactorily completed what he had begun. The problem, according to Saddler, was that Herc would literally "pick up the needle and drop it on the vinyl—first on one turntable and then on the next—taking a chance that he would land on the break." This lack of precision meant that Herc often missed the downbeat, interrupting the flow of the music and momentarily confusing dancers. Saddler remembers that "if you looked at the crowd in that moment between the songs, everybody fell off the beat for a few seconds. They'd get back on it again, but in those few seconds you could see the energy and the magic start to fade from the crowd."[25]

In response, Saddler began searching for a more exact way to cue up breaks. After much trial and error, he arrived at a method where he could precisely manipulate his records by placing his hands and fingers directly on the vinyl. Holding a recording in place on the rotating turntable, he could now "slip-cue" breaks with precision. By releasing the vinyl to spin at the exact moment the breakbeat on his other turntable was ending, he could transition cleanly into a new break. Using multiple copies of the same recordings, two turntables, and a mixer, a breakbeat could also be "looped," meaning that it could be extended indefinitely and, what is more, stay in the pocket the whole time. Mark Katz neatly summarizes the procedure in his history of hip hop DJing:

- Put two copies of the same record on the turntables with the needles at the beginning of the break.
- Slide the crossfader [of the mixer] to the left position so that only turntable one will sound.
- Using a marked label as a guide, start playing the disc on turntable one at the beginning of the break.
- While turntable one is playing, start turntable two, but hold the disc in place so the needle doesn't move through the grooves.
- Right when the break on turntable one ends, quickly slide the crossfader to the right side and let go of the disc on turntable two.
- While the break is playing on turntable two, manually rotate the disc on turntable one backwards (this is called backspinning) to the beginning of the break and hold the record in place.
- Right when the break on turntable two ends, quickly slide the crossfader back to the left side and let go of the disc on turntable one.
- Continue at your pleasure.[26]

Saddler named this achievement his "quick mix theory."[27] Working to perfect his new approach to spinning breakbeats, he began earning a reputation for the ability to mix faster and cleaner than other DJs. Soon Saddler and his crew were performing at their own events, where he went by the name Grandmaster Flash.[28]

Flash's innovation was key. Manipulating breakbeats with greater accuracy and speed allowed him to create a more reliable rhythmic framework for dancers, and for his MCs to launch increasingly elaborate rap routines. What is more, Flash's focus on musical technique allowed him greater control of the general atmosphere at his parties. Just as he had first witnessed Kool Herc do at Cedar Park, Flash strategically ordered the records he played to keep his audiences engaged and build toward climactic moments.[29] But in addition to building energy through the ordering of the records he played and the volume at which he played them, Flash capitalized on his precise technique, creating new musical arrangements by virtue of the way in which he looped individual breaks. Looping also served another valuable purpose: by avoiding the parts of songs that might be considered "cheesy" or undesirable for any number of reasons, DJs were able to draw on a much wider palette of sounds.[30] As we will see later in this chapter and throughout this book, the ability to select and repeat parts of a pre-existing recording plays an important role in rap's production of racial identity. By creating a new groove that repeatedly juxtaposes the end of one segment of a recording with its own beginning, quick mix theory "Africanizes" any slice of sound, aligning it with other Afro-diasporic forms, such as funk and Cuban *son*.[31]

AUDUBON ROCK ON

One of the best-preserved recordings of hip hop music prior to 1979 features Grandmaster Flash and the Four MCs (before they added Rahiem and became the Furious Five). The performance took place at the Audubon Ballroom in Harlem on December 23, 1978, almost a full year before the release of "Rapper's Delight." Over the course of the thirty minutes of performance preserved by this audio recording, Flash applies his quick mix theory to eleven different recordings.[32] The timings in table 1 illustrate how he moves through this set. For each artist and song title listed, Flash uses two identical copies of the respective recording to isolate and loop the breaks. But Flash did not simply repeat the breakbeats in unvarying cycles. By choosing exactly *where* and *when* to loop breaks, he created a live "remix" of the prerecorded material.

In graphically representing parts of Grandmaster Flash's routine, I have avoided staff notation in favor of an original method that calls greater attention to the process underlying the sounds captured on this recording. Rather than revealing particular pitches and rhythms, this method gives a measure-by-measure account of how Flash works with *his* fundamental musical unit: the break. There are two good reasons for this approach. First, this method prevents the abstraction of individual parts from a whole that in the world of the DJ never existed as separate entities. To distinguish between individual musical lines or instruments, as in a musical score, would disguise the fact that the sounds we hear come from the manipulation of two copies of a single record.[33] By focusing on Flash's use of particular breaks rather than transcribing the individual lines that can be abstracted from them, this method of transcription calls attention to the musical, which is to say expressive, priorities of the DJ. A second reason, closely

Table 1. Song titles and timings for the breakbeats Grandmaster Flash mixed in his performance at the Audubon Ballroom, December 23, 1978

Group, song title (year)	Time
Fatback Band, "Fatbackin'" (1973)	0:01–0:53
Brooklyn Dreams, "Music, Harmony and Rhythm" (1977)	0:54–4:56
Gaz, "Sing Sing" (1978)	4:57–9:23
Manzel, "Space Funk" (1977) [spun backwards]	9:24–11:08
Dynamic Corvettes, "Funky Music Is the Thing" (1975)	11:09–13:30
Duke Williams and the Extremes, "Chinese Chicken" (1973)	13:31–15:30
All Dyrections, "On Top Of It" (1973)	15:31–19:08
Pleasure, "Let's Dance" (1976)	19:09–22:09
John Davis and the Monster Orchestra, "I Can't Stop" (1976)	22:10–26:22
David Matthews, "Main Theme from *Star Wars*" (1977)	26:23–28:59
The Blackbyrds, "Blackbyrds Theme" (1974)	29:00–29:34

aligned with the first, is that doing so also sets up future analyses of rap songs. Because DJs and DJ techniques continued to play an important part in the development of rap's sound, focusing on the breaks—whether played directly from LPs, interpolated by studio bands, programmed into electronic drum machines, or digitally sampled—can offer insight into rap's formal evolution.

Examining Grandmaster Flash's use of Brooklyn Dreams's "Music, Harmony and Rhythm," which begins at just under a minute into the Audubon recording, we can hear how Flash applies his intimate knowledge of this recording to exploit its musical features. The break that Flash isolates is the song's opening sixteen measures, which can be divided into two eight-measure parts, A and B (fig. 2). Part A features drums and bass guitar, and part B adds a piano. The numbers in the boxes correspond to measures 1–16; I've shaded measures 9–16 to indicate the presence of the piano. Parts A and B each consists of two nearly identical four-measure units. If we label each of these units individually, the entire sixteen-measure break has an AABB form.

By manipulating two copies of this recording, Flash coaxes four minutes of music from a thirty-second break. Although he could have simply looped the entire sixteen measures eight times to supply the same duration, he chooses to work with "Music, Harmony and Rhythm" in tighter, more irregular cycles. Selecting varying points of repetition within the break, he

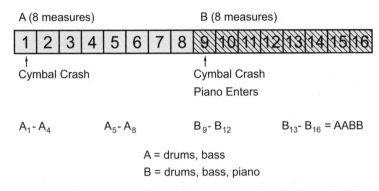

Figure 2. Brooklyn Dreams, "Music, Harmony and Rhythm" (break).

"unlocks" the potential within it to create a new, larger-scale form that differs dramatically from the original song. This portion of Flash's performance is relatively easy to follow because the first four measures of the "Music, Harmony, and Rhythm" break begin with a cymbal crash on the downbeat of the first measure. The transcription in figure 3 reveals the musical arrangement that Flash creates by shuttling between two copies of the break.

Figure 3 begins at 0:54 in the recording, the moment that Flash transitions from the end of the Fatback Band's "Fatbacking" break into "Music, Harmony and Rhythm." Flash begins by playing the opening four measures of the new break, giving him time to replace "Fatbacking" with his duplicate of "Music, Harmony and Rhythm." After these first four measures, however, he builds the next minute of music from the break's first two measures. In fact, he quickly settles into looping the first measure repeatedly, creating a groove that prominently features a cymbal crash on the downbeat of each measure. By concentrating on only the first two measures of the break, Flash effectively "rewrites" the bass line, keeping it fixed on a single, repeating phrase, instead of allowing it to move through the entire four-measure progression. This decision is significant because it adds to the dramatic effect when, nearly two-minutes into his use of the break, he finally allows the record to spin into part B (measures 9–16). Withholding the piano part of the break for this long, Flash delays gratification and heightens the impact of its arrival. The piano's entrance is timed to coincide with the transition between rappers Melle Mel and Kid Creole. In fact, Melle Mel begins introducing Kid Creole at the 2:25 mark, referring to him as the group's "secret weapon" and "the prince of soul." Thus, we could hear Flash's choices as emphasizing the dynamic taking shape between

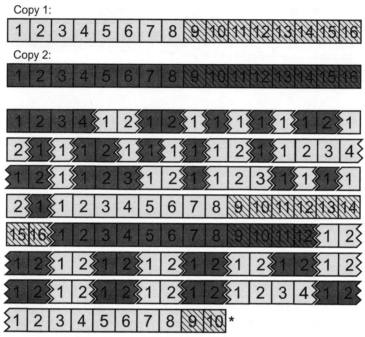

* Coincides with transition to "Sing Sing" break.

Figure 3. Transcription of Grandmaster Flash's use of the "Music, Harmony and Rhythm" break in his performance at the Audubon Ballroom, December 23, 1978.

these MCs, offering the piano's entrance as a kind of bridge between their two routines. This interpretation is supported by the fact that he cuts back to part A soon after Kid Creole begins rapping, and settles back into mixing just the break's first two measures for another minute and a half. The next time Flash lets the break spin into part B, he uses the piano's appearance in the break as a transition into the next recording: Gaz's "Sing Sing."

It is worth stating that there is nothing anomalous about Flash's approach to the "Music, Harmony and Rhythm" break. Every other breakbeat he manipulates on the Audubon recording receives similar treatment. Gaz's "Sing Sing" break, for example, begins with a bass ostinato that repeats four times before a quick three-note pickup leads into a lengthy twenty-two-measure percussion groove. In performance, however, Flash reorders these occurrences, beginning with the percussion groove and only cutting back to the bass ostinato after the break reaches its end. After allowing the ostinato to be heard, Flash returns to playing the percussion groove; only this time he tightens the loop, cutting back repeatedly to the three-note pickup before the percussion groove ends. Then, to create a climactic moment in his use of the break, he loops just the three-note pickup and backspins it rapidly so that only the first note of the bass guitar sounds repeatedly in quarter note bursts. Not only does this quick mixing allow him to effectively improvise a new bass line, but it also introduces the sound of the record being "scratched" as its grooves are pulled back rapidly beneath the stylus.[34]

In the performance preserved on this audio recording, it is clear that Flash's role as a DJ involved more than just replaying prerecorded songs. Quick mix theory allowed him to assert a fair amount of creative control over the sounds coming from his turntables. First, the mixing transcribed in figure 3 suggests that Flash imbued different parts of the break with different functions. For example, part A of "Music, Harmony and Rhythm," without the piano, leaves more open space for the MCs' rapping, and it is not surprising to hear Flash reserve the piano part for dramatic moments in the performance, whether they be a transition between MCs or breakbeats. Secondly, Flash's quick mix theory fostered a sense of drama and created a new musical accompaniment that his MCs actively engaged in their lyrical routines. Because Flash did not always loop breakbeats the same way, the musical surface constantly shifted, and MCs had to adjust their flows to match it. These rapid changes in rhythmic texture—what Tricia Rose would later identify as hip hop's propensity for "rupture"—encouraged MCs to alternate between the delivery of rhyming couplets (what we might hear as short verses) and single-line phrases that allowed them to navigate rapid changes in the musical surface. Consider, for example, Flash's transition between the "Music, Harmony and Rhythm" and "Sing Sing" breaks (fig. 4). Kid Creole is in the middle of a short verse when Flash introduces the new break. Melle Mel quickly takes control of the microphone, using a short, repeated chant, "Let's rock y'all, nonstop y'all," to accustom himself to the new instrumental track before beginning a short verse. As the breakbeat changes, we can hear Melle Mel comport himself to the new rhythm, getting his bearings before launching into a longer, more elaborate verse.

Looking back on these live performances, Flash emphasizes the amount of effort and practice it took for MCs to be able to navigate his beats. "You just didn't get it over night. You had to play with it, develop it, break things, make mistakes, embarrass yourself."[35] To avoid embarrassment and captivate their audiences, Flash and his MCs clearly worked out short routines to capitalize on the musical juxtapositions enabled by quick mix theory. Turning to another bootleg tape recorded in 1978, we can hear Flash and the Four MCs performing at the Bronx's Jackson Housing Projects. At just

Kid Creole:

Hip hop shooby doo Whatcha wanna do
When a boy like me and a girl like you
got a bad case of the boogaloo flu
We called the doctor and the doctor knew
We called the nurse the nurse had it, too
So whatcha wanna do in order to
give everybody the boogaloo flu

Melle Mel:

Rock rock y'all, you don't stop. Keep on.

Let's rock y'all, non stop y'all
Let's rock y'all, non stop y'all

We're two for one, we're twice the fun
We rock you hard from sun to sun
It's the face of the place with the bass in your face
The funk machine, rock the whole place

| Brooklyn Dreams, "Music, Harmony and Rhythm" |
| Introduction of Gaz, "Sing Sing" |

Figure 4. Transition between rappers Kid Creole and Melle Mel. Melle Mel uses a short, repeated phrase to accustom himself to the rhythm of Gaz's "Sing Sing."

under five minutes into the recording, Flash begins alternating between two of the most famous breaks in hip hop and rap music history: the Incredible Bongo Band's "Apache" and the 20th Century Steel Band's "Heaven and Hell Is On Earth." Here, Flash mixes the opening two measures of "Apache" with the opening two measures of "Heaven and Hell" to create a new four-measure loop. Although "Apache" is pure percussion, "Heaven and Hell" features vocals that make it unsuitable as an accompaniment to rapping. Thus, Flash and his four MCs created a routine—a call and response of sorts—between these breaks. The MCs remain silent during the two measures of "Heaven and Hell" which feature vocals, and they respond with their own couplets when Flash switches to "Apache." Trading measures two at a time, this section recalls the interaction between jazz instrumentalists:

"APACHE" + MELLE MEL: Yes, yes y'all! Freak, freak y'all!
You say hit it Flash!

"HEAVEN AND HELL": Children growing, women producing,
men go working, some go stealing.

"APACHE" + MELLE MEL: *[rest]*
Hit it Flash!

"HEAVEN AND HELL": Children growing, women producing,
men go working, some go stealing.

"APACHE" + MELLE MEL: Melle Mel rocks so well,
From the world trade to the depths of hell.

"HEAVEN AND HELL": Children growing, women producing,
men go working, some go stealing.

"APACHE" + MR. NESS: I'm Mr. Ness and I sound so good
As I rock side-side, I rock side-ways

"HEAVEN AND HELL": Children growing, women producing,
men go working, some go stealing.

"APACHE" + COWBOY: I'm the C-O-W-B-O-Y
The man is bad and you can't deny

"HEAVEN AND HELL": Children growing, women producing,
men go working, some go stealing.

"APACHE" + KID CREOLE: Too hot to handle, too cold to hold
I go by the name of the Kid Creole

Although we hear something that resembles later commercial rap music—namely MCs rapping over beats—there are several aspects of these live performances that distinguish them from later studio-produced music. First, as these examples demonstrate, the DJ controlled the musical texture and set parameters for the MCs to negotiate. Far from a regularized musical backdrop, Flash's accompaniment was constantly in flux. His interaction with the four MCs resembles something akin to a game of musical cat-and-mouse. Although Flash's mixing could create a dialogue with his MCs (as in the most recent example), we also hear him move from one breakbeat to the next with little apparent regard for his rappers. If one of his MCs happens to be in the middle of a verse, so be it; it is up to the MC to adjust his flow and make the most of the transition. Second, much like Flash's approach to DJing, the MCs' rhyming roams freely, an approach sometimes referred to as freestyling. We hear MCs drop out to call attention to what the DJ is doing (particularly at 9:24, when Flash demonstrates his virtuosity by quick-mixing Manzel's "Space Funk" in reverse); we hear them shift into conversational speech to advertise upcoming performances; and we hear them repeat favorite couplets multiple times without any particular fear of sounding unoriginal. It is easy to imagine why such spontaneity and flexibility were necessary. Without any solid assurances about exactly how and when Flash was going to loop the breaks, developing longer verse structures or narrative forms would be a pointless exercise.

A final difference between these live performances and recorded songs is that Flash's application of quick mix theory gives rise to a sense of musical spontaneity that one rarely hears in commercial rap recordings after 1979, even those by Grandmaster Flash and the Furious Five. Although he cuts from one record to another strictly on the downbeat, allowing him to maintain a steady 4/4 rhythm for dancers and MCs, Flash does not seem concerned with repeating cycles of symmetrical length as would become common practice in hip hop music after its translation into rap songs (to be explained shortly). Instead, he improvises how and when he will loop a given break, a practice that gives rise to music with a steady beat, but also much room for variation. The remnants of pre-1979 hip hop music preserved on these audio recordings offer an alternative view of hip hop music, a world where performances unfold over the course of an evening and the musicians emphasize process more than production. No doubt this capacity for spontaneity helps explain why DJs were the focal point in early hip hop. Not only were they in control of *what* music got played, but they developed new and exciting techniques that informed *how* they played it. And in so doing, they commanded MCs, inspired dancers, and enlivened the atmosphere at their events for partygoers. The appropriative and transformative nature of these practices is what led Grandmixer D.ST (one of hip hop's early DJs) to characterize the essence of hip hop as a "genre-less" approach to music.[36] Theoretically speaking, according to this approach, any recording from any genre has the potential to be grist for hip hop's mill. Later sample-based production in hip hop as well as the practices of electronic dance music producers are indebted to this philosophical innovation, which allows producers to assemble new tracks from diverse snippets of sound.

At the Audubon Ballroom and other pre-1979 hip hop performances, DJs took pre-existing records from multiple genres (rock, disco, jazz, funk, etc.) and literally spun new musical forms into existence. Although Grandmaster Flash and the Four MCs' performance does not hang together as a series of songs, we would be mistaken to hear the loose feel of this recording as a sign of sloppiness. The group's job was to maintain control of the vibe at their events, to the keep people dancing and engaged with what the DJ was doing, not to create a coherent work of art. We can imagine MCs and DJs reacting to specific things that were happening in the room at that moment—arguments, somebody wearing a crazy outfit, a drunk person falling down—that by their very nature cannot be understood through audio recordings alone. (In contrast, everything one needs in order to appreciate a commercial recording has to be on the record itself.) Looking back on these live performances, Grandmaster Flash recalls: "If you could tell where one record stopped and the next one began, or where Mel handed off to Cowboy, or if Rahiem rapped the same part of the jam last night as he did tonight, then your ears were better than mine."[37] As Flash makes clear, the lack of beginnings or ends within the set was deliberate. Hip hop's early DJs and MCs were not concerned with crafting songs, only with rocking parties.

FROM GENRE-LESS TO NEW GENRE

Within a year of Grandmaster Flash's Audubon Ballroom and Jackson Projects performances, the first rap songs began hitting the airwaves, clubs, and record shops. Once independent music labels began marketing the first rap singles to a regional, then a national commercial market, the musical practices and priorities of Bronx DJs and MCs were complicated by a new set of concerns and issues related to the (racialized) popular music industry. In attempting to craft hit singles, rap's first producers significantly altered the music as it was heard in New York's clubs. Nearly all were inspired by the success of the Sugharhill Gang's "Rapper's Delight," the influential single that relied on the recording studio to translate live hip hop into a rap song. In this context, the music producer—a central figure in the history of recorded popular music—enters our story to challenge the sovereignty of the hip hop DJ. By examining this first stage in rap music production beginning in 1979, a period that has sometimes been referred to as "disco rap," we can begin to understand how rap's reliance on breakbeats helped give rise to new racial meanings.

Hip hop music is often colloquially referred to as the art of beats and rhymes. But in 1979, no standard procedures existed for making beats. There was no recorded rap tradition to provide guidance, and Sugar Hill producer Sylvia Robinson's arrangement for "Rapper's Delight" departed significantly from the practices of DJs such as Grandmaster Flash. As already mentioned, instead of employing a DJ with two turntables and a mixer, Robinson directed the musicians in her studio to record the song's backing track. Yet, even under these new circumstances, the break remained an important organizing concept. In fact, the instrumental track for "Rapper's Delight" was a composite of *two* breaks. The song opens with an eight-measure vamp derived from a portion of Love De-Luxe's "Here Comes That Sound Again" (1979), a mostly forgotten track from the disco years. This groove, whose relationship to "Here Comes That Sound" is most clearly audible in the vamp's piano part, is abruptly interrupted

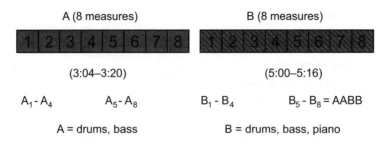

Figure 5. Two different eight-measure sections of the instrumental break from Chic's "Good Times."

(almost like a DJ cutting from one record to the next) to give way to the main beat that the MCs rap over. The source of this second interpolation is well known as one of the hottest singles of the disco years: Chic's 1979 megahit, "Good Times." What is not commonly acknowledged, however, is that the studio musicians at Sugar Hill Records based their arrangement on two different portions of the instrumental break that occurs at the three-minute mark of "Good Times" (fig. 5).

Splicing these parts together, Robinson's arrangement for "Rapper's Delight" foreshadows the chopping and looping of sample-based production that would become the industry standard in the late 1980s and early 1990s. The resulting composite break, which the musicians reproduced with remarkable accuracy, consists of two eight-measure units. Part A features drums, bass, and handclaps, and part B adds guitar and piano. Each of these eight-measure units consists of two repeating four-measure units. In fact, the form of this studio interpolation should be familiar: it shares the same structure as the opening sixteen measures of "Music, Harmony and Rhythm" (see fig. 2) that Flash used in his Audubon performance.

Despite maintaining the centrality of breakbeats, however, the way that Robinson treated "Good Times" in the studio marked an important shift in musical priorities. Rather than attempt to "remix" the break as Flash did during his live performances, the musicians settled on a strictly regularized arrangement for the Sugarhill Gang to rap over. They simply repeated the entire sixteen measures without variation for the duration of the song. To emphasize this point, consider figure 6, in which the backing track to "Rapper's Delight" is represented as a function of what a DJ would have to do to achieve the same result using two copies of the same record: simply cut from part A of one record to part B of the other, *ad infinitum.*

The repetitive nature of the arrangement confused, even frightened, some of the musicians who had been called into the studio that day. Chip

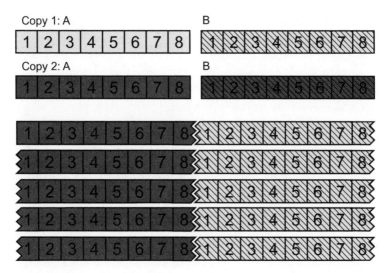

Figure 6. Backing track to "Rapper's Delight" as a function of what a DJ would have to do to achieve the same result using two copies of the same record.

Shearin, then a seventeen-year-old aspiring jazz musician, played bass guitar at the session and remembers being puzzled by Robinson's instructions. Shearin's job was to play the intricate bass line from Chic's "Good Times" for fifteen minutes without stopping or making mistakes. He remembers, "The drummer and I were sweating bullets because that's a long time."[38] Although he was unaware of it at the time, Shearin and his fellow session players were being used to recreate something that approximated a DJ looping portions of Chic's "Good Times." In other words, Robinson translated Flash's quick mix theory into a studio setting—only with a rigidity and evenness that was rarely, if ever, a goal in Flash's live performances! Although the replacement of the DJ with a studio band has been acknowledged and commented on, no one to my knowledge has explored the significant shift in *form* brought about by how this change was implemented.

With "Rapper's Delight" a new kind of stability and symmetry emerged. With no scratching, no rapid transition between breaks, and no ruptures in the musical surface introduced by a DJ, MCs (or rappers as they increasingly became known) were granted an unprecedented amount of space to fill with their vocals. Rather than freestyling loosely as live MCs tended to do, the Sugarhill Gang neatly arranged their verses into four-measure units to correspond with the orderliness of the beat. Of course, the majority of MC couplets and party chants were not designed to fill such long uninterrupted stretches, and such sudden unencumbered freedom might have seemed daunting to live MCs suddenly turned recording artists. Indeed, the majority of the Sugarhill Gang's lyrics sound like a pastiche of an MC's live repertoire, a "mesh of rhymes," as one critic put it.[39] Although "Rapper's Delight" does not develop a particular theme or broadcast a specific message, these longer verse forms eventually enabled the development of more complex narratives as MCs began turning their attention to the process of recording songs. In other words, the practice of matching a stable musical arrangement to a particular set of lyrics granted hip hop lyricists new creative license and eventually led to the thematic diversity, longer narrative forms, and poetic prowess of more recent hip hop and rap music.

If we examine an audio recording of Grandmaster Flash performing together with MCs Melle Mel and Kurtis Blow at the Armory in Jamaica, Queens, on October 6, 1979, we can hear just how different the musical track for "Rapper's Delight" was from live DJ-centered events. Approximately five minutes of their performance that evening featured the MCs rapping over Flash's quick mix of Chic's "Good Times," the same song that had formed the basis for the Sugarhill Gang's "Rapper's Delight." Alternating between different parts of the song, Flash scratches and cuts the recording in dozens of ways, using scratching and quick mix theory to add percussive accents and new rhythms to the mix. Melle Mel actively engages with Flash's mixing. When he hears Flash scratching the title phrase ("good times"), he sets up a call-and-response routine:

> MELLE MEL: "Come on Flash! Let's have a . . . have a . . . have a . . ."
>
> FLASH (VIA CHIC'S RECORD): *"GOOD TIMES!"*

As in the Audubon tape, Flash rearranges the order of musical events on these recordings, highlighting different sections at different times. At times, he plays just the drum-and-bass breakdown section; at other times he cuts to portions that feature singing and Chic's full band. Toward the end of the excerpt, Flash even demonstrates what later became known among hip hop DJs as "beat juggling." Creating entirely new rhythms and melodies by rapidly alternating between the two recordings set out of phase with one another, he spontaneously recomposes Bernard Edwards's iconic bass line.

In retrospect, the Armory recording captures a moment where change hangs in the balance—an instant where Flash and Melle Mel hold up what has been in the face of what would be. As Mark McCord writes about the Armory concert for *Wax Poetics* magazine, "At least for that one night, it didn't matter if there was a record selling in stores all over the country, because it was the guys on the stage that night who were the real stars."[40] Even as "Rapper's Delight" climbed the charts and attracted waves of outsiders who had never heard or cared about live DJs and MCs, Flash's Armory performance exemplifies a dynamism and sense of musical spontaneity absent from Sugar Hill's interpolation of the "Good Times" break.

These differences between live hip hop and recorded rap songs have led some historians, musicians, and critics to treat "Rapper's Delight" as hip hop's original sin, or as what Jeff Chang refers to as its "first death."[41] It is easy (and perhaps even fair) to look back on "Rapper's Delight" as a corruption of hip hop performance practice that exploited the culture for profit. That the Sugarhill Gang was a studio creation, totally unknown within New York's club scene, is an often-repeated fact, and the story of how Sylvia Robinson auditioned and assembled the group herself has been documented in great detail. In fact, the Sugarhill Gang did not perform together live until after they had a hit record; and when they did, they worked through a set of songs, not the kind of spontaneous party music Flash and his MCs specialized in providing. The group's many critics have emphasized their lack of credibility as live performers as well as their "borrowing" of other, more famous MCs' rhymes. Thus, previous accounts tend to highlight the inauthenticity of "Rapper's Delight" as well as the shady, exploitative financial practices of Sugar Hill Records, a bias that tends to shield from view the profound shift in form that accompanied hip hop's translation from live performance to recorded rap.

The musical differences brought about by this transformation had significant consequences for rap music, and it is important that we acknowledge the effect of Robinson's and other early producers' decision to record *songs* rather than attempting to capture or re-create live hip hop practices.[42] Not only did this decision create discrete units that could be sold and played on the radio, but the practice of matching a particular musical arrangement to a particular set of lyrics also unleashed new creative possibilities. Although it is fair to look back on "Rapper's Delight" as a corruption of hip hop practices, the backing tracks of later hip hop and rap songs *all* draw from a similar logic. The basic idea that rap producers should construct stable backing tracks and pair them with particular MC verses to create discrete songs links "Rapper's Delight" to just about every rap song that came after it. Without meaning to, perhaps, Robinson had translated the way DJs and MCs worked with breaks into a new form of songwriting.

Through the force of recording practices, which emphasized efficiency and predictability, Robinson and the producers that followed her changed the relationship between MCs and the musical track, expanding the possibilities for rappers to expound on particular themes. No doubt the regularity and symmetry of the backing track to "Rapper's Delight" had a practical purpose, making it easier for the musicians to coordinate their arrangement and easier for the rappers to deliver their lines cleanly in the pocket. Yet these new recording practices also encouraged hip hop practitioners to begin thinking in terms of discrete units that could be recorded, sold, and played on the radio. Songs need titles; titles suggest themes; themes require lyrical development, and so on. Not surprisingly, the majority of early rap songs, including Grandmaster Flash and the Furious Five's "Super Rappin'" and Kurtis Blow's "The Breaks," turned directly to the practices of live hip hop performance itself for thematic inspiration. Not long after, however, aspiring recording artists began searching for new ways to distinguish themselves, expanding the purview of rap music to include new topics and scenarios, including some, such as "Take My Rap . . . Please," that broadcast distinctly racialized meanings. In rap music's first few years as a commercial genre, MCs took leading roles as songwriters and stars while DJs mostly watched from the sidelines. The late Sylvia Robinson—who Grandmaster Flash still refers to as "the queen," with a mixture of reverence and resentment—had overthrown the kings of the party.

RAP MUSIC AND THE DISCO BACKLASH

The shifts accompanying live hip hop's translation into recorded rap music were more than purely formal. They were inextricably tied to social currents in contemporary U.S. popular music. Early rap music's characteristic sound was not wholly unfamiliar to national audiences, even those ignorant of New York's underground hip hop culture. With its backing track based on Chic's "Good Times," one of the biggest disco recordings of 1979, "Rapper's Delight" combined the novelty of rapping with a musical accompaniment that was recognizable even to those who had never witnessed Kool Herc, Grandmaster Flash, Afrika Bambaataa, or other New York DJs in performance. In fact, before rap came to be understood as a genre in its own right, the industry treated it as a species of disco/R&B recording.

Rap's proximity to disco was not something wholly fabricated by the recording industry. Many of the mixing techniques employed by hip hop DJs, such as slip-cueing, were pioneered by so-called disco DJs. In his autobiography, Grandmaster Flash recalls picking up tips from disco DJ Pete Jones.[43] Moreover, the records that Grandmaster Flash and others spun were often the same recordings featured at downtown disco clubs and marketed by the recording industry as disco records.[44] Although there were differences in how DJs from downtown and the Bronx tended to approach their craft (not to mention profound social distances between the whiter, Manhattan dance clubs and the uptown venues where hip hop flourished), there is no evidence to suggest that in 1979 hip hop and disco represented distinct musical genres.[45] The term *disco* itself indexed a number of overlapping meanings: a commercial music genre, a musical style, a type of dance, a kind of dance club, and a style of DJing. On the Audubon tape, for example, MC Melle Mel repeatedly refers to Grandmaster Flash as "king of the disco mix." And the Armory performance discussed earlier was billed as "The First All-Star Disco Concert." Following this fluidity in usage of the term, rap's first singles were also often conflated with disco releases.

A part of this association was due to obvious musical similarities. Although the modern recording studio would eventually allow rap artists to exploit its technical attributes to "experiment and develop more complex beats and rhythms," the early rap singles that followed "Rapper's Delight" adhered to conventions already familiar to fans of contemporary dance music (i.e., disco), or what Rickey Vincent calls "dance soul."[46] Executives at the independent labels responsible for recording the first wave of rap records encouraged these stylistic trends. Many of them had entered the business to capitalize on the disco boom. As the dance fad fizzled, they recognized rap as a new way to transform recent hits into profit, and many of the first rap singles were, like "Rapper's Delight," covers of existing dance singles.[47] In fact, early creative choices seem to have been dictated by relatively conservative musical tastes and shrewd business sense. In addition to "Good Times," rap producers also seized on Cheryl Lynn's 1978 dance floor anthem, "It's Got To Be Real." Table 2 lists rap singles recorded and released in 1979 that interpolated breaks from pre-existing disco hits, all of which reached No. 1 on the *Billboard* charts.

However, the preference for popular disco records cannot be attributed solely to calculating producers. Hip hop DJs had used these singles with live audiences before they became the foundation for new rap recordings. In

Table 2. Rap singles released in 1979 that were based on pre-existing disco hits

Artist	Title	Covered artist, song title (year)
Sugarhill Gang	"Rapper's Delight"	Chic, "Good Times" (1979)
Xanadu & Sweet Lady	"Rapper's Delight"	Chic, "Good Times" (1979)
Sicle Cell & Rhapazooty	"Rhapazooty in Blue"	Chic, "Good Times" (1979)
Joe Bataan	"Rap-O, Clap-O"	Cheryl Lynn, "Got To Be Real" (1978)
Funky Four Plus One More	"Rappin' and Rockin' the House"	Cheryl Lynn, "Got To Be Real" (1978)
Jazzy 4 MCs	"MC Rock"	Cheryl Lynn, "Got To Be Real" (1978)
Jocko	"Rhythm Talk"	McFadden and Whitehead, "Ain't No Stopping Us Now" (1979)
Mr. Q	"D.J. Style"	Michael Jackson, "Don't Stop 'til You Get Enough" (1979)

fact, it was hearing Lovebug Starski rap over the "Good Times" break at a Harlem club that first inspired Sylvia Robinson to record "Rapper's Delight."[48] Even when rap producers did not copy breaks from extant hit recordings, the original arrangements that they used drew on the stylistic conventions of contemporary dance music. As Richard Taninbaum, the percussionist and co-writer of "Take My Rap . . . Please," put it, the musical formula was simple: "disco with a guy rapping over it."[49]

Rap producers also tried to imbue their studio productions with elements, such as handclaps or the cacophony of overdubbed voices, evoking the atmosphere of the discotheque.[50] Even the packaging of some recordings testifies to rap's close ties to the disco genre. One of the first rap singles recorded in the wake of "Rapper's Delight" was a track called "We Rap More Mellow" by the Younger Generation.[51] Released on the Brass label by Brasilia Records, the single arrived in stores in a package that rendered explicit the connection to disco (fig. 7).

Given these multiple points of overlap, it would be a mistake to assume that rap and disco were immediately understood as distinct and opposed genres. Although some observers frame the birth of hip hop and rap music as a reaction *against* disco,[52] the often-cited animosity between disco and hip hop has been more of a retroactive phenomenon.[53] In fact, printed materials and recorded evidence of hip hop music in the years leading up to "Rapper's Delight" give no indication that "disco versus hip hop" was a

Figure 7. Cover, the Younger Generation, "We Rap More Mellow," Brass Records BRDS 2504, 1979.

meaningful topos. There are numerous examples of hip hop DJs, MCs, and promoters embracing the term "disco" to describe their events and performance practices. These observations are significant when considering rap music's racialization, because its national debut coincided with a growing backlash against disco that was itself saturated with race and gender anxieties. By the time "Rapper's Delight" rose to the top of the charts, a widespread movement against disco's ubiquity was well underway.[54]

The eventual "death of disco" was not really a stylistic change; it was more of a shift in the categories used by the recording industry to market music.[55] As musicologist Jeffrey Kallberg explains, genres—such as disco or rap—represent more than a species of classification. A piece of music's genre identity is not inherent in the music itself, nor is it reducible to a set of particular stylistic traits. Genre is better understood, Kallberg argues, as a relational and hierarchical concept addressing the way that music makers and music listeners negotiate shared expectations and cultural values.[56] In other words, genres serve as sites where music's meanings are contested.

The "disco" genre itself emerged from a live, DJ-centered club scene popular in New York and other urban centers. The name itself simply comes from the location (discotheques) where DJs played records for crowds of dancers. As the phenomenon picked up steam, the music industry translated a fluid, live experience of dancing to pre-existing songs in discos into a genre of recordings for sale. Thanks in large part to the runaway success of the film *Saturday Night Fever* (1977) and its accompanying soundtrack by the Bee Gees, disco became a dominant force in the recording industry. *Saturday Night Fever* brought a wider audience into the genre's folds, and soon disco clubs were popping up in cities and towns nationwide. By 1979, there were over two hundred all-disco radio stations across the county.[57]

It is possible to view the advent of the first rap songs as another round in the commodification of New York's disco scene. In fact, the scene was already selling itself in more ways than one. In May of 1979, months before the release of "Rapper's Delight," Robert Ford, Jr., reported in *Billboard* that New York's "rapping DJs" were recording and selling tapes of their live performances, noting that "tapes of [DJ] Hollywood's raps are considered valuable commodities."[58] In fact, the Audubon and Jackson Projects recordings analyzed earlier in this chapter were products of this local New York market. Looking back on this moment prior to the advent of the first rap songs, DJs Afrika Bambaataa and Grandmaster Flash reminisce about these tapes as their "first albums."[59] In an early example of grass-roots cross-promotion, Flash explains that the tapes were popular with cab drivers and luxury car services: "How it worked is people would call for a car, and if they had a dope [Kool] Herc tape, or a dope Bam[baataa] tape, or a dope [Grandmaster] Flash tape, that particular customer might stay in the cab all day long. So these cab drivers were making extra money and at the same time they were advertising us."[60]

Reaching further from downtown in search of new sales, independent record producers like Sylvia Robinson sought to tap this underground market and translate uptown New York's particular take on the disco scene into hit records. Not surprisingly, "Rapper's Delight" came packaged with a familiar disco beat and a music video featuring the Sugarhill Gang performing in a club, complete with disco ball and costumed, choreographed dancers. Yet, by 1979 disco was experiencing a breathtaking drop in popularity, and being labeled "disco" had become a cause for concern. A look at the *Billboard* Hot 100 singles charts gives an idea of how rapidly the effects of the disco backlash were felt. Halfway through 1979, over half of the top ten tracks in the nation were disco songs; six months later, only one was. Disco declined so fast that Gloria Gaynor's 1980 Grammy Award for "I Will Survive" was the first—and *only*—Grammy Award ever given for Best Disco Recording. After 1980, the term *disco* virtually disappeared from marketing and publicity.[61]

As the disco bubble burst, music industry observers presumed that rap would also be short-lived. Even producers making money from rap records wondered aloud how long it could last.[62] Reactions to early rap music reflected the backlash culture that had grown up around the anti-disco movement. Rap was denigrated as "crap," and, as we have seen, it was parodied and lampooned. What is more, it was marginalized within the recording industry and by radio. Rap—like disco, or as a part of it—was heard *in relation* to "higher" commercial youth genres, such as rock. These genre distinctions helped maintain a musical color line separating black artists and listeners from white ones. As Alice Echols explains, "By the late seventies rock fans understood their music to be implicitly (if not explicitly) white, and pretty much all music by black musicians to be disco."[63] As radio stations converted their formats, abandoning disco and returning to rock, the airwaves became increasingly segregated.

The pressure that this new regime exerted on black musicians was evident in a *Billboard* article on Nile Rodgers and Bernard Edwards. In the issue of December 15, 1979, just one month after their smash hit "Good Times" had inspired the backing track for "Rapper's Delight," the two African American masterminds behind the music of Chic revealed that they were abandoning disco.[64] The attention-grabbing headline seems aimed at surprising readers, given that the group was currently a leading presence in the genre. The next issue of *Billboard*, for example, announced that the magazine had named Chic the top soul artists of the year and that the group's single "Good Times" and album *C'est Chic* had also been ranked No. 1 by *Billboard*.[65] The article reveals that the duo's stance appears to have been motivated by unease about the confluence of racial identity and musical style limiting their creative and financial opportunities. Edwards explained that the group wanted to be able to "to work with a white artist so people could stop tagging us as black producers or disco producers."[66] Edwards's comments, in which he conflates the labels "black" and "disco," are telling, and reflect the growing perception that disco was moribund as a genre as well as the reality that, by the end of the 1970s, the U.S. recording industry had become increasingly segregated. Having been branded as too disco to touch as a solo act, Nile Rodgers retreated into studio work, and became one of the most successful music producers of the 1980s. Crafting hits for white artists David Bowie, Madonna, and Duran Duran, among others, Rodgers continued to shape mainstream dance music away from the public eye.

Rap artists enjoyed no similar alternatives. As a musical form that placed black bodies and black vernacular rhyming at its center, rap songs highlighted the identity of their performers from the very beginning. (Recall how quickly Steve Gordon and the Kosher Five were able to make a rap parody that played on the music's presumed blackness.) As many cultural critics have noted, rap music brought African American street culture to the mainstream with unprecedented force.[67] Highlighting the MC as a new kind of performer, early rap singles put black male stars at center stage. Paired with backing tracks often resembling disco music, "Rapper's Delight" and other "rapping DJ" songs inaugurated a genre situated on the margins of the margins of the industry.[68]

CONCLUSION

As the first rap hit, and a song that today's critics and fans often identify as the beginning of more than three decades of music, "Rapper's Delight" offers a logical starting point for the commercial music genre known today as hip hop and rap music. Although there is undeniable truth to this view (i.e., the song was hugely popular and influenced subsequent producers), the assignment of exact beginnings to musical genres is always retroactive. Rap music did not arrive as a fully formed, self-contained genre. Seeking to make sense of rap's growing popularity for the paper's white, middle-class audience, *New York Times* journalists John Rockwell and Robert Palmer initially wrote rap off as a "novelty phenomenon," or at least hedged their bets by suggesting it could be short-lived.[69] Despite this skepticism about its longevity, from the beginning rap was unmistakably black. Rockwell and Palmer contextualized it as the music of "urban communities" and "black neighborhoods," once even suggesting that their presumably white readership would most likely encounter rap on the subway and in parks as "intrusive noise."[70] Although these early reviews and write-ups were not always in agreement, some general similarities are worth noting. For example, when examining how the *New York Times* and the *Washington Post* connected rap's sonic qualities to identity, the emphasis was clearly on rap's verbal style, with hardly any serious discussion of its backing tracks or beats. The papers described rap as "rhythmic black street chant" with origins in "street slang" and "jive talk."[71] By contrast, the musical accompaniment, if mentioned at all, was described as simple ("rudimentary") and incomplete ("skeletal").[72] In other words, in its first years (roughly 1979 to 1981), rap was certainly identified as black music, but its potential as a genre—in particular, the force of its musical style—was far from knowable.[73]

Concentrating on this liminal moment in music history, the profound difference between DJ and MC club performances and the first commercial rap songs becomes clear. The world of mid-to-late-1970s hip hop music was both musically and conceptually distinct from the commercially released rap recordings that followed it. The tapes of live hip hop performance prior to 1979 provide evidence of how Grandmaster Flash and other DJs transformed pre-existing recordings into something new. Hip hop music was defined not so much by *what* was on the records that DJs played, but by *how* they played them. In using their skills to refashion breaks and reorder the contents of individual songs, DJs found a new way to bring people together on the dance floor. While the primary role of downtown disco DJs was to blend one song's ending into the next song's beginning as smoothly as possible, "eliminating or masking the breaks between songs," Bronx hip hop DJs fostered a style of music and dance that emphasized the breaks within and between songs.[74] Unconcerned with crafting individual songs, hip hop's first performers specialized in moving the crowd, providing a continuous, engaging musical presence that enlivened the party atmosphere of the club, recreation room, or park where their audiences had gathered.[75]

As producers such as Sylvia Robinson translated these practices into shorter, saleable units, however, a new form of songwriting was born. The ten-hour party jam became the ten-minute rap single. But although "Rapper's Delight" differed greatly from live hip-hop music, Robinson and other rap producers relied on the break as a fundamental musical unit. In heavy rotation, the Sugarhill Gang's hit single became the center of a new solar system, pulling other bodies into orbit, inspiring other producers and MCs to try their hands at making records in a similar fashion. In the studio environment of rap's first years, producers used this break-centered approach to craft discrete songs, opening the door for MCs to concentrate on developing new themes and expanding upon them.[76]

In the next chapter, we will examine how, as rap music developed in the 1980s, the success of the genre hinged on changes that its producers made to renegotiate rap's image and push it into new territory. Like Nile Rodgers and Bernard Edwards rejecting the disco label in an attempt to reboot their careers, rap producers, DJs, and MCs in the 1980s sought to free themselves from the constraints of race and genre. Instead of working behind the scenes for mostly white artists, however, rap musicians increasingly sought to own blackness, cultivating new themes, imagery, and sounds that became central to the genre and their artistic strategies. MCs, DJs, and producers might not have been able to escape race, but they could renegotiate what it meant.

2 "Rebel Without a Pause"

Public Enemy Revolutionizes the Break

> We knew we had to make something that was aggressive. Chuck's voice is so powerful and his tone is so rich that you can't put him on smooth, silky, melodic music. It's only fitting to put a hailstorm around him, a tornado behind him, so that when his vocals come across, the two complement each other.[1]
>
> **Hank Shocklee, producer**

Writing for the *New York Times* in 1988, Jon Pareles began his review of Public Enemy's seminal *It Takes a Nation of Millions to Hold Us Back* with a telling observation: "In the last decade, rap has become as much a symbol as a musical style."[2] The review's layout bolstered Pareles's assertion: its text wrapped around an iconic photograph emphasizing the group's status as hip hop's "prophets of rage." Chuck D and Flavor Flav wear their signature clock necklaces and sit, hands folded in front of them. DJ Terminator X stands behind them, and the three core members are surrounded by a detail of S1Ws (the group's dancing security unit) dressed in matching fatigues, berets, and dark sunglasses. The group's members look off into the distance away from the camera. None of them smile (see fig. 8 for a related photo).

As Public Enemy's second Def Jam release, *It Takes a Nation of Millions to Hold Us Back* furthered the group's conception of themselves as rap's rebels, bringing a heightened sense of urgency to the genre. Chuck D's lyrics were peppered with references to the Nation of Islam, Louis Farrakhan, and other black political icons, and their sartorial style and album imagery blended the Black Panthers and contemporary street fashion. Without a doubt, there was no better group at the time on which Pareles could base his claim about the rising importance of symbolism in rap.

For many listeners, *It Takes a Nation of Millions* set a benchmark for politically engaged hip hop music, even marking for some a beginning to the "golden age of rap nationalism."[3] This political orientation has been discussed most extensively through references to the group's lyrics, imagery, and public statements, but looking more closely at Pareles's review

Figure 8. Photo taken by Suzie Gibbons at the same shoot as the one used in the article by Jon Pareles, "Public Enemy: Rap with a Fist in the Air," *New York Times*, July 24, 1988, H25. Used by permission of Getty Images.

shows that the critic did not find Chuck D's lyrics particularly compelling.[4] Instead, he highlighted the album's powerful beats. Characterizing Public Enemy's backing tracks as "clipped" and "abrasive," he singled out the songs "Bring the Noise" and "Rebel Without a Pause," noting that both feature "repeated, nagging, wavering sounds that could probably drill through a foot of soundproofing." This colorful description was not meant as a put-down. Rather, the review acknowledged that Public Enemy's "uncompromisingly confrontational" sound was helping to voice the black community's most pressing concerns.

Of course, not all listeners agreed with Pareles, and my point here is not to diminish the views of those who may have been equally inspired by Chuck D's lyrics. Rather, Pareles's suggestion that the power to symbolize resistance can come from the group's backing tracks provides crucial evidence of rap's ability to *sound race*: to project an image of race "constituted within and projected onto the social through sound."[5] Radano and Bohlman describe such constructions of race as "soundtexts" for the way that they become intelligible through an articulation of sonic and textual discourse.[6] Pareles's *New York Times* review is a case in point because of the way it blends references to Black Power iconography with descriptions of the music's sonic features. Describing the album as having "its fist in the air," Pareles employs a striking visual metaphor (the Black Power salute) to personify the album and explain the significance of its musical style. As a concept symbolizing social conflict—characterized in his review as "urban tension and black anger"—race becomes intelligible through the music's "abrasive noises," which serve as a sonic analogue for black militancy. Yet, what musical practices enabled such associations? How can we better understand the sounds in this soundtext?

A familiar answer to this question is digital sampling. Public Enemy's beat-making team, the Bomb Squad, aptly named for the booming quality of their work, famously employed newly available sampling and sequencing technologies to craft tracks that supported the group's rhetoric.[7] The cacophony that Pareles so vividly describes depended upon the group's prominent use of sampling as well as their commitment to sounding a radical black aesthetic, qualities that have led scholars to make Public Enemy one of the most analyzed groups in rap music.[8] However, despite the wealth of writing about the group, there is good reason to revisit their work here. By historicizing the *process* that gave rise to such iconic music, this chapter emphasizes stylistic change as a motivating force in the production of musical meaning and seeks greater insight into the relationship between aesthetics and racial representation. Although there are a number of ways one might approach such issues, this chapter focuses on the production of rap's backing tracks, colloquially referred to as "beats," which are often overlooked in discussions of the music's political content. Looking back on (and listening to) the evolution of rap music production and stylistic developments in the 1980s, the rap song comes into focus as a sonic force that participates in racial formation—the "sociohistorical process by which racial categories are created, inhabited, transformed, and destroyed."[9]

Although fans and critics often trace the emergence of Public Enemy's mature style to *It Takes a Nation of Millions*, the album's sample-based musical approach was first codified on the single "Rebel Without a Pause." Recorded and released in the summer of 1987, a full year before it was bundled with the other songs on *It Takes a Nation of Millions*, "Rebel" also laid the groundwork for the group's musical approach on its subsequent two albums, *Fear of a Black Planet* (1990) and *Apocalypse 91 ... The Enemy Strikes Black* (1991). Rather than simply providing a canvas for the group's politically charged lyrics and imagery, the group's beats conveyed important content of their own. Building on the techniques and styles of their predecessors while introducing a new way of conceiving of and working

with breakbeats—an innovation I describe as "revolutionizing the break"—
Public Enemy enabled a new sounding of race in popular music.

CULTURAL CONTINUITY AND STYLISTIC CHANGE

The Bomb Squad's approach to production helped earn Public Enemy legions
of fans and inspired numerous imitators. Their dense sound and musical
philosophy, which Hank Shocklee famously refers to as "organized noise,"
bolstered Chuck D's politicized lyrics and brought a new seriousness to the
rap genre.[10] However, rather than jump directly into an analysis of Public
Enemy's music, this chapter returns to where the previous one ended, in rap
music's first years as a commercial genre. Doing so allows us to trace how
Public Enemy's characteristic sound depended on a series of changes in beat
making that occurred over the course rap's first decade. Although tied
directly to the advent of sampling and sequencing technology, these innovations in musical production also depended on techniques and concepts first
introduced by hip hop DJs in the 1970s.

As early as 1994, Tricia Rose explained the connection between Public
Enemy's explosive sonic collages and the turntable techniques of Grandmaster
Flash, whose musical innovations were explored in the previous chapter. In
Black Noise: Rap Music and Black Culture in Contemporary America, Rose
cites Flash's 1981 recording "Adventures on the Wheels of Steel," explaining
that "backspinning" (another term for what Flash called his "quick mix theory") allowed DJs to build new compositions from breakbeat recordings in
ways that are remarkably similar to the practices of contemporary rap producers.[11] Joseph Schloss expands on this idea in his ethnography of hip-hop
producers, cataloguing the numerous historical, social, and conceptual ties
binding hip hop DJing to sample-based production. In the late 1980s and
early 1990s, for example, many DJs transitioned from DJing to production,
and virtually all of rap music's most famous producers began as DJs. In addition, these producers sample many of the same recordings that they originally became familiar with from their work as DJs. Finally, the way that
producers exploit the potential of sampling technology closely mirrors the
practices of cutting and looping first developed by South Bronx DJs in the
1970s.[12]

These linkages are especially relevant in the case of Public Enemy
because the group's production team, the Bomb Squad, first began working
together as a mobile DJ crew named Spectrum City. Hailing from Roosevelt,
on Long Island, Spectrum City began in the mid-1970s as brothers Hank
and Keith Shocklee's sound system. As hip hop music spread throughout

New York City's boroughs, the group added MC Chuck D and began performing at jams, eventually recording the singles "Lies" and "Check Out the Radio" (1984).[13] Thus, Public Enemy's members observed and participated in the transition from live hip hop DJing and MCing to the song-oriented production practices of sample-based rap.[14] Hank Shocklee explicitly connects Public Enemy's sample-based production techniques to the culture of breakbeat DJing, explaining, "It's all about the breaks. . . . I had the entire record collection that we all ended up sampling for the album. I wanted to take the records that I loved, and take the drum breaks that I heard, and mimic that process with the sampler."[15]

There is no reason to doubt that what DJs did with their records—isolating numerous breakbeats to loop, cut, and scratch—informs sample-based approaches to production. One of the arguments made in the previous chapter is that the DJs' conception of the break influenced the production of early rap songs even when no DJ or turntables were present in the studio. What I do wish to point out, however, is the danger of *overemphasizing* the cultural ties between early hip hop and Public Enemy's music. As the previous chapter makes clear, the world of mid-to-late-1970s hip hop was conceptually and musically different from later, studio-produced rap songs. Prior to the release of "Rapper's Delight" in 1979, hip hop performances did not feature individual songs. Instead, DJs looped and mixed a variety of breakbeat records into hours of continuous music while their MCs kept the energy high with their lyrical routines. It was the music industry's intervention that transformed the spontaneous and flexible forms of live performance into discrete, saleable units. In fact, the birth of rap as a musical genre depended on the creation of a new kind of commodity: the rap song.

In the "disco rap" era, singles were marketed and understood as party music, and early rap recordings often featured handclapping, call-and-response chants, and background noises, such as a cacophony of voices that simulated the "vibe" of a live performance.[16] In this context, Grandmaster Flash's "Adventures on the Wheels of Steel" (1981), which Rose compares to Public Enemy's sonic collages released almost a decade later, was an anomaly. Although "Wheels of Steel" is one of the most important recordings in the development of hip hop DJing—if not *the* most important—by the standards at Sugar Hill Records in 1981 it did not represent the way forward for rap music. In the context of contemporary popular music, most listeners heard it—if they heard it at all—as a novelty. In the early 1980s, rap music may have been understood as a genre of black music, but it did not sound like a fist in the air.

To understand how Public Enemy's music sounded race in such powerful ways, we have to explore changes in musical production and meaning across rap's first decade. Interpreting moments of stylistic change as acts of racial rearticulation, this chapter cuts across culturally essentializing arguments that seek to identify and interpret fixed musical qualities particular to hip hop and rap. Such positions have been effective in proving the cultural coherence of hip hop as a cultural practice, but they have come at the expense of more historically nuanced understandings of rap's shifting aesthetics and ideological implications. Rose's influential *Black Noise*, for example, embraces what many contemporary observers regarded as rap's "unconventional" practices. She theorizes the black cultural foundations of sampling and rhythmic repetition—qualities that led some critics to hear rap as unethical and simple-minded—and explains that rap producers deliberately pushed their studio equipment to "unmusical extremes" to achieve results that matched their creative sensibility.[17] Indeed, it is rap's deliberate noisiness, as her book's title implies, that enables the music to challenge authority.[18]

With the benefit of hindsight, many of Rose's assertions might now sound untenable. The highly political and noisy style of production that Public Enemy exemplified was relatively short-lived. In fact, Rose herself seems to have backed away from insinuating that something inherently political or progressive lies at the heart of rap's musical aesthetics. Her more recent book, *The Hip-Hop Wars*, avoids discussing sonic elements altogether, focusing instead on the debates surrounding contemporary rap music's narrow and problematic portrayals of black life.[19] Rather than dismiss Rose's earlier musical analyses outright, however, I suggest that it would be illuminating to historicize her aesthetic arguments with respect to the stylistic transformations occurring in rap while she was conducting research for her book. This was a period some have called "the golden age of hip-hop sampling," a time when rap producers were busy exploiting the capabilities of new sampling technology without the prohibitive costs of modern-day sample clearance practices.[20] Doing so suggests that Rose's musical observations are colored by Public Enemy and other groups that were in fashion at the time of her writing.[21] As rap music went from a novelty associated with the disco boom (and bust) to an established genre in its own right, its style and approaches to production evolved considerably. If rap no longer sounds as progressive and subversive as it did during Public Enemy's heyday, we might look for answers in the *musical* practices of its producers, as well as interrogating the usual suspects: lyrics, video imagery, and influence of corporate sponsors.

In one of the first musicological attempts to grapple with the political implications of rap's sonic aesthetics, Robert Walser built upon some of Rose's arguments and offered a thorough analysis of one of Public Enemy's most densely layered tracks: "Fight the Power" (1989). Using staff notation to transcribe every sound he heard in the track, Walser argued that the song's beat invests Chuck D's lyrics with "affective force." Taking rap's sonic elements more seriously than any previous scholar, he argued that "Public Enemy became influential and successful in part because of what fans perceived as the *extra intensity of their noise* and its significance within the context of their lyrics" (emphasis mine).[22]

Although Walser's transcription is revealing and useful for the arguments that he advances, in abstracting individual musical lines from the recording, Western staff notation obscures the processes of sample-based production that gave rise to these sounds in the first place.[23] The lines that Walser transcribes in example 1 do not represent musical ideas that were conceived one by one by the track's composer. Rather, many of them exist together in the breakbeat recordings that were sampled and looped by the Bomb Squad, a fact that I have highlighted by annotating Walser's transcription. The lines labeled "guitar" and "bass," for example, both come from a recording of "Hot Pants Road" by the J.B.'s—a funk single from the early 1970s that could easily have found its way into the collection of any early hip hop DJ.[24] Thus, Public Enemy's intense layering, which Walser's transcription helps make visible, needs to be understood in light of the two developments to be explored in this chapter: (1) the way producers employed new technologies to continue working with breaks; and (2) the searching out and cultivation of particularly noisy breaks to serve the group's expressive purposes.

To retrace the steps leading to Public Enemy's radical sound, we need to account for both the cultural continuity linking hip hop practices *and* the formal differences that resulted from the way they were put to work in particular contexts. By continuing to focus on the break as a key musical concept, I intend to show how rap producers, including the Bomb Squad, reintroduced aspects of hip hop DJ practice to rap music production, but with effects and meanings that were new to the genre.

RAP GETS "THE MESSAGE"

In rap music's first years as a commercial genre, samplers and sequencers did not exist; or more accurately, the ones that did exist had limited capacities and were prohibitively expensive. Even if such technologies had been

Example 1. Robert Walser's transcription of "Fight the Power," from his "Rhythm, Rhyme, and Rhetoric in the Music of Public Enemy" (1995). I have added annotations indicating the sample source of each line where possible.

readily accessible in 1979, there is no reason to suspect that rap's first producers would have used them. Seeking to replicate the success of "Rapper's Delight" and other early rap singles, such as Kurtis Blow's "The Breaks," producers like Sylvia Robinson of Sugar Hill Records worked with studio musicians to arrange and record beats for MCs to rap over. Translating the way hip hop DJs worked with breakbeats into a new form of songwriting, most producers set out to create a fun and danceable vibe evoking New York's disco and party jam culture.[25] When mainstream news outlets began picking up on the growing popularity of rap recordings, they tended to downplay the music's instrumental features and highlight instead the novelty of its vocal style. In 1982, however, Sugar Hill Records released a rap song of unprecedented force, prompting a reevaluation of the music's sonic elements. As producers began moving away from the "disco rap" sound, musical changes at the level of the song took on greater importance, and journalists sought to understand and interpret the growing significance of the music's beats.

Early in 1981, Sylvia Robinson approached Grandmaster Flash with a tape of something Ed Fletcher, the percussionist in Sugar Hill's house band, had written. Robinson was convinced that the recording held the key to Sugar Hill's next big hit, and she insisted that the group adopt the song and record it as soon as possible. Having recently made the transition from live club group to recordings artists, Flash and his group remained skeptical. He remembers that nobody liked it. "The shit was way too dark, way too edgy, and way too much of a downer. It was the furthest thing from a party rap anyone could imagine."[26] Flash remembers doing his best to forget about the tape. Not one to be deterred, Robinson hounded the group for almost a year until she convinced MC Melle Mel to begin recording the track without Flash's consent.

This inauspicious beginning led to one of the most critically acclaimed songs of 1982 and the most financially successful record for Sugar Hill since "Rapper's Delight." Grandmaster Flash and the Furious Five's 1982 hit single "The Message" provided a stark counterpoint to the party rhymes and call-and-response toasts of previous releases. The song's most memorable phrases—"It's like a jungle sometimes; it makes me wonder how I keep from going under" and "Don't push me 'cause I'm close to the edge"—captured the frustration of those living in America's inner-city neighborhoods. In contrast with previous party-oriented raps featuring light-humored toasting, "The Message" addressed the challenges of inner-city life under Reaganomics. As a song detailing the oppressive conditions of America's ghettos, it marked the beginning of a politically engaged, street-conscious approach to rap and opened the door for the genre to move into new thematic territory. Writing in 1984 about the change that "The Message" helped spawn, Nelson George et al. observed: "Where live rap once consisted of a series of catch-phrases cleverly ad-libbed and strung together, today's recorded raps tend to be story-oriented."[27]

Not surprisingly, "The Message" figures prominently in hip-hop historiography, and it has been discussed as an important political and artistic precedent.[28] Murray Forman explains that by departing from the thematic norms of hip hop's early days as party music, "The Message" signaled a profound shift in the genre's spatial dynamics.[29] By shifting the music's primary locus from the disco to the inner-city streets, the song "helped transform rap as a whole into a powerful cultural vehicle for the description of particular urban conditions of existence."[30] Although I agree with Forman's conclusions, "lyrical content and vocal presentation" alone cannot explain the impact of the recording.[31] "The Message" was not the first rap song to deal explicitly with sociopolitical concerns.[32] Although Forman may be correct in asserting that "The Message" did so with unprecedented clarity and force, it is important to acknowledge the role that musical decisions played in fostering this new seriousness. In addition to the song's politicized lyrics, "The Message" also announced a musical turning point, and its departure from genre-specific expectation was so great that the group did not originally want to record the song.[33] In fact, their objections to it were not only about the song's lyrics, but the musical features of its beat as well. Group member Kid Creole remembers: "When it came to 'The Message,' we were like, 'What in the hell is this? What are we doin' with this?' It's slow, it's plodding . . . the hook . . . what is it? We was used to all of the break records. . . . We was afraid of the song because we didn't think that it would work."[34]

Perhaps it is not surprising that this departure from the party-oriented sound of past recordings began with a song written by an outsider to the group, Sugar Hill studio percussionist Ed "Duke Bootee" Fletcher. Having established themselves as leaders of the Bronx's hip hop scene, Flash and the Furious Five were cultural insiders. As Kid Creole makes clear, their musical ideal revolved around the breakbeats that DJs like Grandmaster Flash spun for partygoers and on which early disco rap tracks were based. As a musician more seasoned in studio work, however, Fletcher seems to have approached songwriting differently. With its repetitive and neatly structured verse-chorus form, "The Message" reflects a more traditional approach to songwriting, compared to other contemporary rap songs that sounded more like excerpts from longer, open-ended party routines. What is more, in terms of sound quality, the track placed a new emphasis on

Example 2. Electronic synthesizer melody that appears repeatedly throughout Grandmaster Flash and the Furious Five's "The Message."

musical expression at the expense of hip hop's dance-oriented ideals. The song broadcast its seriousness through the use of mimetic devices. The opening lyrics, "Broken glass everywhere," are preceded by the sound of breaking glass. Elsewhere in the track, sounds imitating subway trains, screeching car tires, and police sirens help render the imagined urban space more vivid. The song even closes with a skit clearly reminiscent of Stevie Wonder's "Living for the City." As the beat continues to play, the group members act out a confrontation with the NYPD in which they are racially profiled, harassed, and arrested for no apparent reason.

In addition to such word painting and role playing, "The Message" initiated the development of new figurative meanings through its departure from established generic conventions: in this case a move away from disco-influenced dance beats. Jeff Chang characterizes "The Message" as "the grimmest, most downbeat rap ever heard" up to this point.[35] As Chang points out, the song's tempo was slower than other contemporary releases— as he puts it: "too slow to rock a party." At 100 BPM (beats per minute), "The Message" is in fact anywhere from 10 to 25 BPM slower than other contemporary releases, such as Afrika Bambaataa's "Planet Rock" (127 BPM) and the Sugarhill Gang's "Apache" (115 BPM). In addition, the timbres of the beat's elements are qualitatively different from other rap releases. The song's "harder, darker, more metallic sound," achieved in part through the use of synthesizer keyboards and electronic drums, created a vibe as cold as the city streets described in the song's lyrics.[36] Anchored by the synthesizer's slow and hypnotic vamp (transcribed in ex. 2), "The Message" lacks the propulsive dance energy found in disco rap songs, focusing listeners' attention more on the song's lyrics. The minor-key feeling of the track, reinforced by the synthesizer's ascending and descending pentatonic melody, adds to the song's edgy and dark sound.

Instead of boring listeners or scaring them away, as Flash and the Furious Five had feared, the departure from rap's dance-floor imperatives was celebrated by both fans and left-leaning music critics, who began speculating whether rap might end up providing a new vehicle for disenfranchised black youth to voice political concerns. "The Message" took top honors for best song in the *Village Voice*'s annual Pazz & Jop Critics' Poll. Earning praise unprecedented for a rap song, it convinced many skeptical listeners that the genre was more than a cheap fad. Writing for the *New York Times* in 1982, Robert Palmer gave a brief history of rap music culminating with "The Message," which, in his opinion, had "radically expanded the horizons of rap."[37] Writing for the *Washington Post*, Geoffrey Himes concluded: "During this past year of cutbacks and rollbacks, the sharpest cry of protest has come on a 12-inch single from Harlem: 'The Message' by Grandmaster Flash & the Furious Five."[38] Continuing on, Himes explained how the song's musical track symbolized entrapment, its "unwinding synthesizer" adding a "disturbing fatalism to the angry, dryly spoken rhymes."[39] Reviewing a Grandmaster Flash and the Furious Five performance in 1982, *New York Times* critic John Rockwell explained in a somewhat patronizing tone that although rap "has its limits" due to its lack of melodic development, the music cultivated an unusually refined sense of rhythm. By focusing almost exclusively on rhythm, he maintained, rap music fulfilled "what had been implied in so much earlier soul, disco and funk." It is no coincidence that this insight occurred to Rockwell at a concert where "The Message" served as the climactic number, which he describes as a "graphic depiction of the frustrations and anger of an urban black [audience]."[40]

Embedded within Rockwell's summation are two key ideas about rap music and race. First, through their repetitive rhythms, rap beats distill an undiluted musical blackness. Second, this audible racial difference places rap in a unique position to sound the political alarm for African Americans. Thus, by deliberately moving away from the up-tempo dance grooves of early rap songs, Sylvia Robinson's and Ed Fletcher's musical decisions helped transform how rap could sound black identity. As an example of social conflict projected through sound, "The Message" and its critical reception foreshadow Public Enemy's music and Pareles's writing about it six years later.

THE DRUM MACHINE ERA

By relying on the "harder" timbres of electronic instrumentation to achieve these results, "The Message" helped initiate an important stylistic shift in the genre, and the single suggested a new direction beyond the disco funk of rap's first years. In fact, the other major rap hit of 1982, Afrika Bambaataa's "Planet Rock," also demonstrated that producers were experimenting with new technologies. Working together in a Manhattan studio, Bambaataa, Arthur Baker, and John Robie crafted a futuristic-sounding track that relied on a variety of electronic sounds, including a Roland TR-808 drum machine. They programmed the 808 to match the drum track from "Numbers," a song by German electronic music group Kraftwerk. Robie also played the minor-key melody from another Kraftwerk track, "Trans-Europe Express," on a Fairlight synthesizer to provide the song's most memorable hook.[41] The resulting single spawned dozens of imitators and launched various genres and subgenres, including techno, electro, and Miami bass.

Within a year of "The Message" and "Planet Rock," Run-D.M.C., a young trio from Hollis, in Queens, popularized a "new school" aesthetic that definitively spelled the end of rap's first wave. Moving away from studio bands laying down replays of dance-music hits, Run-D.M.C centered their approach to production on the Oberheim DMX, one of a handful of newly released digital drum machines that were rapidly changing the sound of popular music. The device's maker and model number are significant because to choose a digital drum machine to work with in 1983 was to define in large part the sound of a recording. The sounds produced by an Oberheim DMX, or Roland TR-808, or Linn LM-1 were hard-wired into the equipment. Although the Oberheim DMX boasted a bank of drum sounds that had been sampled directly from acoustic instruments, the 12-bit sampling resolution (low by today's standards) and analog filtering introduced significant distortion. In other words, the preprogrammed sounds of the DMX (and those of its competitors) all had their own distinctive, electronic-sounding character.[42] If a producer wanted a different snare sound, for example, he or she would have to get it from another machine. These limitations would have been a drawback for some, but for rap groups like Run-D.M.C. drum machines provided a means of creatively reimagining aspects of the break-centered musical practice first developed by hip hop's DJ pioneers.

In the late 1970s Grandmaster Flash had developed a "beat box" routine in which he switched from looping breaks on his turntables to tapping out syncopated rhythms on a primitive Vox drum machine. The Vox machine that Flash used was purely electronic and lacked digital sequencing capabilities, meaning that Flash had to play the beats manually in real time. Digital drum machines like the DMX, however, made it possible to program a sequence of drum sounds into the machine's memory. Once loaded into memory, these sequences could be repeated (looped) indefinitely and arranged into any desired order. By pushing the right buttons, Run-D.M.C. producers Larry Smith and Rick Rubin could approximate the short breaks found on classic B-boy records, crafting syncopated rhythms and looping them in ways that mirrored the practices of hip hop's first DJs. Run-D.M.C. were essentially programming the DMX to play breaks, in some cases even copying rhythms directly from classic breakbeat records.

The memory limitations of the DMX—a total capacity of 2,000 "events"—also encouraged an approach to composition that seemed to mirror the hip hop DJ's practice of isolating and looping of breakbeats. Events—the sound of a single snare or hi-hat—could be organized in a variety of ways, from a single 2,000-note sequence to 2,000 different sequences of one note each. Because one song composed entirely as a single sequence could easily exhaust the memory of the machine, the makers of the DMX encouraged producers to think in terms of repeatable units, which could be looped and reconfigured indefinitely without taking up additional memory. In this way, producers could create large-scale forms from a collection of smaller units. As the user manual to the Oberheim DMX suggested: "In general, it is best to take advantage of the repetitive nature of music by constructing songs from short sequences. Each part of a song requires one-third as much memory as a single event in a sequence! A song consisting of one bar repeated eight times uses only one fifth the memory of an eight bar sequence."[43]

The default setting of the DMX was a sequence of two measures in 4/4 time. Although the makers of this early generation of digital drum machines most likely had the repetitive verse–chorus forms of other, more traditional popular music genres in mind, the sequencing capabilities of these machines perfectly suited the tastes and proclivities of rap music producers and hip hop DJs. Programming sequences into the memory banks of the DMX one measure at a time was akin to composing one's own breakbeats, which could then be looped effortlessly and endlessly by the machine. With a precision that might make Grandmaster Flash envious, the digital drum machine could be programmed to execute its own version of quick mix theory. Thus, producers creatively reimagined the break for the drum machine era, displacing the studio musicians who had laid down their own versions of popular breaks and newly written arrangements based on the disco funk of rap's early years.

Embracing both the capabilities and limits of the drum machine, Run-D.M.C. pared their instrumentation down to a minimum, at times featuring little more than the thundering kick and cracking snare of the DMX. As Tom Silverman, owner of Tommy Boy Records and someone who had witnessed at first hand rap's evolution as a commercial genre, explains, Run-D.M.C. had "scrapped the sixteenth-note hi-hats, ringing 9th and

6th chords, and slick vocal inflections that hip hop had carried over from disco." In its place, Silverman explained, were "booming" drums and "hollered" vocals, contributing to "headbanging rap at its hardest."[44] As critic John Leland put it, Run-D.M.C. and other groups that followed in their wake represented "a fierce, dislocating clash between old-school funk/rap and new, electronic hardcore hip hop."[45] The group's 1983 debut single, "It's Like That" b/w "Sucker MCs," introduced this harder sound.

"It's Like That" was the group's obvious and self-conscious attempt to emulate the streetwise social critique of "The Message," and it featured a similar beat, complete with sharp synthesizer stabs and drum machine rolls, not to mention a tempo even *slower* than the Furious Five's seminal hit. But it was the record's B-side, a swaggering toast entitled "Sucker MCs," that generated the most interest from New York radio.[46] For "Sucker MCs" Run-D.M.C.'s producer Larry Smith programmed the DMX to create a four-measure loop consisting of the drum machine's stock sounds: hand-claps, bass kick, snare, and a closing hi-hat (fig. 9).

The only other sound featured in "Sucker MCs" backing track is Jam Master Jay scratching on his turntables, which were connected directly to the studio's mixing console. Thus, Run-D.M.C. pioneered a studio-produced version of Flash's beat box routine while adding a new twist: With Jam Master Jay on the turntables in the studio, the group could add scratching and snippets of other records to the track, suggesting that all of the sounds in the beat, including the drum machine, were under the immediate control of a DJ. Much of the music produced during rap's drum machine era (roughly 1983–86) followed this logic.

To a certain extent the new school brought the DJ back into the music, although now as more sidekick than star. One of Run-D.M.C.'s next singles, "Jam Master Jay" (1983) devoted its lyrics to praising the skills of their DJ and showcased what Jay (and producer Larry Smith) had been able to do in the studio by combining drum machines and turntable-manipulated breaks. Despite a renewed emphasis on turntable skills, these changes were no nostalgic return to the days of old. Run-D.M.C. introduced a fresh mode of self-representation to the genre that was heavily rap-centric, so much so that they are regarded as the originators of the "new school." Their posturing and fashion sense—the cross-armed b-boy stance, athletic suits, leather jackets, and shell-toe sneakers—as well as their sharper, more percussive lyrical flows, helped distance them from the disco era and finalized the relocation of rap music from the clubs to the rough inner-city streets.[47] *Village Voice* writer Gary Jardim described the beats of "It's Like That" b/w

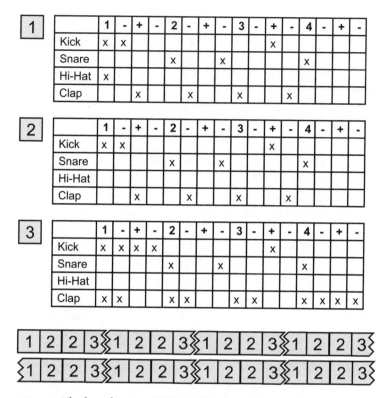

Figure 9. The beat for Run-D.M.C.'s "Sucker MCs," represented as a looped arrangement of three one-measure sequences.

"Sucker MCs" as "battering ram percussion," conjuring an image of the police weapon used to break down doors in a sting operation.[48] This shift in attitude and style was conscious: Russell Simmons (the group's manager and Run's older brother) and the group members themselves often expressed disdain for disco rap's costuming and fantasy play, and the hard-hitting sound of their beats provided the perfect support for their new image.[49] As Run-D.M.C. continued to work with producers in the studio to develop a characteristic sound, Simmons and his associates remained closely attached, developing a marketing plan to broaden the group's fan base. As they experienced breakthrough success in the mid-1980s, Run-D.M.C.'s music (and the critical discourse surrounding it) helped to rebrand rap music and reconfigure the racialized meanings that had become associated with its sound.

BLACK ROCK AND ROLL

Run-D.M.C.'s stylistic departure from disco rap reflected the ambition of the new school, in particular that of budding industry mogul Russell Simmons, who, from the very beginning of his career in music, sought to move his clients beyond the commercial ghetto that had constrained previous rap acts. Simmons's business strategy targeted new audiences and focused on changing public perceptions about the music's cultural value and financial potential. Doing so, however, meant reaching the same market demographics that detested disco, and Simmons's strategy for bridging this gap was clear: rap needed to move in on the space that the popular music industry had reserved for white rockers. By introducing a sparse, drum machine-centered sound, Run-D.M.C. had begun moving the genre in a new direction, and the group's next step was not particularly subtle. Songs such as "Rock Box" (1984) and "King of Rock" (1985) added electric guitar riffs and wailing rock solos to the group's hard drum machine beats. The music video for "King of Rock" even showed the duo bum rushing a fictional Museum of Rock 'n' Roll (staffed by Larry "Bud" Melman, the character creation of comedian Calvert DeForest). Moving through the exhibit, Run-D.M.C. irreverently mock rock and roll pioneers, including not only white singer Buddy Holly but also Michael Jackson, whose dance hits carried a disco sensibility into the heart of 1980s pop. This self-conscious engagement with rock music culminated with "Walk This Way," the group's best-selling single from *Raising Hell* (1986) and a rap remake of white rock group Aerosmith's song of the same name.[50] A Boston-bred, blues-based hard rock group, Aerosmith's popularity had peaked in the mid-1970s, and the stylistic fusion of "Walk This Way" simultaneously reinvigorated their career and opened the door for rap music to reach a larger, whiter audience.

By engaging rock music directly, Run-D.M.C. did more than bring black music to a white audience. They helped scramble racialized genre codes to transform what rap songs could mean and to whom they could direct their messages. Although many listeners heard the collaboration between the black rappers and white rockers as a novelty, Aerosmith's song was no stranger to hip hop circles. The song's break—its opening two measures featuring only drums and then four measures adding Joe Perry's signature guitar riff—had been used in clubs by hip hop DJs since the 1970s (fig. 10).

Some have gone as far as to claim that "Walk This Way" was not a departure from past practices within the culture at all, but instead reflected hip hop's long engagement with a variety of sound sources.[51] To look upon

Guitar Enters

Figure 10. Break (first six measures)
from Aerosmith's "Walk This Way."

Run-D.M.C.'s collaboration with Aerosmith as a return to the "genre-less" days of early hip hop, however, would be a mistake.[52] As I will argue, the imagery of the song's music video as well as its sonic elements were deliberately crafted to suggest a meeting and reconciliation between two distinct racialized genres: rap and rock.

In the music video, which received ample airplay on MTV, Run-D.M.C. attempt to rehearse in a room adjacent to Aerosmith, whose noisy performance distracts and annoys the DJ and two rappers. The members of Aerosmith remain oblivious to their neighbors' plight until Run-D.M.C. devise an appropriate response: Jam Master Jay gets behind the turntables and begins playing a loud drum break, which vocalist Steven Tyler and guitarist Joe Perry instantly seem to recognize as the opening to "Walk This Way." Just as Tyler is about to begin singing, however, the two rappers interrupt him by beginning his verse. Frustrated by this intrusion, Tyler begins using his microphone stand as a battering ram, breaking through the wall separating the two groups just in time to sing the song's chorus. After Tyler both literally and figuratively breaks the wall separating the two groups (and races), Run-D.M.C. return the favor by crashing an Aerosmith concert. The ensuing collaborative performance provides a number of black/white juxtapositions that highlight popular music's generic codes. Tyler exemplifies the long-haired, androgynous style of hard rock. Wearing tight-fitting pants and a jacket that reveals his skinny, bare chest, he dances acrobatically across the stage, contorting his face wildly as he sings. Adopting a cooler, more measured attitude, Run-D.M.C. descend a staircase to the stage dressed in black with leather jackets and Adidas shell-toe sneakers, typifying the street-smart look of black New York. Posing with arms crossed across their chests or gesturing rhythmically as they rap, they present a harder image. The video climaxes with the reconciliation of these visual extremes. Although Tyler initially appears distraught when an electric sign proclaiming "Run-D.M.C." descends onto the stage, he soon relents, joining the two rappers in their verse. The three performers even engage in some choreographed dancing, moving together to the music for the first time in the video. By depicting both groups triumphantly sharing the stage (and audience), the video symbolizes rap's transgression of racialized musical boundaries.

In conjunction with such visual symbolism, the music of "Walk This Way" and other songs on *Raising Hell* did more than embody the transcendence of genre categories. Through their mixture of racialized sounds, Run-D.M.C.'s production sought to expand the cultural meanings and significance attached to rap as a genre. This hybridization of sonic signifiers was at the heart of the song's conception: Run-D.M.C.'s recording of "Walk This Way" is a rapped version of a rock song that follows the verse–chorus form of the original scrupulously. (For what it is worth, Joe Perry's guitar solo is even longer on the Run-D.M.C. version than on the Aerosmith original.) However, despite the electric guitar, vocals, and structure inherited from the Aerosmith version, producer Rick Rubin and Jam Master Jay assembled the backing track in such a way as to privilege rap music aesthetics and highlight the importance of the break.

Compare, for example, the opening of Run-D.M.C.'s "Walk This Way" to Aerosmith's original. Rather than have Aerosmith's drummer, Joey Kramer, replay the opening live in the studio, Rick Rubin programmed the DMX to emulate the break's rhythm. Then Aerosmith's Joe Perry and Steven Tyler rerecorded the song's signature guitar riff and vocals *over* this new drum machine track. In other words, Run-D.M.C.'s cover of "Walk This Way" retains the characteristic drum machine timbres and rhythmic feel of the group's other songs.[53] Rather than have two black MCs simply rap over a rock track, the rock song was rebuilt from the ground up and translated into a rap song. As he did in other tracks like "Sucker MCs," Jam Master Jay overdubbed scratches that suggest that the entire beat was itself under the control of a DJ. We can hear this musical illusion clearly in the five-minute album version of the song, whose opening measures extend the break and loop it multiple times before the entrance of the guitar riff. Joe Perry even adds a three-note pickup to the beginning of his signature guitar riff, giving his performance a stuttering effect that sounds like a DJ rhythmically "cutting" a small portion from the third measure of the break before allowing the record to play (fig. 11).

Will Fulton, a former producer and A&R (artists and repertoire) executive for Profile Records, witnessed the techniques that gave rise to these effects. By the 1990s, when Fulton worked with Run-D.M.C., sampling and sequencing devices, such as the E-mu SP-1200 and Akai MPC 60, had already revolutionized rap music production, but Run-D.M.C. still preferred to make music "the old way," like they had for the *Raising Hell*

Figure 11. Opening of Run-D.M.C.'s "Walk This Way" represented as a function of the original Aerosmith break as if manipulated by a DJ using two copies of the recording. (Wavy black lines indicate scratching.)

album.[54] Fulton explains that the sound engineer reserved two of the studio's twenty-four tracks for Jam Master Jay's turntables. This way Jay could use overdubbing to precisely loop a breakbeat, scratch percussive accents, or "punch in" snippets of sound from his record collection.[55] Jam Master Jay exploits this technique in "Walk This Way," looping the original drum break directly from Aerosmith's original to provide a beat for the song's second verse. Although this approach drew on the foundational DJ practice of looping breakbeats, Run-D.M.C.'s sound was not a purist's attempt to take hip hop back to its origins. Using drum machines and contemporary studio technology, the group created something that had not been heard before. In addition to Run-D.M.C.'s rapped verses, Rick Rubin and Jam Master Jay blended genre-specific stylistic features, such as the electric guitar and turntable scratching. This musical hybridization not only transformed "Walk This Way" into a rap song but suggested that rap was more like rock (and vice versa) than many listeners might have previously thought.

The strategy of mixing rap and rock (read as black and white) musical signifiers pervades the album and reaches far beyond the highly visible collaboration between Run-D.M.C. and Aerosmith. In addition to "Walk This Way," the songs "It's Tricky" and "Raising Hell" from the *Raising Hell* album also prominently feature distortion-laced electric guitars. The chorus of "It's Tricky" even includes a similarly famous guitar riff from the Knack's hit "My Sharona," which Jam Master Jay cut into the studio mix on his turntables.[56] In contrast, however, other songs on *Raising Hell*, such as "Peter Piper," "My Adidas," and "Proud to Be Black" eschewed the timbre of the electric guitar in favor of funky breakbeats that harkened directly back to hip hop's earliest days. The track "Peter Piper," for example, combines the DMX drum machine and portions of Bob James's "Take Me To the Mardi Gras," a recording whose funky bell pattern made it a favorite of b-boys and DJs in hip hop's early years.[57]

If this mixture of rock and rap signifiers worked to expand Run-D.M.C.'s appeal with white audiences, then it is telling that the same strategy was employed to launch Russell Simmons' and Rick Rubin's other crossover success of 1986: the Beastie Boys' album *Licensed to Ill*. The Beastie Boys, who for a time were the highest-selling act in the history of rap as well as the first commercially successful white rap group, managed to appeal to both black and white fans with a similar blend of sounds. The group's plat-inum-selling *Licensed to Ill* featured songs that mixed drum machines and electric guitars, including "Rhymin and Stealin," "She's Crafty," and "No Sleep Till Brooklyn"; while other songs on the album, including "The New Style," "Posse In Effect," "Paul Revere," and "Hold It Now, Hit It," sounded like a pastiche of classic breakbeat records, as had Run-D.M.C.'s "Peter Piper."[58]

It would be simplistic to assume that the blend of stylistic elements in Run-D.M.C.'s and the Beastie Boys' albums were successful because white audiences liked electric guitars and black audiences liked drums (a proposi-tion comedian Dave Chappelle hilariously satirizes in one of his comedic sketches).[59] The sounds that these albums mixed were associated with racially coded genre expectations, not tied to human bodies in any essential way. By mixing drum machines, electric guitars, breakbeats, and scratching, the Beastie Boys and Run-D.M.C. were renegotiating what rap could *mean*. *Raising Hell* and *Licensed to Ill* encouraged listeners to hear breakbeats as capturing the same defiant, youthful, and care-free attitude that electric guitars had long symbolized. As a genre, rap moved decisively away from the perceived decadence and fantasy of disco clubs and toward an in-your-face attitude and antiestablishment rebelliousness that had been heretofore reserved for white rockers. And by doing so they reached back even further, reclaiming for black artists a place in U.S. popular culture which owed its very existence to African American musicians.

As producer and Def Jam co-owner Rick Rubin argued in explaining the logic behind the new school's sound, "Rap records are really black rock and roll records, the antithesis of disco."[60] Rubin's use of the adjective "black" reveals the irony that by the mid-1980s rock and roll, which has its roots in black rhythm and blues, now seemed to exclude African American perform-ers. Also ironic is his identification of rap as the polar opposite of disco (see chapter 1). In doing so, Rubin sought to elevate rap's standing by appealing to the same anti-disco sentiments that had pigeonholed black musicians in rap's first years as a commercial genre. Elaborating on this strategy to cast rap as rock reborn, Def Jam publicist Bill Adler sought to decouple rock's privileged genre positioning from its particular sonic signifiers, explaining: "Rappers make rock and roll. My notion of rock and roll isn't pegged to a big, noisy guitar. I think rock and roll has always been about attitude and rhythm; it's about aggression, rebellion, sex, and a big beat."[61]

Critics certainly did not miss the musical messaging, and they helped confirm rap's reconstructed significance. In his 1986 review of *Raising Hell*, for example, J. D. Considine described Run-D.M.C.'s work as proof that rap can be as "loud and aggressive as any [heavy] metal act."[62] Robert Palmer followed with a lengthy feature for the *New York Times* outlining the similarities between rap music and early rock and roll. "The rock hits of the 50's had a rawer, more abrasive sound than the period's mainstream pop; think of Jerry Lee Lewis's 'Great Balls of Fire' compared to Patti Page's 'How Much Is That Doggie in the Window.' The Lewis record created excitement and made its point with minimal instrumentation, just drums, piano and a voice. Similarly, rap is a sparse, stripped-down style, mostly performed by one or more vocalists, a disk jockey and an electronic drum machine."[63] As a blues historian and rock aficionado himself, Palmer was well aware of the source of Jerry Lee Lewis's "rawness." In comparing the abrasiveness of early rock and roll to rap, he was aligning the culture of contemporary inner-city streets to the "deep" African American origins of rock music in the south. Even if the connection was not meant so literally, Palmer's message was clear: like rock and roll pioneers before them, rap musicians were bringing an authentic, raw (read as black) form of expression into mainstream U.S. culture.

As the racialized language of marketing and music criticism reveals, *Raising Hell* and *Licensed to Ill* helped reconfigure the generic expectations that listeners held for rap, promoting the idea that rapping, drum machines, and breakbeats could serve the same audiences as rock. The success of *Licensed to Ill* and *Raising Hell* was not in the way they exploited existing genre boundaries, but rather the way they redefined what rap meant, how it could sound, and to whom it could appeal. Def Jam's two most popular groups put forward a bold musical argument that challenged previous understandings of genre and race: *Rap is the new rock.*

This mainstreaming of rap occurred at precisely the same moment that the news media, law enforcement agencies, and state and federal politics began turning attention toward inner-city gangs and the crack cocaine "epidemic," two related issues racially coded in public discourse as black. Just as these issues were being constructed as an imminent danger in need of containment, a Run-D.M.C. concert in Long Beach, California was marred by gang fights that escalated into a small-scale riot. Some mainstream media outlets, such as *People* magazine, seized on the event and suggested that rap was at least partly responsible for attracting violent "ghettobred street gangs" to public venues.[64] Run-D.M.C. adamantly denied such charges, arguing that their music had a positive, anti-gang message. They cast the blame instead on the lack of security personnel and on the gang members themselves who instigated the violence.[65] Despite their arguments, the association between rap and the threat of violence stuck, leading some venues to limit or stop booking rap acts, in part because of the higher insurance costs associated with them in the wake of the Long Beach melee. As Rose explains, "rap-related violence" became another "facet of the contemporary 'urban crisis' that consists of a 'rampant drug culture' and 'wilding gangs' of black and Hispanic youths."[66]

Run-D.M.C., Russell Simmons, Bill Adler, and others in the industry issued statements protesting such characterizations as not only unfair but also part of the ongoing history of racial oppression in the United States. Writing for *The Washington Post*, Richard Harrington agreed, portraying the group as hardworking musicians on tour simply doing their best to cope with the country's hostile racial environment.[67] Yet there was a certain irony to Run-D.M.C.'s predicament, given that their publicists and staunchest defenders were the same people currently praising and promoting rap as "aggressive," the kind of music that "says 'fuck you' to society," an "authentically rebellious" alternative at a moment when rock and roll had become "sleepy" and "safe."[68] By basing their promotion of rap music in a discourse extolling its raw power and antisocial attitude, Russell Simmons, Def Jam Records, and other proponents of the new school left themselves vulnerable to discourses that constructed blackness as a threat. In short, the new rap authenticity came with a price. In the following two years, Run-D.M.C.'s hard-edged sound would be adopted and transformed by Public Enemy, a group Russell Simmons once incidentally described as "Black punk rock."[69] Where Run-D.M.C. sought to diffuse the perception that their music was dangerous and threatening, Public Enemy would not. As their name suggests, they were more than willing to embrace their role as the enemy.

REVOLUTIONIZING THE BREAK

"Bring the Noise," the first song on Public Enemy's critically acclaimed 1988 album *It Takes a Nation of Millions to Hold Us Back*, begins with the sound of Malcolm X's voice. The group sampled two phrases from a recording of his speech, "Message to the Grassroots," which was delivered in Detroit, Michigan, on November 10, 1963. Public Enemy was drawn to two excerpts from the following passage: "The same white element that put Kennedy in power—labor, the Catholics, the Jews, and liberal Protestants; [the] same clique that put Kennedy in power, joined the march on Washington. It's just like when you've got some coffee that's too black, which means it's too strong. What you do? You integrate it with cream; you make it weak. If you pour too much cream in, you won't even know you ever had coffee."[70]

In this part of the speech, Malcolm X critiques the influence of white interests on the civil rights agenda. Using the image of coffee being diluted with cream, he argues for stronger, more independent black leadership, reflecting the growing division between civil rights and black power organizations at the time. Zeroing in on just four words from this passage, Public Enemy extracted the phrases "too black" and "too strong," arranging them into a new, succinct statement. Rendering these phrases in tandem and repeating them, the group transformed Malcolm X's metaphor about political leadership into a forceful summation of their identity as artists: "too black, too strong; too black, too strong."

Public Enemy's digital manipulation of Malcolm X's voice was more than a game of semantics; it also spoke to the group's approach to music production. By "chopping" and looping a recording of "Message to the Grassroots," they had creatively hijacked Malcolm X's words, redirecting them to suit their immediate needs.[71] Placing these two short phrases in relief, the group heightened their impact, not by amplifying Malcolm's original point (only a small percentage of contemporary listeners would identify the speech's original context), but by bringing out the qualities and associations listeners immediately had with Malcolm's voice and his words in their new configuration. In just seconds, Public Enemy demonstrate exactly how they plan on manipulating breakbeats.

Similarly to Run-D.M.C., Public Enemy's approach to music production revolved around a creative reconceptualization of the break. In addition to recordings of Malcolm X and other political leaders, the Bomb Squad revisited many of the same breakbeat records used by hip hop's first DJs. Employing digital sampling to isolate and assemble relatively brief sonic events into a new collage, Public Enemy helped redefine which parts of these records could count as breaks. Their music combined aspects of Run-D.M.C.'s heavy, drum machine sound with dense vertical layering, repositioning the break as a noisy signifier of resistance and confrontation.

To arrive at their characteristic sound, Public Enemy drew directly on a technique pioneered by Queensbridge, New York–based producer Marley Marl. Marl, who rose to prominence as a main player in two early hip hop "beefs" (the Bridge Wars between MC Shan and KRS-One, and the Roxanne Wars), was the first to realize that newly available sampling technology could allow producers to move beyond the limitations of a drum machine's stock sounds. Marl realized that sampling and sequencing technology allowed him to capture drum sounds from any recording, radically expanding his sonic palette. Taking aim at the style popularized by Run-D.M.C., he quipped that his innovation meant "no more of that dull DMX shit."[72]

As early as 1984, Marl began mining the drum sounds in his collection of breakbeat records, rearranging them with a digital sequencer to create new rhythm tracks.[73] On singles such as "Eric B Is President" and "I Know You Got Soul," he used the E-Mu SP-12 sampler-sequencer (the predecessor to the more powerful and popular SP-1200) to assemble beats by layering snatches of sound from different records.[74] Consider the beat for "I Know You Got Soul," which blended the drums from the opening measures of Funkadelic's "You'll Like It Too" with a break from Bobby Byrd's "I Know You Got Soul."[75]

The four-measure drum break from "You'll Like It Too" begins with a half-measure fill. To create a looped sequence that repeats every four measures, Marl truncated the fourth measure of the break, cutting back to the opening half-measure drum fill on the third beat of the fourth measure.[76] In essence, he composed a new drum pattern in which the beginning of the break begins to function as its end, becoming a turnaround that leads us back to the break's beginning (fig. 12). Schloss describes effects such as these as fundamental to sample-based hip hop: the way a loop "automatically recasts any musical material it touches, insofar as the end of a phrase is repeatedly juxtaposed with its beginning in a way that was not intended by the original musician."[77] In a sense, this manipulation of a break to give rise to new patterns harkens back to Grandmaster Flash's Audobon performance (explored in the previous chapter). But instead of repeatedly shifting how the break is looped to create a spontaneous "remix," Marl locks the loop into place as the foundation for the entire song, allowing it to take on its own "air of inevitability."[78]

On top of this loop, Marl adds another break that he sampled from the opening of Bobby Byrd's "I Know You Got Soul," a single measure that features a prominent guitar riff and drums. He loops this short break evenly so that it repeats continuously on the downbeat of every measure. Layering

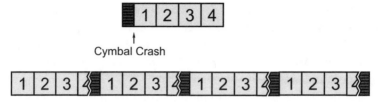

Figure 12. Funkadelic's "You'll Like It Too" break and the new loop Marley Marl created from it. (The shaded portion represents the half-measure drum fill.)

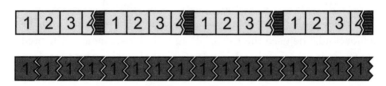

Figure 13. Marley Marl's composite break for Eric B and Rakim's "I Know You Got Soul," featuring the breaks from Funkadelic's "You'll Like It Too" and Bobby Byrd's "I Know You Got Soul."

these two samples gives rise to a composite break that forms the backbone of Eric B and Rakim's "I Know You Got Soul" (fig. 13).

Although not technically impossible before the advent of sampling and sequencing devices, constructing beats like this one the "old way" (à la Run-D.M.C.'s Jam Master Jay, Larry Smith, and Rick Rubin) would have involved laborious overdubbing. Using sampling and sequencing technology, however, producers could render any snippet of sound endlessly repeatable. This new method meant that producers could draw directly from breakbeat records and loop their samples perfectly without time-consuming studio acrobatics. What is more, sampling helped reveal new possibilities, such as truncating and repeating samples like the drum break from "You'll Like It Too," that producers quickly embraced as fundamental to the compositional process. Freeing producers from the rhythmic rigidity and sonic limitations of digital drum machines like the Oberheim DMX or Roland TR-808, Marley Marl's beats helped usher in a new stylistic era where the distinctive timbres and "live" rhythmic feel of 1960s and 1970s soul and funk recordings permeated rap music. Yet, the introduction of sampling and sequencing did not amount to a complete departure from the

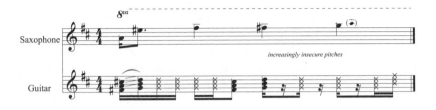

The J.B.'s, "The Grunt, Pt. 1"

James Brown, "Funky Drummer, Pt. 1"

Figure 14. One-measure breaks looped in Public Enemy's "Rebel Without a Pause."

practices and sounds of the recent past. As we have seen, Run-D.M.C.'s Jam Master Jay had already begun mixing breakbeat records with programmed drum machine beats and live studio instrumentation in tracks such as "Walk This Way" and "Peter Piper." Public Enemy's celebrated style arose from an intensification and transformation of this approach, which was enabled by the new technology.

Public Enemy reportedly conceived of their song "Rebel Without a Pause" as the "evil twin" of Eric B and Rakim's "I Know You Got Soul."[79] To build the track for the song, the Bomb Squad combined electronic drum machine sounds and turntable scratching with a variety of sampled loops (fig. 14): one taken from James Brown's "Funky Drummer" and another featuring the squealing saxophone glissando from the opening of the J.B.s'

"The Grunt."[80] For the song's chorus, DJ Terminator X used turntables to cut in vocals from Chubb Rock's "Rock 'n' Roll Dude," adding yet another layer to an already dense groove.[81] Noting these various layers of sound in "Rebel Without a Pause" helps to explain why Chuck D once described the Bomb Squad's aesthetic as putting "loops on top of loops on top of loops."[82]

As has already been mentioned, the way digital sampling was used to construct new cyclical grooves mirrors the practice of cutting and looping developed by the Bronx's first hip hop DJs. Moreover, the samples themselves—in this case two recordings featuring James Brown's exceptionally funky band—come from breakbeat records that would have been a part of any early hip hop DJ's collection.[83]

Although prior DJ practices and earlier approaches to beat making clearly influenced Public Enemy's single, it is also clear that the Bomb Squad set out to use these techniques to create a particular effect important to "Rebel Without a Pause," whose main theme is the rebelliousness of Chuck D (and by extension, Public Enemy). Compared to the song's predecessors discussed earlier in this chapter—"The Message," "Sucker MCs," "Walk This Way," and "I Know You Got Soul"—the groove for "Rebel Without a Pause" is the most tightly wound; its most prominent features—the high-pitched saxophone and drum break—repeat relentlessly every measure. What is more, the sounds that the group selected have qualities that suit the group's expressive goals. The song's harsh timbres and clashing rhythms gave rise to the sound of insistence that Pareles described as "uncompromisingly confrontational" and that the group itself referred to in song titles such as "Bring the Noise," "Louder Than a Bomb," and "Countdown To Armageddon." Listening to "Rebel Without a Pause" in the broader context of rap music's first decade reveals both a continuity of practice—hip hop's obsession with breakbeats—and specific details about how these practices change and are strategically deployed to create specific effects and meanings. It is the dialectical relationship between these two features—cultural influence and creative agency—that is critical to understanding how Public Enemy arrived at its sound.

For example, a key creative difference between earlier hip hop and rap music and "Rebel Without a Pause" resulted from the selection of breaks on these records and the duration and frequency with which they were looped. The saxophone glissando from "The Grunt" (transcribed in fig. 14), which forms the most prominent element in the groove (likely one of the elements Jon Pareles had in mind when discussing the album's "repeated, nagging, wavering sounds that could probably drill through a foot of sound-proofing"), differed dramatically from the breakbeats looped by earlier DJs and producers. Earlier hip hop DJs and rap producers had primarily sought out breaks featuring percussion grooves that could be looped or interpolated to form the foundation of a new track. It is difficult to imagine anyone before Public Enemy selecting something like the piercing opening measure of "The Grunt" as a viable break. That they conceived of "Rebel Without a Pause" as the "evil twin" of Eric B and Rakim's "I Know You Got Soul" gives us a clue as to the expressive intent behind the selection of such a noisy break. In addition, early sampling technology was predisposed to favor selections of short duration. Although producers could arrange these samples in any way they saw fit or loop them continuously throughout a track with ease, the limited memory capacity of early samplers meant that not much more than two seconds of any break could be captured at a time. The two samples in Public Enemy's "Rebel Without a Pause," each just one measure in length, adapted these limitations to the fundamental logic of rap production.[84] As the Bomb Squad's chief producer, Hank Shocklee, recalls: "'Rebel' is interesting because that was originally done with the only sampler that I had at the time, which was the [Ensoniq] Mirage. And the Mirage, if you know the Mirage, it's a 4-bit sampler that gives you three seconds of sample time and that's it. And it was [as if] the stars lined it up for me. I was doing this thing . . . and I was trying to catch it, and I caught the right piece of it in three seconds."[85]

Of course memory capacity alone did not determine the shape that rap music would adopt. Like Run-D.M.C. working with drum machines before them, Public Enemy applied the new technology to hip hop cultural paradigms in a way that suited their musical tastes and expressive needs. Where Run-D.M.C. had drawn upon the sound of distorted electric guitars to match their defiant attitude, Public Enemy cultivated a sample-based approach to conveying a similarly rebellious sensibility. The "The Grunt" loop demonstrates how the hip hop DJ's library of breakbeat records could be mined to forge a new take on the black rock and roll sound. By finding, redeploying, and looping short snippets of sound from breakbeat records— especially those parts that previous DJs might have heard as too noisy or brief to be useful—Public Enemy redefined what parts of their records could count as breaks. This innovation allowed the group to develop its characteristically intense sounding style, and it also dramatically expanded the possibilities for future producers working with breaks. For sample-based producers after Public Enemy, "a break [was] any expanse of music that is *thought of as a break* by a producer."[86] Although they were not the first musicians to use sampling technology to chop and loop preexisting records, Public Enemy revolutionized the break as a concept that encompassed a wider world of sound types. At the same time, their use of breaks to support and amplify their militant imagery and lyrics also brought a black radical sensibility to rap music.

The emergence of such intensely politicized rap at the end of the 1980s testified to the contradictions facing black Americans in post–civil rights America. African Americans who came of age just after the civil rights and Black Power movements lived in a world where the rhetoric of racial equality had been adopted by numerous institutions, but severe racial disparities in health, housing, employment, and education remained.[87] "Impeach the president/Pulling out the ray-gun," Chuck D rapped on "Rebel Without a Pause," creating a pun that connected the Honey Drippers' widely sampled breakbeat to the current president of the United States.[88] Coming at the end of Ronald Reagan's second term, "Rebel Without a Pause" was released into a context where the United States had rolled back public spending and eliminated social programs that sought to ameliorate the effects of poverty and joblessness. The song hit the airwaves in a country where the so-called War on Drugs targeted inner-city communities and where African Americans made up a disproportionate number of those arrested and incarcerated for nonviolent drug crimes. (In fact, the U.S. prison population—today the world's largest—doubled under the Reagan administration.) Public Enemy sought to sound an alarm about these and other problems. Their logo, an image of a black man caught in the crosshairs of a rifle scope, spoke to Chuck D's belief that "Black people in America are at war."[89] With highly publicized cases of African Americans dying at the hands of police and white vigilantes echoing in the media, such sentiments need to be understood as more than paranoia.

Public Enemy's music, Jeff Chang explains, entered a world hungry for black leadership. Jesse Jackson's 1984 bid for the U.S. presidency under the slogan "Keep Hope Alive" had promised "a grand synthesis of the civil rights and Black power agendas," but eventually ran aground amid charges of anti-Semitism.[90] The demise of Jackson's Rainbow Coalition created a political vacuum for strong leadership on questions of race and inequality, and Public Enemy's music seemed to reanimate the black radicalism suppressed through more traditional political avenues. Name-checking the Black Panthers and the Nation of Islam, the group reintroduced political symbols and slogans to a generation too young to have participated directly in the civil rights and Black Power movements. With his booming baritone voice, Chuck D embodied the role of a leader, a new image of blackness that was harder, more serious, and more politically engaged than any previous

MC. Public Enemy's lyrics and iconography sampled and remixed various strands of black politics and culture. The group invoked the African American past (e.g., Malcolm X and the Black Panthers), while also referencing contemporary leaders, such as Jesse Jackson and Minister Louis Farrakhan. Drawing on iconic political images and imbuing them with new meaning, the group sought to reanimate Black Nationalism for contemporary audiences. Writing for the *New York Times,* Stephen Holden argued that Public Enemy's call to bring the noise "is not just the sound of boom boxes blaring out rap on American city streets, but angry, organized black separatism."[91]

In their work on racial formation, Michael Omi and Howard Winant introduce the Gramscian term "rearticulation," which they define as "the processes of redefinition of political interests and identities, through a process of recombination of familiar ideas and values in hitherto unrecognized ways."[92] By historicizing Public Enemy's musical style, which was first codified in the single "Rebel Without a Pause," we have been tracing a process that I believe we can hear as the musical analogue to processes of racial formation. The recordings and DJ-derived musical practices that Public Enemy used had been a part of hip hop since DJs first spun breakbeat records in the 1970s. Using sampling technology, drum machines, and turntables to extend and transform the approaches to beat making pioneered by earlier groups, Public Enemy was able to redeploy these sounds and concepts in ways that would have been difficult to imagine just a few years earlier. Their unique approach to sound also distinguished them from their contemporaries. Many groups released critically acclaimed albums in 1988 that featured sample-based musical tracks, but none attracted the kind of attention that Public Enemy did. Reading through accounts of their music, one finds that they attracted attention not just for their fashion sense or pro-black lyrics, but also for something that was audible in their "all-out assault on the eardrums."[93] And this new sonic portrayal of black identity emerged from the way that familiar techniques and ideas were recombined in "hitherto unrecognized ways." Although rap music's stylistic evolution from 1979 onward depended on the way producers worked with breakbeats, the quality of sounds that producers sought out and the vibe they created with them differed markedly. These musical developments form part of the process by which race has been "rearticulated" by rap artists.

Similarly to their appropriation of Nation of Islam rhetoric and Black Panther uniforms, Public Enemy's particular approach to sample-based production sought to remix aspects of the black musical past. Consider Bomb Squad member Hank Shocklee's explanation of the relationship between James Brown's music and the tracks that he helped craft for Public Enemy:

> What was really cool about the James Brown records was the fact that he controlled the band. He was a conductor at the same time as he was a singer. . . The other part that made him really incredible was he created a signature scream. I bought James Brown, not because of the groove and the beat, but because I was waiting to hear him scream in the record. And that was the highlight for me. And that scream is the characteristic trait of his signature. You knew his records out of anybody's records that you heard that were playing on the radio. That scream is to me what got me to replicate that same vibration with Public Enemy. Because now instead of it being a scream, I wanted to use an instrument that created that same scream. So this way, you could know that this was a different record from anything else.[94]

Shocklee provocatively equates the construction of sample-based rap music with Brown's role as the conductor of his band. And he calls attention to the scream, an utterance of distinctive timbre, as a marker of musical difference that can be remade and updated for expressive purposes. These ideas align well with Afrocentric discourse about black musical difference, theorized by musicians and scholars, including Olly Wilson, Amiri Baraka, and Samuel Floyd, Jr.[95] For example, arguing for cultural continuities between Afro-American and African music, composer and scholar Olly Wilson writes: "The essence of their Africanness is not a static body of something which can be depleted but rather a conceptual approach, the manifestations of which are infinite. The common core of this Africanness consists of the way of doing something, not simply something that is done."[96] To support his thesis regarding the "heterogeneous sound ideal," Wilson defines a number of characteristically black approaches to musicking, including timbral diversity, sonic density, and polyrhythm.[97] By crafting beats that were more timbrally diverse, sonically dense, and funkily polyrhythmic than anything that had preceded them, Public Enemy constructed a sonic analogue of cultural nationalism to match their lyrics and imagery. Public Enemy's music didn't just confirm a black aesthetic; like Amiri Baraka's description of black music's "changing same," it reimagined and reinscribed one.[98]

A constant element in rap music, from "Rapper's Delight" to "Rebel Without a Pause," has been the break, both as raw musical material and as a concept organizing how producers conceive of songwriting. Over the course of rap's first ten years, the practices of early hip hop DJs manipulating breaks were reintroduced and reimagined in a variety of rap styles. Although this chapter has focused on Public Enemy's characteristic sound, other artists in the late 1980s developed different approaches to selecting and manipulating breaks that helped to distinguish their work.[99] Artists including Arrested Development, A Tribe Called Quest, Biz Markie, De La Soul, DJ Jazzy Jeff and the Fresh Prince, MC Lyte, and Queen Latifah, to name only a few, worked within hip hop's culture of breakbeat sampling to generate diverse musical identities.[100] As will be discussed in the next chapter, gangsta rap group N.W.A. was quick to combine Public Enemy's musical style with different lyrics and imagery to activate an equally powerful but ideologically distinct form of expression.

The ability to strike back (or "strike black," as Public Enemy put it) is one that developed from a long chain of musical innovations. By subverting conventions and reworking the sounds and approaches of past music, rap producers cultivated new expressive powers. Historicizing Public Enemy's influential approach to production allows us to better understand how the formal aspects of rap music and music making contribute to the genre's representations of race. In outlining some of the developments that led to Public Enemy's sample-based approach to beat making, we have seen that rap's ability to render race audible has existed since the genre's earliest years. Yet, as an unstable social construct, race in rap has changed dramatically over time. To rearticulate Jon Pareles's observation about rap's first decade, the story of how Public Enemy's music could suddenly seem to have "its fist in the air" is the story of how a musical style itself became a symbol.

PART II

Rearticulating Race in the Neoliberal Nineties

3 "Let Me Ride"

Gangsta Rap's Drive into the Popular Mainstream

> The real city, one might say, produces only criminals; the imaginary city produces the gangster.[1]
>
> **Robert Warshow**

> Straight outta Compton is a crazy motherfucker named Ice Cube From a gang called Niggaz Wit Attitudes.[2]
>
> **Ice Cube**

Writing about the infamous genre of gangsta rap in the wake of the 1992 Los Angeles Uprising, Robin D. G. Kelley offered a political reading of rappers' outlaw theatrics. By inflating their reputations for starting trouble and inflicting pain on those who dared to get in their way, he argued that rap artists cultivated "badass" identities that allowed them to stand up, symbolically at least, to the powers that be.[3] Kelley explained that by inverting conventional morality and racial hierarchy through their irreverent and boastful signifying, gangsta rappers had carved out a space where they could critique the police brutality, racial profiling, and socioeconomic forces criminalizing black youth.[4] However, reminding readers that rap is primarily "produced and purchased to drive to, rock to, chill to, drink to, and occasionally dance to," Kelley also maintained that rap's sociological implications should not prevent us from acknowledging the music's aesthetic value, explaining that it would be a gross misunderstanding of rap music and hip hop culture to ignore the pleasure that listeners find in gangsta beats and rhymes.[5]

Kelley's call to balance politics and aesthetics in writing about rap provides a useful starting-point for this chapter, which compares the way that lyrics, sound, and imagery work together in Los Angeles–based gangsta rap. Building on the previous chapter's exploration of Public Enemy's revolutionary black aesthetic, I compare producer Dr. Dre's work with pioneering gangsta group N.W.A. (Niggaz Wit Attitudes) to hit singles from his later solo album, *The Chronic,* to explain how changes in sound lead to differing ideas about race and politics. Although gangsta rap is often discussed (and denounced) as a singular entity, the stylistic evolution of the subgenre, as well as the internal tensions within it, have been largely overlooked.[6] Comparing two different iterations of so-called gangsta rap, this chapter focuses attention on the aesthetic features of individual songs, including the *music* that Kelley reminds us should not be forgotten.

Although Dr. Dre's production for N.W.A.'s *Straight Outta Compton*, the influential 1988 album that brought West Coast rappers to the attention of national audiences, evoked the frenetic atmosphere of inner-city Los Angeles, the hit singles from his 1992 solo debut *The Chronic* seem more relaxed and fluid, a style that Dre called "G-funk." Celebrating *The Chronic* as one of the most influential and popular rap albums in history, numerous critics and fans praise Dr. Dre's meticulous approach to beat making. However, a vocal minority have long countered that Dr. Dre and his protégé Snoop Doggy Dog depoliticized gangsta rap, veering dangerously into exploitative misogyny and senseless violence. Rather than treat these contrasting opinions as separate issues (e.g., good music but bad lyrics), this chapter explores how Dr. Dre's musical innovations as a producer were central to *The Chronic*'s sounding of black politics.

As Robert Warshow explains in the epigram to this chapter, the gangsta is a uniquely urban archetype, a product of the "imaginary city." Hailing from Compton, California, an inner suburb known as the Hub City for its proximity to downtown Los Angeles, Dr. Dre and the other members of N.W.A. made place a central element in their musical strategy. In comparing the music of N.W.A. to Dr. Dre's G-funk, I consider how musical aesthetics contribute to two different representations of identity, as well as two contrasting experiences of the city.[7] By reconceiving the gangsta's relationship to urban space, Dr. Dre rearticulated blackness not as conflict and rebellion but as transcendence and mobility.

RAPPING AND MAPPING

In recent years, scholars have become increasingly attuned to the spatial character of musical practices. Analyzing the dynamics of space and place at the heart of the genre's growth and expansion, Murray Forman explains that rappers often cultivate an aura of authenticity tied to their respective 'hoods.[8] Making Compton, California, a central part of their identity as a group, N.W.A. encoded experiences of black Los Angeles in their rap recordings. Writing for the *Washington Post*, music critic Richard Harrington picked up on such meanings when he described N.W.A.'s album *Straight*

Outta Compton as a chronicle of "the crack- and crime-ridden black community of L.A."[9]

Despite this tendency toward spatial thinking, however, it is important to emphasize that music derives much of its power from the way it structures temporal experience. To understand how music "maps" a particular space, one must also deal with the fact that music is experienced in time. As we have seen in previous chapters, rap producers create cyclic arrangements built on repeated passages of music (sampled or otherwise). These repeating musical loops, derived from the breaks that hip hop's first DJs worked with, can vary considerably with respect to expressive character, breaking up time in different ways for vastly different effects. The challenge is to translate these temporal dimensions of rap music into a greater understanding of how gangsta rap portrays the urban space, highlighting the potential disjuncture between some people's imagined ideas of a place and other people's lived realities. *Pace* Chuck D of Public Enemy (who once famously referred to rap music as the "black CNN"), gangsta rap does not aspire to objectively reflect the city in a documentary manner.[10] Rather, N.W.A. and Dr. Dre envisioned Compton (and the larger geography of Los Angeles) in particular ways for particular purposes at a particular time. If the metaphor most appropriate for understanding music's spatial character is that of a map—an aural cartography—then we must acknowledge that different maps can lead to very different understandings of urban space. Maps are designed to reveal certain things, but they always conceal others in return.

As the founder of the "L.A. School" of postmodern geography, Edward Soja has brought increased attention to the forces that contribute to the fabrication of social space. Drawing on the theoretical insights of Henri Lefebvre, Soja refuses to see space as a neutral or blank grid against which social activity occurs. Instead, he interprets the city's spatial dimensions against the forces of capital, creating opportunities and setting limitations on development and growth. Soja's *Postmodern Geographies* contains a lengthy chapter on Los Angeles, and he dubbed the city *the* "paradigmatic place" to witness the effect of capital on the production of social space.[11] Although Soja did not explicitly consider popular music, his analysis reveals many of the social and economic conditions that set the stage for 1980s gangsta rap. Published in 1989, the year in which *Straight Outta Compton* captured a national audience, Soja's work provides a useful counterpoint to N.W.A.'s musical representation of urban space. In fact, his analysis of Los Angeles's socioeconomic conditions opens a hermeneutic window for understanding N.W.A.'s aesthetic strategies.[12]

In the period stretching from World War II to the early 1960s, the area sprawling southward from downtown Los Angeles toward the port city of Long Beach was one of the largest urban industrial centers in the world. The heavily segregated area—African Americans were only allowed to inhabit a thin section west of Alameda Boulevard—became the third-largest black ghetto in the country. Despite the deleterious effects of segregation and systematic racism, blue-collar South Central Los Angeles presented opportunities for upward mobility, making the area an attractive destination for thousands of African Americans who moved to Southern California from Alabama, Texas, and other parts of the country.

By the 1960s, however, South Central Los Angeles was beginning its precipitous decline as factories began closing and laying off employees. Paradoxically, other regions of the metropolitan area were experiencing high levels of growth, leapfrogging south into Orange County and northwest into the outer San Fernando Valley. From 1970 to 1980, Los Angeles's population grew by 1,300,000, and non-agricultural wage and salary workers increased by an even greater number—1,315,000—making Los Angeles the largest job machine in the country.[13] Soja analyzes this differential growth and contraction in Los Angeles's economy as a kaleidoscopic mix of highly educated and skilled labor at the top and a poorly paid immigrant workforce at the bottom.[14] For example, while the high technology and military sectors were hectically booming thanks to the Reagan-era defense build-up, older industries such as rubber, steel, and auto manufacturing were losing their place in the global economic order. For Compton and South Central Los Angeles, this deindustrialization, which also meant the decline of labor unions and union wages, was coupled to the growth of an informal underground economy, led by a gang-controlled drug trade.

Los Angeles was both enabled by and particularly vulnerable to the mobility of capital.[15] According to Soja, the city was prone to rapid demographic and economic change because it was not built around the centralized industrial districts characteristic of nineteenth-century modes of production. By the time Los Angeles began its industrialization, the more decentralized practices of early-twentieth-century capitalism were already well under way, enabled by one of Los Angeles's defining symbols: the automobile. Indeed, the sprawling metropolis with its arterial network of freeways has been the most automobile-oriented region of the United States, excepting Detroit itself. The automobile industry boomed in Los Angeles throughout the Great Depression, and cars played a central role in Southern California's postwar economic expansion.[16] As residential suburbs and "satellite cities" continued to grow, the automobile shuttled commuters between their homes and places of work.

Although daily users often describe Los Angeles's freeway system as a gridlocked prison, its origins lie in a dream of freedom. Its postwar boosters billed the construction of Los Angeles's freeways as central to the suburban good life. Over the protests of the inner-city residents whose lives and neighborhoods were vulnerable to the destructive effects of freeway construction, proponents of the freeways presented the city as "the sum of its attractions," emphasizing that Los Angeles's freeway system would make it possible for the average middle-class car owner to take advantage of all the Southland had to offer.[17] By viewing the city as a "collection of isolated sites, each severed from its sociohistorical context," freeway developers tapped into a vision of decentralized Los Angeles that had long been enshrined in the city's planning.[18] Streetcars and rail lines, for example, had served the sprawling metropolis for decades before the rise of freeways. The new freeways were, in fact, a solution for suburban commuters dissatisfied with the high cost and poor efficiency of the rail system.[19]

Like the streetcars and rail lines before them, the freeways allowed commuters to traverse the long distance from home to office, and they enabled sightseers and middle-class families to enjoy a wide variety of activities spread across a wide expanse of land. Yet they also contributed to the isolation and invisibility of many poorer Los Angeles communities, including South Central Los Angeles. Thousands of people passed through the city's black neighborhoods each day on their way to work, but the conditions in these areas were hidden behind the freeway's walls. What is more, the freeways reinforced patterns of segregation and marked physical boundaries cutting African Americans off from other parts of the city. Figure 15 illustrates roughly the area of South Central Los Angeles and neighboring black communities (including Compton) circumscribed by Interstates 10, 110, and 710 and State Route 91. As houses were razed and large swaths of earth cut open to make way for these roads, communities were divided by cul-de-sac streets that dead-ended into towering sound walls. For those without easy access to automobiles, the freeways and inadequate public transit system make movement across Los Angeles's vast expanse difficult. Many activists and community members have charged Los Angeles with supporting a "transit apartheid" in which the ability to move through urban space remains contingent upon class and color.[20]

N.W.A.'s *Straight Outta Compton* responded to the conditions of neglect and segregation plaguing Los Angeles's black community, creating and disseminating a ghetto-based understanding of the city's spatial dynamics.

Figure 15. Boundaries of South Los Angeles neighborhoods (c. 1986), reinforced by Interstates 10, 110, and 710 and State Route 91.

Scholars Robin Kelley and Eithne Quinn, for example, both interpret the very ethos of early gangsta rap, which celebrated the ruthless, individualistic pursuit of profit, as a cultural strategy for opting out of the low-skill, low-wage service economy that Soja describes in *Postmodern Geographies*.[21] N.W.A. was inspired by the crime, violence, and chaotic atmosphere surrounding the underground drug trade, which had flourished in the void created by massive layoffs and high rates of unemployment. The rise of gangs that fought bitterly for control of the lucrative drug economy was met with a heavy-handed response from the Los Angeles Police Department (LAPD). Despite being chemically identical to powder cocaine, which was associated with wealthy white users, the news media and law enforcement agencies exaggerated the dangerous effects of smoking "crack" cocaine. In this context of public panic over the crack cocaine "epidemic," the U.S. Congress passed the Anti-Drug Abuse Act of 1986, which allowed crack possession to be punished at a rate *one hundred times greater* than that for powder cocaine and stipulated new mandatory minimum sentencing guidelines for drug crimes that previously would not have resulted in imprisonment.[22] These measures disproportionately affected African Americans who lived in communities where street dealers made easy prey for law enforcement, and the LAPD response to the drug-and-gang problem was particularly aggressive. With names like "Operation Hammer," the LAPD's actions included roundups of suspected gang members and destructive search-and-seizure missions whose purposes were not only to find contraband but also to intimidate. The War on Drugs provided a pretext for the LAPD to adopt paramilitary equipment such as the "batter ram," a small tank whose purpose was to break down the doors and walls of suspected crack houses in dramatic fashion.

Exploiting the stereotypes and popular imagery of the ghetto as a violent and troubled "no-go" zone, gangsta rappers found a way to make infamy pay. By embodying outlaw personae through first-person gangsta narratives, N.W.A. developed a sophisticated cultural hustle that allowed them to profit from the very system conspiring to contain them. This artistic strategy had a powerful—and somewhat ironic—musical component. The sound of *Straight Outta Compton*, which supports N.W.A.'s grassroots mapping of South Central Los Angeles as a place where black residents are economically and physically cut off from other parts of the city, depended on musical techniques imported from New York and transposed onto remarkably similar post-industrial conditions.

COMPTON VIA NEW YORK

Before the rise of West Coast gangsta rappers, New York City's MCs were the uncontested trendsetters in rap music. Not only did the most famous rap artists hail from the city, but New York was also the center of production for managers, record labels, and recording studios. Although few might have thought of it in such terms at the time, the national sound of rap music in the early-to-mid-1980s was actually a regional one. Virtually everything in rap, including the music's sound, slang, and sense of fashion, came from New York. MC Chip, an original member of N.W.A., recalls, "Early, early West Coast hip-hop, before it became gangsta, we were looking for an identity."[23]

Evidence of the group's search for an identity can be found on *N.W.A. and the Posse* (1987). Released by Macola Records (apparently without the group's consent), the uneven and stylistically diverse album provides a snapshot of what Los Angeles–based rap music sounded like prior to N.W.A.'s breakthrough, *Straight Outta Compton* (1988). As manager Jerry Heller recalls, the album was "the product of a loose amalgamation of DJs, musicians and MCs," and captured the group at a moment when the direction of their musical careers had not been fully set.[24] Indeed, for those familiar with N.W.A.'s later albums, one of the greatest outliers on *N.W.A and the Posse* is "Panic Zone," a song in the L.A.-based "electro rap" style.

One of many regional styles spawned by Afrika Bambaataa's powerful 1982 hit single "Planet Rock," electro dominated Los Angeles–based rap in the years before N.W.A.'s rise, roughly 1983–1988.[25] Like their counterparts in cities across the country, electro groups began as mobile DJ units, displaying a flashy and ostentatious style associated with the nightclub scene. Dr. Dre, for example, began his music career with the World Class Wreckin' Cru, which also included original N.W.A. member Arabian Prince. Dressed in bright sequined shirts and with a stethoscope draped around his neck, Dre used turntables (for scratching), electronic keyboard synthesizers, and drum machines to help craft electro's futuristic-sounding world of fantasy and sexual innuendo. "Panic Zone," a song whose minor-key riffs, percussive synthesizer stabs, and bleeping electronic drum track bear a strong resemblance to "Planet Rock," reveals Dre's and Arabian Prince's lingering ties to the electro scene. However, unlike "Planet Rock," which aimed itself rhetorically toward a global party audience, the lyrics to "Panic Zone" named specific places of origin for each respective member of the group: L.A., Compton, Inglewood, East L.A., West L.A., Carson, Crenshaw. Thus, the track reflects N.W.A.'s self-conscious concern with place, a strategy that would prove central to the group's breakthrough.

N.W.A. founder Eazy-E, who also cofounded the group's label, Ruthless Records, with Jerry Heller, was known to dismiss electro groups as "corny."[26] Like Run-D.M.C. and Public Enemy, discussed in the previous chapter, N.W.A. would build its identity in opposition to the flamboyant costuming and dance-floor orientation of its predecessors. Eazy-E's first task was to convince Dr. Dre and the other members of the group to focus on a more hardcore style of rap. Their first single in this vein was "Boyz–N-the-Hood." The single was written by Ice Cube but rapped by Eazy-E. Set to a sparse drum machine track with a tempo too slow for dancing, the song describes Los Angeles's tough city streets as seen from Eazy-E's 1964 Chevy Impala lowrider. The song's mix of misogyny, violent imagery, and braggadocio was clearly indebted to Philadelphia rapper Schoolly D's "P.S.K. (What Does It Mean?)," a 1985 single widely regarded as the song that gave birth to gangsta rap. It also drew on Ice-T's "6 in the Mornin'" (1986), which was the first West Coast song to adopt the lyrical cadence, defiant attitude, and violent yet humorous boasting of "P.S.K." "Boyz–N-the-Hood" was both thematically and musically similar to these predecessors and helped plot a new course for Los Angeles–based rap.

With the support of Los Angeles's AM 1580 KDAY, the city's first all-rap radio station, "Boyz-N-the-Hood" was a hit. While manager Jerry Heller signed the group to a national distribution deal with upstart Priority Records, N.W.A. continued work on their first album as well as Eazy-E's solo project *Eazy-Duz-It*. According to Chuck D, Public Enemy's musical style directly influenced Dre's work on these albums, and he recalls giving the first two copies of *It Takes a Nation of Millions to Hold Us Back* to Dr. Dre and Eazy-E prior to the album's official release.[27] The recorded evidence supports Chuck D's recollection. For many of the tracks on *Straight Outta Compton*, Dr. Dre seems to have borrowed from the "loops on top of loops" style of Public Enemy's Bomb Squad.[28] N.W.A.'s breakthrough was finding a way to put a distinctive spin on these influences, and the artistic strategy that they arrived at for their first Ruthless Records release was designed to put them on the map—both literally and figuratively.[29]

Rather than shout out the multiplicity of neighborhoods where their members were actually from (as they had done in "Panic Zone"), N.W.A. chose to center their identity around Dr. Dre and Eazy-E's hometown of Compton, California. The sound of Compton as Dr. Dre imagined it, however, drew on musical practices and artistic decisions similar to those found in Public Enemy's "Rebel Without a Pause." To construct the rhythmic foundation of "Straight Outta Compton," Dre looped the breakbeat from the Winstons' "Amen Brother" (1969) (ex. 3a).[30] Like other heavily sampled breaks from this era, the one-measure loop features a syncopated interlocking of snare and bass hits that is reminiscent of James Brown's "Funky Drummer." As if he were following the Bomb Squad's exact formula, Dr. Dre layered a drum machine (a Roland TR-808) over this break (ex. 3b). The 808 was programmed to add its characteristic bass boom to the first two drum kicks of the "Amen" loop, and to tick off a 16-count hi-hat pulse with a closing hi-hat clasp on the downbeat of every other measure. The "Amen" break and the two hi-hat parts provide the rhythmic foundation around which Dr. Dre places numerous other repeating sounds. Two other ingredients stand out in this beat: a guitar ostinato and a low drone on what sounds like a baritone sax or trombone (or perhaps a downwardly pitched sample of another instrument). The guitar ostinato, which plays straight eighth notes on E-flat except for a one-step descent to D-flat on the "and" of every fourth beat, churns out tight one-measure units of sound (ex. 3c). The horn drone (also on E-flat) has a raw, muddled quality, and casts an ominous cloud over the track.

Unlike the "Amen" breakbeat, the guitar riff and drone sound are not samples taken from other recordings—or at least if they are, they have

Example 3

(a) Looped portion of the break from the Winstons' "Amen Brother" (1969).

(b) Roland TR-808 drum sequence from "Straight Outta Compton."

	1	-	+	-	2	-	+	-	3	-	+	-	4	-	+	-
Hi-hat	o	x	x	x	x	x	x	x	x	x	x	x	x	x	x	x
Kick	k		k													

(c) Looped guitar riff.

never been identified. Instead, it is likely that Stan "The Guitar Man" Jones performed the guitar part in studio. Recalling his experiences with N.W.A., Jones explains, "they were using the sample records [but] they couldn't control the samples. If you wanted to turn the bass up or the guitar up, you couldn't handle the controls because it was all in samples. That's when Dr. Dre asked me to replay some of those parts and that's how I got involved."[31] Although it is unclear what, if any, pre-existing sample Jones imitated for "Straight Outta Compton," Dr. Dre is known for having studio musicians replay portions of pre-existing records because it allows him greater artistic control over his sources. As Jones implies, by sampling the performances of studio musicians, Dre could manipulate individual lines in his mix (e.g., make the bass louder, or add reverb to the guitar) in ways that he could not accomplish with samples from records. What is more, such an approach to production also made financial sense. Paying musicians a one-time fee for their work in the studio, N.W.A. avoided the expensive master rights ("mechanical royalties") associated with sampling directly from pre-existing recordings.[32]

Table 3. Comparison of layers of looped sound in Public Enemy's "Rebel Without a Pause" and N.W.A.'s "Straight Outta Compton"

"Rebel Without a Pause"	*"Straight Outta Compton"*
Akai drum machine	Roland TR-808 drum machine
"Funky Drummer" (looped breakbeat)	"Amen Brother" (looped breakbeat)
"The Grunt, Pt. 1" (saxophone glissando and guitar)	Low-pitched horn drone and guitar riff

Despite Dre's use of live instrumentation, it is important to note Jones's acknowledgment that traditional instrumentation in N.W.A.'s recording process was a way of achieving greater control over sample-based production, not a departure from it. Although a live guitarist probably recorded this part, Dr. Dre placed the guitar line in the track as a repeating loop, similarly to how another producer might work with a breakbeat taken from a vinyl record. By combining these layers with the dense percussion track, Dre created a tightly packed funk groove with many sonic similarities to the work of Public Enemy's Bomb Squad. Like "Rebel Without a Pause," the track to "Straight Outta Compton" features tight one-measure loops stacked on top of one another to create a thick and intense sound (table 3).

Except for the drone, most of the elements in the track have a punchy feel, full of rhythmic stabs and staccato attacks, including the automatic gunfire that Dre samples to follow Ice Cube's reference to an AK-47 assault rifle. Due to the "noisiness" of the beat, the way sonic space seems filled to maximum capacity, the members of N.W.A.—like Public Enemy's Chuck D and Flavor Flav—practically yell their verses, as if they must raise their voices to be heard over the cacophony. Even before the actual words to "Straight Outta Compton" are digested, the sound of the track and the group's vocals evoke the palpable tension of imminent conflict, which reinforces the theme of violent confrontation in the song's lyrics. For the chorus of "Straight Outta Compton," Dr. Dre strings together a series of samples with rapid-fire precision. The sound of screeching car tires from Davy DMX's "One for the Treble" is followed by turntable scratching; the scratching leads directly to a choppy sample of the words "City of Compton" from Ronnie Hudson's "West Coast Poplock," followed by more scratching. The whole chain of musical events is deployed over the breakbeat from Funkadelic's "You'll Like It Too," which Dr. Dre splices into the beat just for the chorus.[33] The rapid cutting from one sample to the next exemplifies the "rupture" Tricia Rose identifies as fundamental to hip hop's post-industrial aesthetic.[34]

The music and lyrics for "Straight Outta Compton" depict the city as a place of extremes, where things happen fast and change is sudden and complete. It is a place where one is either equipped to deal or left behind. In this way, Dr. Dre exploited the spatial characteristics encoded in Public Enemy's music to depict Compton as place. The sonic characteristics that animated Public Enemy's militant blackness were rerouted and effectively transposed onto N.W.A.'s depiction of Los Angeles gangstas. In place of Public Enemy's political theater, however, stood another kind of spectacle that capitalized on the "too black, too strong" sound. As David Toop puts it, N.W.A. had crafted "a nightmarish record, its sound effects of police sirens, gunshots, and screeching tires depicting a generation virtually in the throes of war."[35] Casting their 'hood as a place of chaos and rage, "Straight Outta Compton" scared and titillated audiences with its sensational portrayal of ghetto life.

COMPTON AS CONFRONTATION AND CONTESTATION

Although the lyrics and sound of "Straight Outta Compton" portray the members of N.W.A. as dominant aggressors, the song's music video, directed by Rupert Wainwright, both amplifies and subverts this impression.[36] Ice Cube begins his verse, for example, by referring to himself as a "crazy motherfucker" who will respond violently to anyone who gets in his way. Ren's verse goes further, challenging the authority of police officers with their "silly clubs" and "fake-ass badges," and detailing how he would "blast" them with his gun if given the chance. The music video's opening scenes support this imagery as the group stomps aggressively through the Compton streets. Later, however, N.W.A. is pictured fleeing unsuccessfully from an LAPD squad intent on locking them up. Pursued through back alleys and over chain-link fences, the group members are captured one by one and forced into submission, arms twisted behind their backs, guns pointed at their heads. Taken together, the contrast between these images emphasizes the tightly circumscribed area of Compton and positions N.W.A.'s members as rebels engaged in a turf war with the authorities. In fact, the video opens with a statement critiquing the LAPD's heavy-handed "gang sweeps."[37]

In the music video for "Straight Outta Compton," the balance of power between the LAPD and N.W.A. is portrayed effectively by a quintessential image of the Southern Californian lifestyle: the automobile. The members of N.W.A. always appear on foot, marching through Compton or fleeing

Figure 16. Still image of walking feet from the music video for "Straight Outta Compton," emphasizing N.W.A. members' proximity to the street.

Figure 17. Still image of rotating tires from the music video for "Straight Outta Compton," emphasizing the mobility and power of the LAPD.

from the police (fig. 16); the police, who presumably do not live in the 'hood, ride in cars that carry them freely in and out of Compton in pursuit of the group (fig. 17). On the one hand, images of the group's members walking and running through the city's streets work well to emphasize their connection to place; we are literally getting a "man on the street" perspective. On the other hand, the contrast between these images and those of police cars on the prowl emphasizes the sense of entrapment felt by African Americans living in South Central Los Angeles. Without cars of

Figure 18. Still image of the police surveying a map, with a bold outline around the area of Compton, from the music video for "Straight Outta Compton." (Note the coffee and donut.)

their own, the group make easy targets for the police, and the video ends with them locked up inside a police van.

The editing of the video intensifies the theme of conflict, matching the sonic intensity of the song with its rapid pace. The video jumps between images once, twice, even four times per measure. Often, the video juxtaposes the members of N.W.A. and their LAPD adversaries, heightening the tension and sense of imminent conflict. The idea that we are witnessing two rival groups squaring off in a contest over urban space is brought home by a clever use of spatial imagery: the police stand over a map of Compton with its borders inked by a heavy red marker (fig. 18).[38]

This image of the map, which returns at the song's chorus, emphasizes the tightly circumscribed area of Compton and the sense of surveillance and limited mobility felt by its inhabitants. Thus, the construction of musical space through sound and imagery portrays the spatial relations of Los Angeles as confining and oppressive to African American residents. The city map, which in another setting might simply function as a means of navigating through the city's streets, finds itself deployed here as a symbol with sinister implications. Like the ubiquitous "war room" scenes in military-themed movies, the police seem to be strategizing their attack on the people of Compton. In sum, the aesthetics of the music video reflect João Costa Vargas's observation that South Los Angeles's ghetto is "the result of widespread social forces galvanized against Black spatial mobility."[39]

The aesthetic formula Dr. Dre and N.W.A. created for "Straight Outta Compton" proved a lucrative one. Their follow-up album, *Niggaz4Life*

(1991), which debuted at No. 2 on the *Billboard* charts and reached No. 1 in its second week, featured the single "100 Miles and Running." The song recycles the imagery and general sensibility of "Straight Outta Compton." The emcees yell their verses—a "fusillade of threats, obscenities and gunshots"—over a tightly packed, "ferocious" rhythm track.[40] The lyrics emphasize the group's domineering posture, and the music video depicts N.W.A. fleeing from but eventually outsmarting the law.[41] Despite the group's continued success, however, Dr. Dre broke with Eazy-E and manager Jerry Heller soon after the album's debut, spelling the end of N.W.A. Feeling that his responsibility for generating the music behind the hits warranted a larger share of the profits, Dre sought out a new arrangement with Death Row Records CEO, Suge Knight. In addition to a new, more favorable business arrangement, the beginning of Dr. Dre's solo career brought about a change in musical aesthetics. Comparing the music and music video of N.W.A's "Straight Outta Compton" and "100 Miles and Running" to the hit singles "Let Me Ride" and "Nuthin' But a 'G' Thang" from Dr. Dre's solo debut *The Chronic* reveals a profound change in direction, reimagining how the gangsta could navigate Los Angeles's urban geography.

PRODUCING G-FUNK IN POST-RIOT LOS ANGELES

Released in the final weeks of 1992, *The Chronic* established Dr. Dre as a viable solo artist. Emphasizing his break with N.W.A., the "Intro" to the album features Snoop Doggy Dogg harshly dismissing Dre's former associates: "Niggaz Wit Attitudes? Naw, loc. [*Loc* is a term of casual address, like *man* or *dude*.] Niggaz on a mutherfuckin' mission." Snoop continues, referring to manager Jerry Heller and rapper Eazy-E derisively as "Mr. Rourke and Tattoo," references to two characters from the television sitcom *Fantasy Island*.[42] For the music video to one of the album's three singles, "Wit Dre Day," Dre ruthlessly parodied, lampooned, and denigrated his two former associates. In the song's music video, actors playing the roles of "Sleazy-E" and "Jerry" portray Ruthless Records—the partnership between the young African American from Compton and the middle-aged Jew from Cleveland—as exploitative and racist. Jerry refers to Sleazy repeatedly as "boy" and dismissively tells him to "go find some rappers." The video portrays Eazy-E as a dancing minstrel and wannabe gangsta, mugging for the camera in a vain attempt to make money. The hostile attack vented Dr. Dre's frustration with Ruthless Records, but more importantly, it provided him with a good vehicle for casting himself and Snoop Doggy Dogg as everything that he claimed Eazy-E was not: authentic. Such

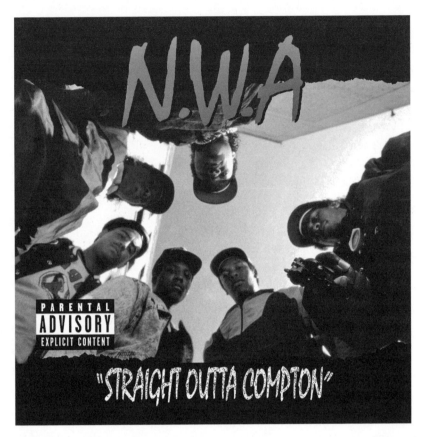

Figure 19. Album covers for N.W.A.'s *Straight Outta Compton* (1988; above) and Dr. Dre's *The Chronic* (1992; opposite).

accusations, however, would have rung hollow if not for a new artistic vision Dr. Dre introduced after joining Death Row Records. By putting forward an updated version of gangsta cool, *The Chronic* reached out to new audiences and increased hardcore rap music's popularity.

This new accessibility is readily visible by comparing the album imagery of *The Chronic* to that of *Straight Outta Compton* (fig. 19). On one album cover, Eazy-E stands over the camera with a pistol; on the other, Dr. Dre's face appears in a design evoking Zig-Zag rolling papers. Potential consumers go from being on the wrong side of a smoking gun to equating the experience of Dr. Dre's music with the smoking of high-quality marijuana. As Jeff Chang succinctly puts it, "The Black Thing you once couldn't understand became the 'G' Thang you could buy into."[43]

Examining *The Chronic*'s hit singles "Nuthing But a 'G' Thang" and "Let Me Ride" in greater detail shows that these differences were also amplified by a change in Dr. Dre's musical style and video imagery that cast life in the 'hood as less about violent struggle and more about the celebration of a certain kind of freedom and mobility. In fact, analyzing lyrics alone might lead one to miss these changes within the genre. Consider, for example, the lyrics of "Straight Outta Compton" and "Let Me Ride," both of which stress the gangsterish qualities of their respective protagonists.

N.W.A.'s "Straight Outta Compton" begins with a verse from Ice Cube describing himself as a "crazy motherfucker" with a "sawed off" shotgun who will destroy anyone who gets in his way: "squeeze the trigger, and bodies are hauled off."[44] Similarly, Dr. Dre begins "Let Me Ride" by revealing that he's holding a "Glock" pistol and that the headless bodies of his adversaries are "being found on Greenleaf [street]."[45] Taken at face value, both lyrics stress the violence-prone nature of the MCs' personas and emphasize the perilous nature of life in inner-city Los Angeles. However, there is a subtle difference between the characters portrayed in these songs. In "Straight Outta Compton," Ice Cube threatens to commit violent acts directly, but in "Let Me Ride" Dr. Dre portrays himself as a gangster of stature. He asserts that he can "make a phone call" to dispose of any unwanted adversaries. In other words, Dre has the ability to have someone killed on demand from afar. In a sense, this shift in perspective reflects the distance traveled by Dr. Dre from his relatively powerless position with N.W.A. to his role as an established hit maker and business partner in Death Row Records. Rather than having to scrap for his daily bread, he now occupies a comfortable seat at the table.

In keeping with this improvement in his circumstances, the music video of "Let Me Ride" portrays Dr. Dre as someone who is able to overcome the geographic challenges posed by Los Angeles, *not* as someone who remains caught up within its oppressive spatial logic. Rather than running from the police, Dr. Dre spends his time leisurely cruising from liquor store, to bar-beque, to car wash, to house party, and so on. "Let Me Ride" and "Nuthin' But a 'G' Thang" repackage gangsta rap as part of a consumable lifestyle that includes marijuana, classic cars, and compliant women. Instead of a turf war with LAPD officers or FBI agents, Dr. Dre and Snoop Doggy Dogg appear at the scene of mundane, yet stereotypically Los Angeles events. What is more, the locations in which they are pictured are not restricted to Compton or South Central Los Angeles. In fact, many of the park and street scenes featured in the video were shot in the middle-class enclaves of Baldwin Hills and the Crenshaw District, areas that represented upward mobility in black Los Angeles.[46] By picturing an experience of Los Angeles rooted in the freedom enabled by the automobile, *The Chronic* represented Dr. Dre's upward trajectory and invited viewers to identify with it.

But what did this new gangsta cool *sound* like?

"NUTHIN' BUT A 'G' THANG" AND "LET ME RIDE"

The short answer is, it sounded freaky. The musical track to *The Chronic's* most popular single, "Nuthin' But a 'G' Thang," was based on Leon Haywood's 1975 hit "I Wanna Do Something Freaky To You." Released in 1975, Haywood's song reached No. 7 and No. 15 on the R&B and Pop charts, respectively. The six-minute track, whose orgasmic moaning vocals leave little to the imagination about what this "something freaky" actually is, opens with a relaxed groove featuring drums and wah-wah guitar. The tension begins to build almost immediately as instrumental layers—bass, winds, conga drums, horns, and so on—are introduced one after another. After about a minute of steady accretion, the implied state of arousal increases dramatically with a shift into a new double-time drum pattern.

However, for "Nuthin' But a 'G' Thang," Dre avoided this double-time section completely. Basing his beat on the opening measures of "Freaky" before the song begins reaching toward climax, Dre focused on looping a relatively sparse break that departed significantly from the frenetic energy of the "Funky Drummer" and "Amen"–style breakbeats popular during his tenure with N.W.A. By looping the opening portion of Haywood's song, Dre locks into place a relaxed groove anchored by a kick-drum pattern that resembles the "and-one, and-three" feel of what many musicians today regard as a basic bossa nova (ex. 4a). Listening closely to the opening of "I Wanna Do Something Freaky To You" and "Nuthin' But a 'G' Thang," however, reveals something surprising: Dr. Dre doesn't sample Haywood's recording, at least not in any straightforward manner. Leading session players in covering Leon Haywood's original track, Dr. Dre used an Akai MPC 2000 to sample the live studio musicians and create his own interpolation of Haywood's groove. This decision had an aesthetic purpose: Dre recreates the original Haywood arrangement—only better. The bass is more booming and the snare is more cracking. Indeed, in a genre where timbre is one of the most important musical parameters, hip hop producers are well known for their connoisseurship and obsession with getting just the right sounds for their drums and other instrumental parts. As he did when employing Stan "The Guitar Man" for *Straight Outta Compton*, Dre departed from a purely sample-based approach. Instead of limiting himself to sounds he could grab from pre-existing records, he sampled live musicians and subjected these recordings to studio manipulation. This practice gave rise to an incredible clarity in the stereo field—very high highs and extremely low lows. Every register of sonic space is filled, without the track sounding muddled.[47]

Dr. Dre and his session musicians also added something else to Haywood's groove: more percussion. First, a studio musician used a tambourine to lay down a steady flow of swinging sixteenth notes, which lend the track a compelling and danceable "live" rhythmic feel. Second, they also added the vibraslap, whose rattling announces the downbeat of every fourth measure. The resulting beat for "Nuthin' But a 'G' Thang," with its lilting swing and laid-back drum beat (ex. 4b), sounds less noisy and rigid than the musical track for "Straight Outta Compton," whose rhythmic foundation

Example 4. Comparison of basic bossa nova pattern with the looped drum break and percussion elements in Dr. Dre's "Nuthin' But a 'G' Thang."

(a)

(b)

consisted of a looped funk break overlaid with a drum machine sequence. This smoother, more open approach gave rise to a beat that allowed Dr. Dre and Snoop Doggy Dogg to deliver their lyrics in a more relaxed, conversational fashion that contrasts dramatically with the nearly shouting vocals one hears on N.W.A.'s tracks.

Furthermore, unlike the beat for "Straight Outta Compton," whose most prominent elements subdivide the groove into tight one-measure units, the keyboard melodies for "Nuthin' But a 'G' Thang" and "Let Me Ride" imply two- and even four-measure subdivisions of time (ex. 5).[48] These melodies, played on one of Dr. Dre's vintage Minimoog synthesizers, became the characteristic sound of G-funk. The pure whine of the electronically produced sine wave was a timbre well suited to reimagining gangsta rap as more open and accessible than its predecessors. In measure 27 of "Nuthin' But a 'G' Thang" (ex. 5a), the synthesizer plays the song's anthemic melodic hook, which Dre interpolated directly from Haywood's "I Wanna Do Something Freaky To You." In Haywood's version, however, this melody is played by string instruments in a lush style similar to disco-soul pioneers Philadelphia International Records. The difference in timbre is striking. The luxurious orchestral timbre of Haywood's version, replete

Example 5. Melodic lines on the synthesizer from "Nuthin' But a 'G' Thang" and "Let Me Ride."

(a) "Nuthin' But a 'G' Thang"

(b) "Let Me Ride"

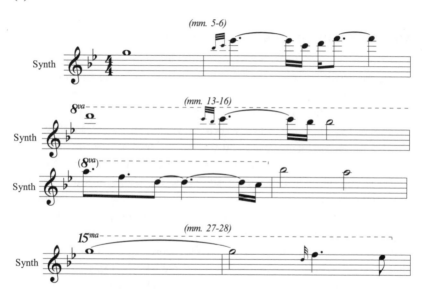

with the overtones of multiple vibrating strings, contrasts dramatically with the Moog synthesizer's electronically generated pure sine waves. By making this simple change, Dre maintained the relaxed melodicism of Haywood's original without evoking any directly audible connection to the disco era. In this way, he was able to open gangsta cool to a laid-back, *sensual* soundscape without conjuring any images of the polyester tackiness or sexual ambiguity still associated with the fallen genre. As contemporary observers noted, it was this smoother, more pop-oriented sound that opened the door to mainstream radio airplay.[49]

Dr. Dre's adoption of the Minimoog also enabled him to evoke the Afro-futurist sound of Parliament-Funkadelic keyboardist Bernie Worrell. George Clinton's P-Funk collective—from which Dr. Dre adopted "G-funk" to describe his new sound—is central to understanding the way in which *The Chronic's* hit singles reimagined gangsta rap, and Worrell's synthesizer work is prominent on the majority of Parliament's most popular songs. Throughout the 1970s, he played on and helped arrange numerous hits, including "Mothership Connection (Star Child)" and "Give Up the Funk (Tear the Roof Off the Sucker)." For *The Chronic's* two hit singles, "Nuthin' But a 'G' Thang" and "Let Me Ride," Dre consciously sought to engage P-Funk's outer-space sound and imagery. Turning to the music and video for "Let Me Ride" illustrates how Parliament-Funkadelic's Mothership provided a useful point of reference for Dr. Dre's rearticulation of race.

THE "MOTHERSHIP CONNECTION" CONNECTION

Describing the Grammy Award–winning single in a 2010 retrospective, music critic Josh Tyrangiel mused, "'Let Me Ride' feels like dusk on a wide-open L.A. boulevard, full of possibility and menace."[50] Tyrangiel's car metaphor is no accident. Like "Nuthin' But a 'G' Thang," the imagery of the video for "Let Me Ride," and the style in which it is edited, amplify these themes, emphasizing a relaxed and fluid experience of city life. Instead of stuck on the streets battling it out with police, as in the video for "Straight Outta Compton," Dr. Dre spends the video for "Let Me Ride" cruising around the city in his vintage lowrider, a convertible 1964 Chevrolet Impala. The video opens with Dr. Dre cruising in his car. Close-up shots of the spinning wheels gleaming with chrome emphasize Dr. Dre's ability to move throughout the city with style (fig. 20). Dre shows off the hydraulic system that makes his car bounce and rise up on three wheels (fig. 21).

These images are juxtaposed with others of Dr. Dre rapping amongst a co-ed crowd of dancing partygoers. The imagery of "Straight Outta Compton," which cast the urban environment as a site of violent contestation, is replaced by a portrayal of a Los Angeles that offers ample opportunity for pleasure and celebration. For example, the interchange of the I-10 and I-110 freeways (a built feature that helps mark the northwestern boundary of South Central Los Angeles) is pictured in the video for "Let Me Ride" from high above (fig. 22). Rather than evoking the surveillance of police helicopters as one might expect from the gangsta genre, the image of the freeway intersection cross-fades to another shot of Dr. Dre cruising

Figure 20. Still image of spinning chrome wheels from the music video for Dr. Dre's "Let Me Ride."

Figure 21. Still image of Dre's 1964 Chevrolet Impala rising up on three wheels, from the music video for Dr. Dre's "Let Me Ride."

Figure 22. Still image of the I-10/I-110 interchange from the music video for Dr. Dre's "Let Me Ride." This image slowly fades into another shot of Dre cruising in his car.

in his car. Such effects emphasize the mobility of the gangsta within the quintessential Los Angeles experience of automobile travel.

N.W.A.'s "Straight Outta Compton" used no such fade-ins or fade-outs to transition between images. Rather, the video's editors employed sharp jump cuts, which emphasize the conflict between the police and members of the group. In the video for "Let Me Ride," fade-ins and fade-outs present smooth transitions between images. These effects imply that Dr. Dre moves fluidly between activities, riding in his car, rapping in the streets, shopping at the liquor store, and so on. The pace of the editing also matches the more relaxed feel of the musical track. Cutting between images occurs at a pace of about once per measure, and in some places even less frequently. The video's emphasis on mobility is amplified by the song's chorus, which features lengthy samples drawn from Parliament's "Mothership Connection (Star Child)." One of these samples comes from live footage of a P-Funk concert, where the song was used at the climax of the performance to signal the arrival of the Mothership.[51]

At the height of their popularity (1976–77), George Clinton's Parliament-Funkadelic collective toured the United States with an elaborate costumed stage show animating the group's funky mythology, including a giant spaceship that descended from above carrying Dr. Funkenstein (played by group leader George Clinton, of course).[52] P-Funk lore posited an Afrocentric universe with black people at the center of history. As Rickey Vincent explains, "Clinton and crew developed their own creation myths and their own black science-fiction in which the values and attributes alluded to by The Funk constituted the resolution of each tale."[53] At the point in the concert preceding the Mothership's arrival, the performers encouraged the audience to join in singing the refrain, "Swing down sweet chariot, stop, and let me ride." After intoning these words for several minutes, the band produced the Mothership, which descended from the rafters with Clinton aboard. The preeminent symbol of Clinton's "Afro-futurist" imagination, the Mothership symbolized the African American drive for freedom through a playful evocation of space travel.[54]

Rather than use samples to break up time into a quick succession of discrete musical events (as in the chorus of "Straight Outta Compton"), the chorus of "Let Me Ride" features a lengthy loop of "Mothership Connection (Star Child)" that repeats four times without interruption. Taking the sound and imagery of the music video together, we can easily imagine this chorus as music being played through the sound system in Dre's 1964 Impala. We even hear Dr. Dre's voice respond enthusiastically to each repetition of "swing down sweet chariot, stop and let me ride" with the phrase "Hell yeah," creating an uncanny call-and-response between the sample and Dre's "live" performance: his words, which could be directed at listeners—but more likely at the Parliament hook itself—imply a performance within a performance and grant a sudden authority to the sampled material. It is as if in this instance, Dr. Dre relinquishes the spotlight as the rap star and calls our attention to the power of "Mothership Connection (Star Child)" and its promise of transcendence.

Dr. Dre's particular use of "Mothership Connection" can be best characterized as "reverse troping," a practice that musicologist Felicia Miyakawa describes as "[using] snippets of borrowed material to comment on new texts and music."[55] Although hip hop producers often manipulate samples with little regard for their original contexts or meanings—what we might consider a purely formalist approach to sound collage—Miyakawa's work reminds us that beat makers also choose samples that comment on lyrics and amplify other elements within a musical track. The chorus of "Let Me Ride" ("swing down sweet chariot, stop and let me ride") is a clear example of such practices. Dr. Dre's sampling does not reflect a "pure" aestheticism unconcerned with the original meaning of the P-Funk sample; it reflects, instead, a deliberate attempt to make a thematic and symbolic connection to the sampled source. This view is confirmed by the music video for "Let Me

Ride," which ends with the splicing in of footage from a live P-Funk concert. As George Clinton (playing the role of Dr. Funkenstein) disappears
into the Mothership behind a white veil of artificial fog, Dr. Dre's face is
superimposed over the concert footage where Clinton was standing. This
creative decision might seem overly grandiose and presumptuous, but it
also suggests we take seriously the connection between the imagery and
aesthetics of "Mothership Connection (Star Child)" and "Let Me Ride."

G-funk's new drive to spatial transcendence comes into clearer focus if
we examine "Let Me Ride" and "Nuthin' But a 'G' Thang" from the perspective of cultural insiders. The "sweet chariot" that forms the subject of
the chorus to "Let Me Ride" touches on a trope with roots deep in the
African American past.[56] In fact, references to celestial chariots of various
types had already become standard practice in earlier African American
musical genres, and the celestial chariots of the bible had already been
recast as real-world vehicles in numerous blues, gospel, and funk songs.[57]
As Robin Kelley traces the badass pose and bawdy lyrics of gangsta rap back
to African American folk tales of Stagger Lee and various off-color blues
numbers, we can also identify an equally rich pedigree underlying Dr. Dre's
decision to cast his 1964 Chevrolet Impala as a vehicle with transcendental
powers.

In many ways, George Clinton's wacky P-Funk mythology reads like a
parody of the Nation of Islam's cosmogony as explained by the honorable
Elijah Mohammed. The Nation of Islam's foundational myth recasts U.S.
race relations as the result of an ancient experiment by an evil "big-head
scientist," Yakub, who created the white race through genetic experimenta-
tion. The white race went on to enslave and oppress the black man through
lies and trickery, and the Nation of Islam strives to bring about the end of
the white race's rule, freeing the black man.[58] Freedom is imagined to be
possible through the divine intervention of the Mother Plane. With Elijah
Mohammed seated as a rider in this divine chariot, the Mother Plane enacts
"apocalyptic retribution" against the sins of the white race, destroying the
world created by the white race and restoring order to the universe.[59]

In an exploration of the biblical roots of the Nation of Islam's cosmogony, Michael Lieb interprets Mohammed's vision of the Mother Plane as a
revision of the biblical story of Ezekiel's wheel: a vision of God's power
symbolized by turning, levitating, burning wheels.[60] Lieb argues that
Ezekiel's wheel informs numerous aspects of U.S. culture, particularly those
points at which the uses and abuses of technology become suffused with
divine character. In other words, the story of Ezekiel's wheel has become a
trope for the human race's attempts to harness the power of God through

technological means. Often the appropriation of divine technology leads to the compulsion to use heavenly powers to triumph over all those who stand in one's way. Not surprisingly, perhaps, the apocalyptic scenario Elijah Mohammed envisioned was especially attractive to an African American community deeply oppressed by a white majority.

As Lieb points out, however, Mohammed's narrative was not without precedent in African American culture. The brilliance of his vision lies in the way he titrated a new reading of Ezekiel's wheel with themes already circulating within black culture. For example, there are a numerous spirituals that make reference to the divine chariots of the Bible. The most famous, of course, is "Swing Low, Sweet Chariot," which is actually about Elijah's chariot (Kings 2:11). In other songs, the chariot was equated with a train, a form of mechanized technology that became a symbol of mobility and freedom for black southerners during the Great Migration. In fact, George Clinton may have borrowed the hook for the chorus of "Mothership Connection (Star Child)" from one such spiritual: "Train coming, oh let me ride/. . . Oh low down the chariot and let me ride."[61] Reimagining the death-dealing Mother Plane as an intergalactic party machine, P-Funk mythology offered listeners a vision of dance-floor transcendence with racialized religious overtones. Dr. Dre's 1964 Impala represents the next link in this signifying chain.

Robert Farris Thompson has written about the long tradition of automobiles, trains, and wheels representing transcendence in African American culture. Thompson recounts poet Daniel G. Hoffman's characterization of the train whistle as the distinctive symbol of black yearning, invoking themes of space, distance, and movement.[62] In more recent times, Thompson argues that the "locomotive wail" has given way to an appreciation of the "beauty of travel and transcendence" in "revolving, shining hubcaps" and the "turning of a rubber tire."[63] In Thompson's words, "automotive flash" has superseded the train whistle as the preeminent symbol of "black quest."[64] The sense of freedom and mobility portrayed in The Chronic's two singles "Let Me Ride" and "Nuthin' But a 'G' Thang" draw from this symbolic history.

Yet, it has been difficult for some critics to accept G-funk's "Afro-futurist" elements. In an article responding to the rise of outer-space themes in Lil Wayne's music, Jonah Weiner contends that until Lil Wayne began describing himself in extraterrestrial terms, gangsta rap had turned its back on Afro-futurism, planting itself firmly in the earthbound contexts of the 'hood. Under Dr. Dre's influence, according to Weiner, "cosmic journeys became fanciful departures from hip-hop's so-called 'true' locus, the flesh-and-blood, asphalt-and-concrete street."[65] Although there is some truth to

Weiner's assertion about gangsta authenticity being firmly planted in the 'hood, we have also seen the extent to which Dr. Dre relied on the music of George Clinton's Parliament-Funkadelic, the Afro-futurist group *par excellence*. In the case of G-funk, the Afro-futurist impulse was not jettisoned; it was selectively tapped for a new purpose. Dr. Dre's 1964 Impala represents the sweet chariot–cum–Mother Ship rearticulated for the new millennium. The irony of Dr. Dre's songs "Let Me Ride" and "Nuthin' But a 'G' Thang" is that they used the cultural resources of 1970s Afro-futurism to help promote what many regard as a negative, materialistic turn in rap music.[66] Dr. Dre appropriated the Mothership as a symbol of mobility, translating Clinton's funky ideology of freedom and collective salvation into a means of individual transcendence. The collective will and striving of a people symbolized by Mohammed's sweeping religious narrative (and Clinton's funky parody) finds itself recast as an earthbound vehicle seemingly directed at nothing more than the assertion of individual, which is to say gangsta, agency.

THE SOUND OF POST-SOUL SPACE

Reflecting on conceptions of freedom as they are expressed through African American cultural forms, Paul Gilroy has criticized the emergence of "automotivity" as a central trope of late-twentieth- and early-twenty-first-century black striving. Although Gilroy remains sensitive to the history of "racial terror, brutal confinement, and coerced labour" that makes the car so attractive as a symbol of black escape, he ultimately concludes that the investment in expensive, shiny automobiles—like other forms of conspicuous consumption—offers only a simulation of liberation.[67] In fact, given the individualistic nature of cars as commodities, he asserts that the automobile has become "the instrument of segregation and privatization, not an aid to their overcoming."[68] Gilroy's concerns are motivated, not surprisingly, by his appraisal of the state of hip hop culture and rap music at the dawn of the new millennium. Titling the chapter from which the previous quotes were drawn "Get Free or Die Tryin'," he makes a play on rapper 50 Cent's *Get Rich or Die Tryin'* (2003), the multi-platinum-selling debut album produced by none other than Dr. Dre.[69] Taking aim at "bling" style, Gilroy decries the celebration of material gain and consumptive practices that have replaced previous (read as civil rights–era) metaphors for human freedom and equality in black popular culture.

Making this departure from more collective, community-centered ideas about freedom and success central to her analysis of gangsta rap, Eithne

Quinn casts the sound, imagery, and lyrics of G-funk as the musical equivalent of what Nelson George terms a "post-soul" sensibility. According to George, the post-soul sensibility encompasses the "death of politics," materialism, individualism, and an anti-romantic attitude toward sex.[70] Quinn finds this ideology crystallized in G-funk's main themes: cruising, marijuana, money making, and casual sex.[71] Yet, she avoids pinning the blame for these attitudes on gangsta rappers themselves and insists that we examine them against the political backdrop of neoliberal economic and social policy. Turning our attention to the articulation of G-funk's sound and imagery and their reception suggests that Dr. Dre's "Nuthin' But a 'G' Thang" and "Let Me Ride" sounded race as black neoliberalism.

David Harvey explains that "neoliberalism is in the first instance a theory of political economic practices that proposes that human well-being can best be advanced by liberating individual entrepreneurial freedoms and skills within an institutional framework characterized by strong private property rights, free markets, and free trade."[72] Gaining traction in the late 1970s and 1980s, neoliberal policies, such as the North American Free Trade Agreement (NAFTA), sought to dismantle barriers to free trade and investment. They also took aim at state programs, such as welfare and other social services, deemed to be impeding entrepreneurial freedom and economic activity. In the United States, such policies tend to favor private capital over public institutions, and the 1980s and 1990s witnessed the steady erosion of programs set up in the mid-twentieth century to ensure public well-being. Welfare reform, the defunding and privatization of public services, and the deregulation of industry are all facets of neoliberal policy. As critics of neoliberalism (including Harvey) argue, the human costs of applying market-based logic to economically vulnerable communities have been severe. Welfare reform might *in principle* seek to decrease dependency and "liberate" the workforce, but by stripping citizens of institutional protections, neoliberal economic policy leaves few choices to the economically disadvantaged, whether they are living in 1980s Compton or present-day Bangladesh.

Yet, one of neoliberal ideology's main strengths has been the ease with which it is absorbed by the culture at large, affecting how people view themselves as workers and consumers. As Harvey notes, neoliberalism has worked its way into our habits of thought to become "the common-sense way many of us interpret, live in, and understand the world."[73] By attaching itself to political ideals of "human dignity" and "personal freedom," neoliberalism has been embraced even by those whose well-being has suffered the most under its policies. Thus, rather than understand gangsta rap's individualistic ethos as a pathology of underclass black youth—as many critics of the music have done—it is better to interpret the post-soul sensibility in G-funk as a political strategy of economic survivalism. As Quinn explains, "Gangsta's governing ethic of aggressive economic self-determination is clearly legible when seen as a tactical response to the steady depletion of resources, rights, and modes of resistance."[74] In other words, the economic and social policies of the Reagan-Bush years created an environment that necessitated and rewarded the adoption of a survival-of-the-fittest mentality.[75] Analyzing Dr. Dre's and Snoop Doggy Dogg's lyrics as primary evidence, Quinn claims that "much of the social significance [of G-funk] derived from its ability to articulate post–civil rights ideas about family, work, masculinity, and advancement."[76]

Examining another set of lyrics from "Let Me Ride," we can clearly see how G-funk rejected previous forms of black politics centered on collective action. Promising "no medallions, dreadlocks, or black fists," Dre names and rejects three symbols of black collectivity and resistance: the African medallions made popular by neonationalist group Public Enemy, dreadlocks symbolizing Rastafarianism, and black fists associated with the Black Power movement of the late 1960s and 1970s. These symbols of black freedom find themselves supplanted by the gangsta, whose ruthless entrepreneurial activity through rap leads to financial success ("that gangsta shit that makes me gangs of snaps"), coded here as the true form of liberation. What role do Dr. Dre's musical choices play in advancing this neoliberal attitude toward culture and politics?

Quinn briefly characterizes the musical aesthetics of G-funk as "laid-back," "low metabolism" beats mirroring the nonchalant attitude of G-funk artists.[77] There is some truth to this description: it is difficult to imagine Snoop Doggy Dogg seated on a porch—as he is in the video for "Who Am I (What's My Name)?"—delivering his smooth Calabama drawl over the frenetic beat from "Straight Outta Compton." But I am skeptical about her assertion that Dr. Dre's sampling of Parliament-Funkadelic, as well as other soul artists of the 1960s and 1970s, was an act of nostalgia signaling the genre's deepening engagement with its parent culture.[78] The problem with this explanation is that Dr. Dre—like virtually all hip hop producers active in the late 1980s and early 1990s—had been sampling the soul music of the 1960s and 1970s throughout his tenure with N.W.A. What had changed by 1993 was not necessarily the artists he chose to sample, but rather the kinds of breaks that he chose and the way that he manipulated them to curate an overall vibe that differed from his previous work.

Rather than simply hearing the music as a nostalgic yearning for community that counter-balances harsh lyrics and imagery, it is also plausible to hear Dr. Dre's rearticulation of P-Funk's transcendental hippie vibe as complementary to the ruthless individualism of post-soul politics. The relaxed groove of "Nuthin' But a 'G' Thang" and the spacious soundscape of "Let Me Ride" helped portray the gangsta as a sophisticated entrepreneur able to rise above his surroundings to conquer the dog-eat-dog world of the ghetto. What our close look at the sound and imagery of these songs reveals is the extent to which the aesthetics of G-funk draw, refashion, and rearticulate soul music's collectivist project for the neoliberal era. The music is not simply a nostalgic or ironic background against which we witness the same old portrayals of gangsta identity. Instead, the music is an active player, just as important as the lyrics, publicity imagery, reception discourse, and political context that Quinn so astutely analyzes. Indeed, it is the musical "mapping" of urban space in "Let Me Ride" and "Nuthin' But a 'G' Thang" that helps reflect gangsta rap's acceptance of neoliberal hegemony.

CONCLUSION: BIRTH OF THE BLING

The sound of *The Chronic*'s hit singles differed remarkably from that of N.W.A.'s *Straight Outta Compton* or *Niggaz4Life*, shifting from a frenetic and noisy aesthetic to one that sounds significantly more open and relaxed. In contrast to N.W.A.'s music videos, which featured the group's members under police surveillance and being chased through South Central L.A.'s streets, the videos for *The Chronic*'s "Nuthin' But a 'G' Thang" and "Let Me Ride" evoked a new sense of mobility and freedom for the gangsta. Rather than presenting the 'hood as a place of conflict and struggle, the gangsta experience was offered up as a site of pleasure one might comfortably attempt to re-create within the confines of one's own car or suburban home. Drawing on a variety of cultural resources, Dr. Dre crafted an aesthetic that detached the image of the gangsta from its embattled origins in the ghetto and made him a symbol of unfettered mobility thanks to entrepreneurial striving. *The Chronic*'s commercial success thus foreshadowed a change taking place in the music and advertising industries: the gangsta would soon leave the world of malt liquor and blue-collar fashion behind, becoming by the end of the twentieth century one of the dominant models of conspicuous consumption.

A glance at more recent popular culture shows just how far gangsta has come. By the end of the 1990s, rap music symbolized a level of economic success and lavish consumption unimaginable at the time of the genre's birth. In a 2008 comedy sketch on *The Daily Show with Jon Stewart*, Stewart, who is white, and African American cast member Wyatt Cenac played a fake game show entitled "Rapper or Republican?" The skit's punch lines involved Stewart's being unable to tell the difference between various rap artists and famous conservatives. After hearing clues about their various business dealings, Stewart ends up confusing Ice-T and Fred Thompson, DJ Quik and Larry Craig, and 50 Cent and Mitt Romney.[79] In the 1980s, a satirist might have skewered Donald Trump or Leona Helmsley as signs of ultraconservatism and materialistic excess; in the 2000s, rap musicians made equally inviting targets. Gangsta rap has thus become a metaphor for the ruthless profit-seeking and seductive pleasures of capitalism.[80]

These shifts in political and aesthetic orientation help explain the conflicting assessments of *The Chronic* by fans, critics, and historians. Even Robin D. G. Kelley, whose analysis of gangsta rap remains one of the most sympathetic and thoughtful explorations of the genre's significance, seemed disturbed by the "senseless, banal nihilism" and misogyny he hears in Dr. Dre and Snoop Doggy Dogg's music.[81] Assessing the state of gangsta rap at the end of 1993, Kelley feared that rap music was not taking the progressive turn many had hoped for. Far from it—the music seemed reduced to, as he put it, "nihilism for nihilism's sake."[82] Writing for the *Village Voice*, Robert Christgau also refused to buy into the hype, dismissing *The Chronic*'s "conscienceless" violence and smooth style of production as "sociopathic easy-listening."[83] However, for many others the arrival of Dr. Dre's solo album took hip hop to new heights. *The Source* magazine praised *The Chronic* as an "innovative and progressive hip hop package," awarding the album four and a half microphones (out of five).[84] Seemingly unconcerned with the album's casual violence and misogyny, the review heaped praise on Dr. Dre's music production.

Rather than understand these appraisals of *The Chronic*'s worth simply as contradicting opinions, I want to suggest that they represent two sides of the same coin. The political and aesthetic dimensions of the album are both critical to the way that Dr. Dre presents his vision of the good life. If *Straight Outta Compton* was designed to force listeners to confront the harsh, hidden realities of inner city life, *The Chronic*'s two hit singles seemed intent on meeting suburban listeners closer to home. As a final example, consider Dr. Dre and Snoop Doggy Dogg's appearance with host Fab Five Freddy in a 1993 episode of *Yo! MTV Raps*. The episode was set, not in the inner city neighborhood of Compton, but in the back yard of Dr. Dre's expansive suburban Woodland Hills home.[85] Conducting the interview with Fab Five Freddy at a poolside barbeque replete with nameless, bikini-clad "honies," the duo presented a vision of the gangsta lifestyle filled with endless sunshine, objectified women, and hedonistic consumption. Discussing his obsessive studio work ethic, *The Chronic's* multi-platinum sales, and Snoop's forthcoming solo debut *Doggystyle,* Dr. Dre also jokes with the young ladies, exhorting them to "keep hope alive" and asking them "Why can't we all get along?" Signifying on the iconic words of Jesse Jackson and Rodney King, respectively, these utterances perform a dual function: flirting with the "honies" while also trolling the naive optimism of civil rights–era politics. The easy way that Dr. Dre and Snoop Doggy Dogg conduct themselves in front of the camera—much like their G-funk musical style—suggests a cool and cynical accommodation with the realities of the neoliberal era.[86] Sociopathic easy-listening indeed.

The Chronic's sounding of race as gangsta cool encapsulates our culture's ambivalence regarding the promises and pitfalls of capitalism. In introducing a new sense of rap authenticity, Dr. Dre set the tone for the genre's commercial expansion in the 1990s as a fantasy world of champagne, SUVs, and private jets. Adam Krims argues that rap music's turn toward "bling" and conspicuous consumption in the mid-1990s reflected and participated in the middle- and upper-class "reconquest of the American metropolis," more commonly known as "gentrification."[87] If N.W.A.'s music predicted the riots, mapping the hostile terrain where African American youth confronted the LAPD, then perhaps Dr. Dre's *The Chronic* foreshadowed the gradual gentrification of urban space in post-riot Los Angeles. This new style of consumption was accompanied and abetted by a new musical mapping of Los Angeles. Thus, *The Chronic* and Dr. Dre's drive into the popular mainstream was tied to a spatial project that far exceeded the boundaries of the recording industry.

4 "My Name Is"

Signifying Whiteness, Rearticulating Race

> Black music centers blackness, yet it does so in continual relation to
> the category and experience of whiteness in America. If black music
> supplies a supplementary difference to whiteness, so does it
> complicate white racial fixity.[1]
>
> **Ronald Radano**

In the closing weeks of 1998, *Billboard* magazine celebrated rap music's commercial success with an article entitled "Rap Rips Up the Charts."[2] The author,
Shawnee Smith, noted with satisfaction that the "increasing and steady presence" of rap songs on the Billboard 200 chart was a clear indication that hip
hop music was nowhere near its end and had firmly ensconced itself within
the industry as a major presence. What is more, she emphasized that artists
whose songs were charting and reaching a mainstream audience were the
ones bringing a more "severe" form of hip hop, the ones who "just expect us
to accept them as they are, no matter how ghetto, country, or vulgar they
may be."[3] In other words, far from "going pop" as some observers had feared,
rap music had generated increasing profits and extended its cultural influence
while embracing its ties to the 'hood—a spatial construct associated with
some of the poorest and most socially marginalized members of U.S. society.[4]
As Smith explained, Def Jam had scored the biggest upset of the year when
hardcore rapper DMX knocked Garth Brooks off the top of the Billboard 200,
and the rise of Southern rap led by New Orleans–bred Master P's No Limit
Records seemed to make no concessions to middle-class sensibilities.[5] As hip
hop and rap music became integrated into a vast mass communications network that included music production, film, television, and various other marketing and advertising ventures, platinum-selling artists including the
Wu-Tang Clan, DMX, Jay-Z, Snoop Doggy Dogg, the Notorious B.I.G., and
Tupac Shakur, among others, emphasized their "realness" and refusal to "sell
out." The tragic feud between Tupac and Biggie Smalls was in many ways
fueled by competing claims of hip hop authenticity: whose ties to the 'hood
were more "real?" Which coast (East or West) was the best?

Examining the genre's evolution from a communication-studies framework, Murray Forman notes that, heading into the mid-1990s, rap musicians were defining themselves with increasingly specific references to place. The generalized ghetto landscape portrayed in Grandmaster Flash and the Furious Five's "The Message" had given way to more detailed representations of urban space, such as N.W.A.'s "Straight Outta Compton." Other groups, like those associated with No Limit Records, followed suit, seeking to stake out a claim for their respective blocks. The previous chapter explored how Dr. Dre's rearticulation of gangsta identity depended in large part on the way his music and music videos depicted a particular relationship to Los Angeles's urban environment. As Forman put it in the title of his study, in hip hop and rap music "the 'hood comes first."

For these reasons, the sudden success of Eminem—the white rapper who first rose to prominence in 1999 with *The Slim Shady LP*, an album that often called direct attention to his racial identity—invites our attention. Eminem was not the first white rapper to sell well or to attract a large following. But unlike previous white artists such as the Beastie Boys or 3rd Bass, he did so at a time when the genre had become dominated by a ghetto-centric ethos of "keeping it real." Seemingly aware of these racial and spatial politics, the 2002 film *8 Mile*, whose title refers to the Detroit road separating the chocolate city from its vanilla suburbs, gives a semi-autobiographical account of Eminem as a marginalized character seeking to break through rap's racially defined standards of authenticity. Yet, how did a genre whose modes of representation had become so thoroughly committed to the production of blackness help give rise to a viable white identity?

The answer to this question lies in this chapter's epigram in which Ronald Radano explains the relationship between black identity and white identity as reciprocal in nature. Since whiteness has been constructed in opposition to and as essentially different from blackness, Radano explains that changes in black music ultimately have a destabilizing effect on "white racial fixity." In this chapter I examine how Eminem's success depended upon the particular way his music made whiteness audible *in relation to* musical blackness, proving that rap producers could also manipulate breaks to articulate non-black identity.

In the closing decades of the twentieth century, popular music was one area of U.S. culture in which the meanings and significance of whiteness were undergoing transformation. Writing on the subject in 1998, Cameron McCarthy declared that American society had entered "new racial times, new racial circumstances," and that there existed among the white middle class a "growing anxiety and restlessness."[6] Numerous other scholars agreed, pointing to a number of developments in U.S. society since the 1960s that had contributed to a "crisis of whiteness," including the civil rights movement, global anticolonial struggles, immigration reform, feminism, and deindustrialization.[7] By the turn of the century, it appeared that the nature and meaning of whiteness was undergoing a historic transformation.

To make a somewhat crude distinction, whiteness in the pre–civil rights era operated as a norm, an everywhere-but-nowhere canvas upon which social life was painted. Under these circumstances, white identity was defined more by what it was not—a racialized minority identity—than by what it was. White ethnics and other racialized groups who wanted to enjoy the benefits afforded by whiteness worked to shed their difference, hoping to pass into the great majority. In the last decades of the twentieth century, however, the presumed invisibility of whiteness was becoming increasingly untenable. Although racism and the legacy of discriminatory practices continued to be defining features of U.S. society, whiteness was also becoming visible in new ways. The rise of multiculturalism in coalition politics and academic institutions subjected white supremacy to critique. In popular culture, some post-1960s African American performers were emboldened to openly critique the attitudes and behaviors of whites. Comedians such as Eddie Murphy and Chris Rock used high-pitched nasal voices and stiff posturing of their bodies to poke fun at supposed white mannerisms. At the same time, new forms of black expressivity such as hip hop and rap music saturated mainstream culture without first having to be remade as white, redefining for a generation of youth what it meant to be "cool." In this context, where the meaning of racial difference was being challenged and renegotiated, Eminem's rise to stardom promises to tell us something about the evolution of whiteness.

Rather than simply transcending racial boundaries, Eminem had to negotiate them in ways that made sense to his audiences. To examine Eminem's performances is to understand something about the dynamic nature of racial categories, to begin mapping how notions of whiteness were changing, both within rap music and outside it. Tracing his artistic evolution, particularly the distance between his first, independently produced album, *Infinite* (1996), and his mainstream debut single, "My Name Is" (1999), reveals that to become successful in a genre coded as black, Eminem had to resolve his own "crisis of whiteness."[8] His mainstream debut presents us with an opportunity to understand white identity not as a fixed essence but as a dynamic construct that is constantly undergoing change. By making whiteness audible in new ways, Eminem's music sounded various hopes and fears regarding race's significance at the close of the twentieth century.

EMINEM'S "CRISIS OF WHITENESS"

Eminem's two hit albums, *The Slim Shady LP* (1999) and *The Marshall Mathers LP* (2000), established him as one of the biggest rap stars of the new millennium.[9] Although Eminem seemed to appear on the radio and cable television fully formed, the artistic strategy that proved to be such a potent force took years to develop. The artifice behind Eminem's infamous celebrity did not occur to him immediately; rather, it was born from his experiences as a young white male struggling to become a successful rapper. In fact, his early attempts to make a name for himself in the music industry appear to have backfired. As we will soon see, developing a style of music that showcased his virtuosic rapping skills and familiarity with urban street life failed to impress listeners and confirmed that his whiteness could be a dangerous professional liability.

Growing up in the Detroit area on the outskirts of the African American sections of town, Marshall Mathers III spent his teenage years working in the local hip hop scene as the rapper Eminem, a name derived from the spelling of his initials, "M&M." As biographer Anthony Bozza explains, while struggling to support himself by working a series of minimum-wage jobs, Mathers borrowed $1,500 from music producers Mark and Jeff Bass to press 500 copies of his first album, *Infinite* (1996).[10] The independently produced album showcased Eminem's smooth lyrical flow, and Mathers hoped it might gain him some much-needed recognition in the local hip hop scene, eventually landing him a recording contract. *Infinite* contains eleven tracks covering some of the common tropes found in 1990s rap music. In the songs "313" and "Open Mic," for example, Eminem flexes his wit by demonstrating his adeptness at boasting and signifying. Battling an unnamed foe, he uses a series of intricate rhymes and violent metaphors to symbolically dominate the opposition. The album also contains more serious and autobiographical musings. In "Never Too Far," which begins by staging an impromptu conversation at a cold Detroit bus stop, Eminem and a friend commiserate about their financial difficulties. Following this introduction, Eminem raps about staying inspired and achieving his dreams so that he can do right by his family. Finally, *Infinite* also features two adolescent love songs: "Jealousy Woes" recounts the troubles Eminem is having with an unnamed female who mistreats him despite how hard he tries to impress her; "Searchin" features Eminem rapping tenderly about "snuggling," "kissing," and "hugging" an unnamed lover. Although the songs on *Infinite* exemplify various hip hop archetypes, they differ in an important way from his later commercial releases: throughout the course of the album, Eminem never once mentions his racial identity.

By choosing not to call attention to his whiteness, Eminem was following the example of previous white MCs who had adopted a particular strategy for dealing with their status as racial outsiders. In the mid-1980s through the early-1990s, groups such as the Beastie Boys, 3rd Bass, and Marky Mark and the Funky Bunch employed a strategy of "immersion" to communicate their proximity to African Americans and black culture.[11] These rappers rarely, if ever, mentioned their whiteness. Instead, they emphasized their familiarity with hip hop music, their support of antiracist politics, or other characteristics that helped to establish their credibility with fans.[12] In a similar way, Eminem's efforts on *Infinite* avoided his racial difference, emphasizing instead his lyrical skills and awareness of prevailing hip hop trends.

In addition to the immersive content of Eminem's lyrics, the formal properties of his music—his lyrical flow, rhyme schemes, and beats—also conformed to contemporary trends in rap music, particularly the sound of mid-1990s New York–based rap. To begin with, Eminem's imaginative internal rhyming and complex rhythmic flow were associated with the work of AZ, Jay-Z, Lord Finesse, and Nas. The first two lines of the example below demonstrate these types of rhyme schemes (table 4). Eminem rhymes homonyms "beat commence" (referring to the musical track of the song) and "beat the sense" (referring to striking an object). He also rhymes clusters of words (e.g., "meat to mince" and "feet to rinse," "burial of Jesus" and "venereal diseases"). Rather than just rhyming the last syllable or the last word of every measure—the standard practice in much old school hip hop—Eminem creates churning internal rhymes that break up the monotony of standard four-measure phrasing. Such rhyme schemes allow his lyrics to spill over the measure lines (enjambment), creating phrases whose rhythms and rhymes often cadence well before or after the downbeat. Such musical features represented what contemporary critics termed the "faster cadences" and "new rhyme patterns" of certain mid-1990s emcees.[13] Adam Krims coined the term "speech-percussive" to describe such virtuosic flows, arguing that they became emblematic of "reality rap" from New York City in the 1990s.[14]

This style of rhyming was most often paired with a stripped-down, back-to-basics musical aesthetic. In fact, the beats that Detroit producers Mark and Jeff Bass created to underpin Eminem's rapping also drew upon the sound of New York City, whose artists emphasized a more "minimalist" and "cerebral" approach than the dense, funk-inspired sound of Los Angeles–based gangsta rap producer Dr. Dre.[15] In general, this sparse New York sound was characterized by beats featuring eight-count hi-hats, interlocking snare and kick drum breaks, and the layering of samples culled from 1960s jazz and soul recordings. All of the musical tracks on Eminem's

Table 4. Rhyming words and phrases in the first verse and chorus of "Infinite" (Eminem, *Infinite*, bootleg, 1996)

	Internal and multiple-word rhymes
Verse 2	
mm. 1–2	beat commence, beat the sense; meat to mince, feet to rinse
mm. 3–5	spoil loyal fans, foil plans, oil pans, coiled hands
mm. 5–6	are lethal, cerebral, jeep full of people, are feeble
mm. 11–12	burial of Jesus, venereal diseases
mm. 13–14	thesis, pieces, releases, masterpieces, telekinesis
Chorus	
mm. 1–2	infinite, sent from it, I went to it
m. 2	serving a sentence, murdering instruments
mm. 3–4	repent from it, attempt at it, infinite

Infinite are indebted to this aesthetic. What gives these tracks an even more distinctive New York flavor is the way that the interlocking snare and kick-drum beats appear to be set to a swinging scale of sixteenth-note triplets—a common practice for New York hip hop producers of this era, including Ski Beatz, Q-Tip, Premier, and Lord Finesse, among others.[16] Thus, the tracks on *Infinite* share a groove, a feel, with numerous New York–based rap albums of the time.[17]

Despite its demonstrating great lyrical skill and an awareness of prevailing musical trends in the rap music industry, *Infinite's* impact was infinitesimal: it was ignored by local radio, music retailers, critics, and talent scouts alike. The problem may have been the album's relatively low production values; the beats created by the Bass brothers sound amateurish next to those of contemporary commercial releases. But the album's lack of success may also have stemmed in part from the way Mathers positioned himself artistically. Remarking on *Infinite*, Bozza explains that Eminem "was an able rhymer in 1996, but he wasn't angry, fed up, or at wit's end. He was just trying to fit in; just rhyming intricate words because he could."[18] Certainly, the album is almost completely devoid of the signature humor and politically incorrect aggression that would make Eminem famous in later years. But we might understand more about Eminem's lack of success by placing his immersive artistic strategy in the context of 1996, only a few years removed from the dramatic rise and fall of another white rapper: Vanilla Ice.

Vanilla Ice's mainstream debut *To the Extreme* arrived in record stores on August 28, 1990.[19] The album's first single, "Ice Ice Baby," got heavy radio play and its video was featured prominently on MTV. With a sleek chorus built around a sample from Queen and David Bowie's "Under Pressure," the single propelled the album to No. 1 on the pop charts for sixteen weeks. Vanilla Ice's good fortune, however, was short-lived. After a group of enterprising high school student reporters from Miami uncovered his real name in school district records and learned that Robert Van Winkle had grown up in a stable, upper-middle-class suburban home, his street credibility was ruined. Even before this discovery, however, the tough image he attempted to project in music videos, public appearances, and even a full-length feature film seemed to many a hollow and exploitative imitation of black hip hop. Hip hop insiders agonized over the fate of the genre, wondering aloud whether Vanilla Ice's popularity signaled that rap was going to go pop. Capitalizing on the backlash against Vanilla Ice's sudden popularity, white rap group 3rd Bass released "Pop Goes the Weasel," a polemical song that— much like the group's earlier hit "The Gas Face"—railed against commercially oriented rappers and positioned themselves as true keepers of hip hop authenticity. Seeking to distance their group from Vanilla Ice, the song's music video features a character dressed flamboyantly as the white rapper who is mocked and then mercilessly beaten by 3rd Bass.[20]

The failure of Vanilla Ice's "imitative" strategy had a chilling effect on the prospects facing other white rappers who hoped to broker a major record deal.[21] From Vanilla Ice's fall to Eminem's successful debut at the end of the decade, no new white rap acts were able to establish themselves in the genre. Eminem's early efforts were evaluated in this context, and his imitation of mid-1990s East Coast style did not ring true to listeners. His critics were quick to point out that the album sounded more like a demo tape from New York than one from Detroit, and this seeming lack of originality resulted in Eminem being labeled an imitator and unfavorably compared to African American rappers. Eminem remembers the way he was dismissed by some of his African American peers: "'I caught a lot of flak: 'You're trying to sound like Nas. You're trying to sound like AZ. You're trying to sound like somebody from New York. And you're white. You shouldn't rap. You should go into rock 'n' roll.'"[22]

RESOLVING THE CRISIS, SIGNIFYING WHITENESS

The irony of condemning Eminem as an imitator and suggesting that he "go into rock 'n' roll" is of course that it assumes rock and roll to be a "white" musical genre. In fact, the rock and roll phenomenon began as a way for the music industry to market black rhythm and blues to white teenagers.[23] Eventually, white performers were able to move to the forefront of the genre, displacing African American musicians and enjoying greater fame and financial rewards. In this way, rock became "white," just like swing (Bennie Goodman as "the King of Swing") and early jazz (Paul Whiteman as "the King of Jazz"). Eminem's stardom cannot be detached from this long problematic history of white performers profiting from their proximity to musical blackness. In fact, Eminem has used his music to display an awareness of this history, comparing himself (satirically) to the white "King of Rock and Roll," Elvis Presley.[24] The difference in Eminem's case is that unlike rock and swing, rap never became white. In the wake of the Vanilla Ice controversy, the genre's racial boundaries seemed to grow even less permeable as people in the recording industry refused to risk their reputations and resources on nonblack performers. Dr. Dre, who eventually helped introduce Eminem to a mainstream audience and produced his debut single, reports being cautioned by friends and business associates not to risk his reputation by backing a white rapper.

These dynamics forced Eminem and his team of producers to cultivate a musical strategy that would be capable of transforming his whiteness from a liability into an asset. By the release of *The Slim Shady LP* (1999), Eminem had arrived at a formula for dealing with his racial identity in a productive way. He had to do more than simply fit in with and match the talent of his African American peers; he had to transform how whiteness mattered in rap. To make a place for himself in the music industry, he employed an approach that rap scholar Mickey Hess labels "inversion." Parodying common understandings of whiteness, Eminem advanced a white identity both at ease with black culture and humble before it.[25] He also emphasized the contradictions in whiteness, particularly with respect to class, allowing him to recast himself as the ultimate underdog.

The vehicle for this strategy was the debut single from *The Slim Shady LP*, "My Name Is." In an interview around the time of the album's release, Eminem announced that the song would be "like my introduction to the world. ["My Name Is"] is going to be the record that, like, promotes the album before it comes out and, like, gets it up to where it needs to be. You know what I mean? For me to, like, establish my following throughout the world."[26] The song was a huge success, paving the way for Eminem to reach international stardom. "A hummable anthem that trademarked Eminem in just one song," as Bozza put it, "My Name Is" spent eleven weeks on Billboard's Rap Singles chart, peaking at No. 10.[27] However, the Billboard charts only tell a part of the story. In an age in which music video does as much as, and often more than, radio airplay to introduce new artists to the public, the video for the single received nonstop attention from MTV. As the first song and video to introduce him to the public at large, "My Name Is" was carefully crafted and chosen for this exact purpose by producer Dr. Dre.

Although Dr. Dre became widely known to the public as his producer, "My Name Is" was one of just three songs he produced, out of twenty on the album.[28] In this song, Dr. Dre followed the same strategy he had used with his previous protégé, Snoop Doggy Dogg, whose debut single was entitled "Who Am I (What's My Name?)."[29] The remarkable quality of both of these singles is the way they serve a utilitarian advertising purpose of introducing the artists' names by repeating them *ad nauseum*, while also managing to sound as confident as if the artists were already superstars. Dr. Dre also co-directed the video for "My Name Is," and its carefully crafted synergy of image, sound, and text reveals a well-conceived strategy for taking a preemptive swipe at Eminem's whiteness, accomplishing what sociologist Edward G. Armstrong describes as "a self-conscious parody of rap's racially based authenticity."[30] Turning his whiteness into a humorous act, Eminem anticipated possible criticism about his racial identity and turned the tables on would-be critics.

In her expansive work on art, literature, and music, Linda Hutcheon encourages scholars to cast a wide net in theorizing how parody functions across a variety of contexts. Hutcheon defines parody broadly as "a form of repetition with ironic critical distance, marking difference rather than similarity."[31] By this definition, one can observe parody at work in numerous rap music contexts. For example, De La Soul's "Ego Trippin' (Part Two)" and the music video for the Roots' "What They Do" each serves as a way for "underground" rappers to satirize the materialistic, misogynistic exploits of more successful "mainstream" ones.[32] In other cases, African American rappers have taken aim at whites, satirizing record executives (e.g., Dr. Dre's brutal sendup of former manager Jerry Heller in the video for "Wit Dre Day") and law enforcement agents (e.g., N.W.A.'s videos for "Straight Outta Compton" and "100 Miles and Running").[33] Perhaps the closest point of comparison to Eminem's use of parody, however, can be found in the crossover success of the first platinum-selling rap album in history: the Beastie Boys' *License to Ill* (1986). In the songs "No Sleep Till Brooklyn" and "Fight For Your Right (To Party)," the group delivered their raps over a simple rock backbeat and distorted electric guitar, the stereotypical sound of white youth culture in the 1980s.[34] The content of these songs, particularly "Fight For Your Right (To Party)," seemed to take an ironic stab at the apathy and narcissism of privileged white youth. (How many of their young listeners were in on the

Figure 23. Cover of Eminem's debut single, "My Name Is" (Interscope Records 97470, 1999).

joke is another question.) In any case, the strategy paid off by attracting young white fans to rap music and helping the group avoid charges that they were simply imitating African American performers. As African American rapper Q-Tip once explained, "You know why I could fuck with [the Beastie Boys]? They don't try to be black. They're just themselves."[35]

In a somewhat similar fashion, "My Name Is" imitates and comments upon numerous faces of whiteness—the suburban white male, the politician, the rock star, and so on. Thus, it offers a prime example of how the aesthetic strategy of parody can work together in lyrics, images, and sound. Although Eminem never explicitly states his racial identity, the lyrics of the song continuously play with various tropes of whiteness. To begin with, the chorus of the song repeats the phrase, "Hi, my name is," which is about as "square" and "standard" a way as one could introduce oneself. Eminem's "Hi," enthusiastically shouted on the downbeat, seems coated in forced sincerity. The image printed on the jacket of the single drives home the joke, featuring the kind of name tag one would wear at a business event, or another stereotypically "white" engagement such as a PTA meeting (fig. 23).

The lyrics of the first verse make ample reference to white popular cultural icons such as the industrial rock band Nine Inch Nails, the pop group the Spice Girls, and television star Pamela Anderson Lee.[36] But the way Eminem makes these references distances him from mainstream (read as "white") culture. For example, he mocks the band Nine Inch Nails by taking its name literally as a set of objects to be poked through his eyelids. The Spice Girls and Pamela Anderson Lee serve a similar function as easy targets of adolescent male aggression. By claiming to "impregnate" a Spice Girl and "rip Pamela Lee's tits off," Eminem's violent, cartoonish, and misogynistic humor consciously distances him from conventional representations of whiteness, positioning him as a social rebel on par with, but clearly not the same as, his African American counterparts. As *New York Times* critic Jon Pareles put it: "Eminem isn't a gangsta rapper, because he's got no gang; he's a friendless troublemaker who insults or attacks everyone he meets."[37]

Yet, above all else, Eminem is rapping. As the title of this chapter suggests, he demonstrates a white version of signifying, playing with language to emphasize his verbal creativity. In doing so, Eminem creates an unexpected "call and response" with hip hop and rap music tradition.[38] He drops in a humorous reference to earlier commercial fads when he claims he "knocked [Pamela Lee's] clothes backwards like Kriss Kross," a pop rap act that launched a short-lived fad in 1992 by wearing their clothing backwards. Although his rhythmic and verbal complexity is more restrained and measured than in the songs on the *Infinite* album, his characteristic propensity for internal rhyme remains intact (e.g., he rhymes "dead weight" with "head straight" and "impregnate"; see table 5). The key to the success of "My Name Is" lies in the way Eminem masters the formal elements of rap music (i.e., rhythmic flow and rhyme scheme) while introducing content that is new and unfamiliar to the genre. For example, he avoids relying on stock images and phrases from the hip hop lexicon: when he mentions marijuana, which by the late 1990s was strongly associated with rap music, he does so by choosing the white, hippie-derived term *grass*, rather than the *weed* or *chronic* favored by African American rappers.

Reflecting on Eminem's creative vision, rapper Ice-T succinctly described him as "Jerry Springer to music."[39] Like that daytime television talk show, "My Name Is" offers up a feast of dysfunctional behavior for the world to see. Slim Shady reveals to his listeners that his mom does drugs and that he has flunked out of junior high school several times. He even commits self-inflicted violence, shooting and hanging himself. In this fashion, the video, co-directed by Dr. Dre, conjures stock images of whiteness to expose and transform them. To construct its visual parody of whiteness, the video for "My Name Is" begins

Table 5. Rhyming words and phrases in the first verse of "My Name Is" (Eminem, *The Slim Shady LP,* Interscope Records 90287, 1999)

	Internal and multiple-word rhymes
Verse 1	
mm. 1–2	hi kids, violence, eyelids
mm. 5–6	dead weight, head straight, impregnate
mm. 7–8	basehead, face red, wasted
mm. 10–11	pissed off, tits off, Kriss Kross
mm. 14–15	that's my girl dog, piss the world off

by toying with middle America, crystallized in the image of its most cherished leisure activity: television. Eminem appears on a living room television set and begins performing the song using various costumes that represent white stereotypes. Opening in black and white—perhaps an ironic reference to an older time in American entertainment when racial representation was very different—the video pans slowly across the front lawn of a suburban home. The caption, in smooth, white (!) cursive writing, reads "The Slim Shady Show." The camera comes to a stop on an image of Eminem, dressed in a suit and tie as the father from *Leave It to Beaver,* standing rigidly and waving at the camera from his front porch in short jerky motions.[40] He flinches stiffly as a newspaper flies by, nearly hitting him in the head. The television image then shifts in a way that suggests that the reception is going bad, cycling quickly through two new images: Eminem dressed as a nerdy professor with spiky white hair and then as a game show host in plaid pants and a bright-red blazer.[41] By focusing the viewer's attention immediately on exaggerated images of normative whiteness, the video implies that Eminem represents the polar opposite of such representations.

The parade of white images continues: Eminem as a mental patient in a straitjacket (Dr. Dre as his psychiatrist); Eminem as the entire Brady Bunch; Eminem as a ventriloquist's dummy; Eminem as a flasher in a trenchcoat; Eminem as "white trash" appearing in boxers and a white T-shirt in front of a trailer home; Eminem as the president of the United States, Bill Clinton; Eminem as shock-rocker Marilyn Manson; Eminem as a drunk driver being arrested on the TV show *Cops.* Some of these images are clear references to recent popular culture, while others refer back to the 1950s and 1960s, and at least one—the ventriloquist's dummy—harks even further back, to the age of vaudeville. All told, we witness a kitchen-sink parody that takes aim at white identity. The critical distance between Eminem and these costumed images is reinforced several times as Eminem appears in normal street clothes rapping the lyrics to the song. Dressed in baggy hip hop–styled clothing (loose-fit sagging jeans and an oversized jacket), Eminem's comportment shifts dramatically as he adopts the conventional body language of a rapper: low to the ground, bending his knees, swaying loosely with the beat, and gesturing rhythmically with an open hand as he delivers his rhymes. Taken together, these various images of Eminem vacillate between sameness and difference, positioning him solidly in the rap genre, while constantly reminding viewers that he is no mere imitation of a black rapper.

Furthermore, the ironic parody of white identity is reinforced by the sound of Eminem's single through its implicit commentary on the musical conventions of rap. Produced by Dr. Dre, the musical track is built primarily out of a large looped section, nearly eight measures total, of black, British, openly gay soul singer Labi Siffre's 1975 "I Got The . . ."[42] Looping a selective portion of the groove, Dr. Dre creates a sparse beat that parodies musical whiteness. The idea of attaching concepts like "parody" and "irony" to rap's beats has a very specific application here. As ethnomusicologist Joseph Schloss has persuasively argued, academic critics overly committed to hearing sampling as primarily about ironic recontexutalization have misapplied the concept of "parody" in assuming that producers intend their samples to be recognized and interpreted as a commentary upon their original sources (see my discussion of this issue in the book's introduction).[43] Thus, instead of centering an interpretation of "My Name Is" on the original intent or meaning of Siffre's song—which is actually quite ironic given Eminem's alleged homophobia—it is more appropriate to concentrate on the particular "vibe" that this sample allows Dr. Dre to create.

In the case of Eminem's "My Name Is," the parameters in need of examination involve the set of expectations and conventions to which rap music producers adhere in constructing the rhythmic foundation for their tracks. As Adam Krims points out, rap music often implicitly or explicitly comments upon or evokes itself and its own history.[44] In the 1990s, platinum-selling West Coast artists such as Dr. Dre, Snoop Doggy Dogg, and Tupac Shakur, and East Coast rappers such as the Notorious B.I.G., Nas, and Jay-Z, helped establish representations of inner-city black subjectivity as a crucial marker of authenticity. Accompanying the gritty, documentary style of rap lyrics in this period are some specific musical constructions of inner-city space. In general, the majority of rap beats in the 1990s drew upon the generic conventions of funk music, featuring eight- or sixteen-count hi-hats with syncopated snare/kick drum patterns, often resembling the

	1	-	+	-	2	-	+	-	3	-	+	-	4	-	+	-	
Shaker	x	x	x	x	x	x	x	x	x	x	x	x	x	x	x	x	16-count
Snare					s								s				
Kick	k					k			k					k			

Figure 24. Rhythmic foundation for the musical track of "Nuthin' But a 'G' Thang," on Dr. Dre, *The Chronic,* Death Row 63000, 1992.

	1	-	+	-	2	-	+	-	3	-	+	-	4	-	+	-	
Hi-hat	x		x		x		x		x		x		x		x		8-count
Snare					s								s				
Kick	k		k				k	k		k					k		

Figure 25. Rhythmic foundation for the musical track of "The World Is Yours," on Nas, *Illmatic,* Columbia 57684, 1994.

	1	-	+	-	2	-	+	-	3	-	+	-	4	-	+	-	
Hi-hat	x				x				x				x				4-count
Snare					s								s				
Kick	k								k								

Figure 26. Rhythmic foundation for the musical track of "My Name Is," on Eminem, *The Slim Shady LP,* Interscope Records 90287, 1999.

grooves of James Brown's band or George Clinton's Parliament-Funkadelic collective. Even when the hi-hat does not evenly subdivide the beat, syncopated ostinato patterns in other prominently sounding levels of the groove imply a sixteenth-note subdivision.[45]

The looped section of Labi Siffre's "I Got The . . ." that makes up the beat for "My Name Is" departs from most sample-based beats in a particularly revealing way. Producers commonly choose samples that feature an eight- or sixteen-count hi-hat, as in the two famous examples shown in figures 24 and 25. The sample Dr. Dre loops to create the beat for "My Name Is," however, has only a four-count hi-hat pattern played evenly in 4/4 time on all main beats (fig. 26).[46] In addition, "My Name Is" contains neither syncopation nor rhythmic tension in the kick drum and snare parts but instead alternates evenly between them to create the obligatory and most rudimentary form of a backbeat. This lack of rhythmic density and absence of syncopation in the hi-hat, kick drum, and snare portion of the beat offer a rhythmic parody of whiteness, toying with the well-known stereotype that white people lack rhythm.

Like the lyrics and music video of "My Name Is," the song's rhythmic backing encodes a palpable distance from conventional representations of blackness. Yet, it does so without pushing Eminem beyond the pale of the rap music genre. After all, the point of this strategy is not to make joke out of Eminem, or rap music for that matter—he is no Steve Gordon (see chapter 1)—but to help him establish a foothold in a genre coded as black. Just as Eminem's virtuosic lyrical signifying and his style of dress remind listeners of his true cultural allegiance, the sampled portion of Siffre's song contains one element of syncopation that keeps the backing track of "My Name Is" from spilling over into satire: the bass line that anticipates the first and third beats of every measure by a swung sixteenth-note gives the track a "droll bounce."[47] Eminem's rapping contributes still another layer of rhythmic complexity. He rhymes in asymmetrical phrases, at times accelerating into dramatic slews of syllables, at other times slowing down to smoothly ride the pocket. Put simply, his flow is anything but "square." Consider, for instance, the song's chorus, in which Eminem delivers the words "my name is" in eighth-note triplets that imply a three-against-two cross-rhythm with the backing track (fig. 27a), or the four lines in the song's third verse in which Eminem's flow dances and weaves around the main beats (fig. 27b). In sum, while certain rhythmic elements of "My Name Is" play with musical stereotypes of whiteness, the song as a whole stops short of a full-blown satire that would overstate Eminem's racial difference and, more importantly, sound boring.

In an age of digital production and sampling where producers can engineer and meticulously design every sound, it is timbre that most betrays the marketing strategy behind "My Name Is."[48] This often-neglected sonic element contributes significantly to the parodic function of the song. Notably, the sounds Dr. Dre layers into the beat of "My Name Is" differ greatly from those he used in the production of his own album, 2001, released six months after Eminem's debut.[49] As the title of one of the tracks on the album promises, Dr. Dre's production for 2001 is "Xxplosive," and his beats feature a powerful bass and kick drum. Loud gunshots are sampled in as percussive accents ("Xxplosive," "Bang Bang," and "Ackrite"), and the instrumental sounds have a grandiose, almost symphonic quality.

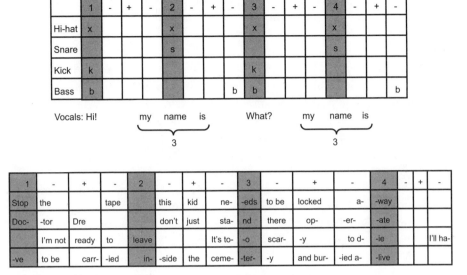

Figure 27. Examples of Eminem's lyrical flow that add rhythmic complexity to an otherwise "square" beat.

Underneath these and other tracks, the sampled sounds of car engines, honking horns, and helicopters evoke the soundscape of South Los Angeles, illustrating Forman's observation that in rap music "the city is an audible presence, explicitly cited and sonically sampled in the reproduction of the aural textures of the urban environment."[50] In direct opposition to this archetypical gangsta sound, Dr. Dre's production on "My Name Is" evokes a light and playful mood, starting with the vocal call-and-response that accompanies Eminem's famously nasal rapping throughout the song.[51]

In the first verse, voices imitating children answer Eminem's questions in a high-pitched, exaggerated tone ("Yeah, yeah, yeah!" and "Uh-uh"). Even the more violent lyrics of "My Name Is" are given a humorous slant by similar call-and-response vocals. When Eminem talks about assaulting his high school teacher, sound effects straight out of "The Three Stooges" emphasize the cartoonish nature of his lyrics. The instrumental sounds on the track also come across as lighter and less ominous than Dr. Dre's *2001*. Writing around the time of *The Slim Shady LP*'s debut, Detroit-based music critic Hobey Echlin got it just right when he described the sound of "My Name Is" as "catchy with its game show-funk hooks."[52] Labi Siffre's electric piano riff, heard during the song's chorus, has a bright tone; a clipped, tinny-sounding synthesizer melody layered into the track changes pitch only on main beats in quarter- or half-note intervals.

Instead of trying to gain acceptance as a rapper by adopting a familiar gangsta persona, Eminem, with help from Dr. Dre, creates a new vision of rap music populated by an unlikely cast of characters. Unlike many of his African American male counterparts who use rap music as a vehicle for hyper-masculine displays of bravado, "My Name Is" offers a humorous portrayal of abjection.[53] At times, Eminem jokingly played up his insecurities during media interviews. In a 2002 conversation with MTV, he confessed, "My insecurities? I'm dumb, I'm stupid, I'm white, I'm ugly, I smell, I'm stupid and I'm white. I have freckles . . . um . . . I'm short, I'm white, I'm not very smart, I wanna kill myself. . . . My nose is crooked. Um . . . my penis is small."[54] In addition to the frequent references to his whiteness, the comment about his genitalia is telling for (among other things) the way it contrasts with the usual way rappers describe their anatomy and the stereotype of the well-endowed black man. In some ways, Eminem's rhetorical strategy parallels that of hard country singers, who, as Barbara Ching describes, foster abject personas as a way of voicing working-class frustration.[55] Certainly this "antihero" stance is part of Eminem's appeal, and it is probably no coincidence that he hails from Detroit, one of the areas hit hardest by post-1960s deindustrialization. In creating an identity that is far removed from normative whiteness, "My Name Is" exposes a class fissure among white people, making race visible in new ways.

This representation of whiteness has proven key to Eminem's positive reception by rap music fans, many of them African American. As the case of Vanilla Ice's spectacular rise and fall illustrates, white rappers had to be careful not to appear as if they were out to "steal" black music. Indeed, even the earlier strategies of authentication adopted by white MCs— "immersion" and "imitation"—attempt to mitigate the appearance of appropriation and exploitation by portraying white rappers as comfortable and familiar with African Americans both personally and culturally. As scholars of whiteness have argued, however, repudiating the privilege associated with white identity is no simple matter. Perhaps sensing this problem and responding to Vanilla Ice's failed commercial strategy, Eminem adopted a different pose. Rather than attempting to shed his whiteness or imitate conventional portrayals of blackness, Eminem emphasized his racial identity in ways that transformed it into something more than a trope of domination. As one Canadian reviewer explained, "Eminem calls himself white trash on record. His protagonists are comic-book caricatures, murdering, popping pills, dosing their dates with psychedelic mushrooms."[56] By focusing on his class identity and various unflattering and outrageous images of whiteness, Eminem positioned himself as an underdog. His direct commentary on whiteness in later songs such as "Who Knew" and "White America" also afforded him the opportunity to acknowledge the extent to which his white skin granted him a commercial advantage, helping him appease his critics and humble himself before black artists.[57]

Although close attention to Eminem's debut single reveals much about the artistic strategy behind his push into the mainstream, it is important not to overstate the centrality of this one song and music video. *The Slim Shady LP* presents numerous faces of whiteness, and the remaining songs on the album do not necessarily eschew conventional funk grooves or portray Eminem as a loser. For example, "Just Don't Give a Fuck" counterbalances "My Name Is" by using a more syncopated beat and positioning Eminem's alter ego Slim Shady as a dangerous and violence-prone character to be feared rather than mocked. Although Eminem's lyrics describe him as "brain dead" from too many drugs, the contrast with "My Name Is" is immediately apparent. In fact, the admission that he has hit bottom only seems to increase his lack of concern for the consequences of his actions. In this song, Slim Shady is free to unleash a torrent of anger and frustration, lambasting his critics with lyrics that demonstrate not only his skills as a rapper but also his apparent lack of concern for causing offense.[58]

On his follow-up album, the highly acclaimed *The Marshal Mathers LP* (2000), Eminem continued to move between the poles of the humorous prankster and the scary psycho-killer. "The Real Slim Shady" opens with familiar signifiers of whiteness as an extremely nasal Eminem intones, "May I have your attention please"—just as "white" a phrase as "Hi, my name is."[59] The song's beat features a looped keyboard riff with a timbre approximating that of a harpsichord, and toward the end of the song a descending melody played on what sounds like a recorder emerges as the final layer of the groove. These timbres, associated of course with "white" classical music, are complemented by the video, which playfully features a chorus of Eminem impersonators that highlight the whiteness of his fan base and brand of musical identity.

On the other hand, the single "Kill You" plays up the darker side of Eminem's creativity. His rapping voice grows extremely gruff and raspy as he rhymes about the numerous ways he can inflict pain and death on his victims. The chorus of the song states Eminem's position clearly: "You don't wanna fuck with Shady, 'cause Shady will fuckin' kill you." Armstrong argues that Eminem employs extreme violence and misogyny to place him in contestation with African American gangsta rappers. In fact, he concludes that Eminem is actually more violent and misogynistic than his black counterparts, "outdoing other gangsta rappers in terms of his violent misogyny."[60] While there is undoubtedly some truth to this assertion, Armstrong's analysis is limited by an unstated assumption that all violent utterances are comparable, overlooking the potential for humor and irony within what Robin Kelley terms rap music's "lyrical ballistics."[61] We miss out on important nuances, including the potential qualitative differences between various forms of lyrical violence. Is Eminem's violence always meant to be taken seriously? Are the subjects of the violence raced, classed, or gendered in particular ways? Even a cursory glance at Eminem's first two albums reveals that he avoids portraying himself as an archetypical gangsta. Instead, he taps into the cultural trope of the cold-blooded psycho-killer most often portrayed in American horror films as a white male. In fact, Eminem often appeared live on stage wearing Jason Voorhees's trade-mark hockey mask from the horror movie series *Friday the 13th,* and "Kill You" invokes the character Norman Bates from the film *Psycho.*[62]

Eminem's particularly literal and visible invocation of white horror film characters and other "white" cultural references added to his preemptive strike against possible criticism about his racial identity, allowing him to carve out a niche in the music industry for his unique brand of rap music. His violent, misogynistic humor and self-characterization as "white trash" con-firm Ingrid Monson's observation that gender and class continue to mediate racial authenticity across U.S. popular music's color line.[63] To many listeners and casual observers, Eminem's humor crossed the line of acceptability, espe-cially because the frequent targets of his lyrical outbursts were women and homosexuals—both long-time victims of discrimination and violence. To other listeners, Eminem's popularity and artistic skill pointed to the various ways hip hop culture and rap music provided young black and white Americans with an unprecedented opportunity for overcoming the legacy of racism. In these and other cases, discussions of Eminem's work commented on the changing meanings of race (and white masculinity) in U.S. society.

REARTICULATING RACE

Unlike the world of electoral politics, popular music does not demand that its practitioners declare their allegiance to specific causes or issues. While some musicians occasionally take a political stand in song lyrics or video imagery, Eminem's first two albums avoided making direct political endorsements. Despite not speaking directly on behalf of specific issues, however, popular culture can offer its consumers timely metaphors for understanding the world. George Lipsitz, Ray Pratt, and Christopher Small, among others, have suggested that popular music can offer listeners "utopian prefigurations" of the kind of society they want to live in and the kind of relationships they want to experience.[64] It seems only reasonable that the opposite must also be true: certain music might symbolize a world gone awry. Indeed, listeners came to very different conclusions about the nature of Eminem's success.

Regardless of one's opinion about Eminem or his music, his popularity made whiteness visible in new ways, an important factor to proponents of critical whiteness studies, who consider how whiteness confers societal privilege and power. During the mid-1990s, while Eminem was honing his skills and developing his artistic strategy, Henry A. Giroux and others were calling for a renewed understanding of whiteness along progressive lines. Seeking to counter the tendency of whiteness to go unnamed and function as a background norm, Giroux argued for a pedagogy of whiteness that considers "the differences in 'whiteness' and the political possibilities that can be opened up through a discourse of 'whiteness' articulated in new forms of identity, new possibilities for democratic practices, and new processes of cultural exchange."[65] Although probably not what Giroux had in mind, Eminem certainly helped to reimagine whiteness as a series of differences and possibilities. By the beginning of the twenty-first century, he had come to embody some of the decade's greatest fears, as well as hopes, regarding the future of American race relations.

One aspect of Eminem's early career that resonated with the politics of his time was the relationship between race and class in his work.[66] The pitting of class against race continued to be a popular political theme in the 1990s, particularly with respect to debates over affirmative action. In 1996, the same year that Eminem recorded *Infinite*, backers of California's Proposition 209 campaigned to abolish state-based affirmative action programs.[67] Proponents of the proposition, including University of California regent Ward Connerly (an African American) and California governor Pete Wilson, employed reasoning that used class to pivot around race, arguing for example that "under the existing racial-preference system, a wealthy doctor's son may receive preference over a dishwasher's daughter simply because he's from an 'underrepresented' race."[68] After Proposition 209 passed in California, Connerly took his campaign to Eminem's home state of Michigan, employing many of the same tactics and arguments to pass another state ban on affirmative action.[69]

In his review of the motion picture *8 Mile*, which mythologized Eminem's struggle to gain acceptance in Detroit's underground rap music scene, R. J. Smith worries that the film suggests that "class trumps race" in contemporary U.S. society.[70] Smith cites the climactic scene of the film, in which Eminem's character Rabbit wins a rap battle against an African American foe by playing up his own status as "white trash" and revealing to the crowd that his opponent is from a middle-class home. (We have already witnessed how important constructions of class identity were in Eminem's early recordings.) In the film, Rabbit uses his status as "white trash" to portray himself as the ultimate victim, flipping the conventional logic of race hierarchy on its head.[71] While this brand of class authenticity might be an attractive proposition, Smith points out that it tends to over-shadow important aspects of Detroit's history, including a legacy of racial terror and white flight. In other words, because it was a fictional movie, *8 Mile's* writers were able to create a villain with the exact racial and class characteristics they needed to make the story work out in Eminem's favor, regardless of whether those characteristics were representative of the actual demographics of Detroit or America in general.

Calls for the elimination of race-based programs and a general turn toward "color-blindness" in political discourse reflect the pervasiveness of neoliberal ideology, which posits that institutional barriers to individual achievement need to be eliminated so that people can be freed to take responsibility for and (presumably) realize their full potential. Rendering ongoing structural inequality and ingrained racism invisible, color-blind rhetoric celebrates meritocratic competition and individual striving as an ultimate good for society. No doubt Eminem's rise to success in a genre coded as black provided no shortage of opportunities for viewers to be swayed by the attractiveness of such propositions. As I observed online soon after *8 Mile's* release, some viewers were doing just that. In a chat forum for *ifilm: The Internet Movie Guide*, a fan shared this breathless review: "This movie was OUTSTANDING! I love how it showed the strug-gle of a young white male trying to make it in a black industry. All he went through. . . . The movie really is a must see for anyone who can appreciate someone who had to fight for what they have and for someone with undy-ing will to get what he or she wants."[72]

This amateur reviewer unwittingly picks up on the way in which the storyline of the film and Eminem's mainstream musical debut intersect with neoliberal rhetoric about race. For example, she praises the movie for foregrounding Eminem's strength of will and work ethic—coincidentally, Rabbit is the only character in the film that seems to possess the motivation to move beyond the small world of urban Detroit. She also takes pleasure in seeing Rabbit succeed in a black cultural world, a pleasure that betrays what could represent for some the soothing reassertion of white privilege in a cultural arena previously off limits. Most problematic of all, the suggestion that Eminem operates in "a black industry" ignores the fact that rap music circulates through the conduits of white-controlled corporations and is heavily dependent on suburban, white teenagers for its revenues. Without an awareness of the history and ongoing legacy of structural racism and inequality, viewers of *8 Mile* could come away believing that because a single white rapper growing up in black Detroit had to struggle for acceptance, it is whites who are equally disadvantaged by U.S. society.

Eminem's underdog status in *8 Mile* and his ironic and playful abjection in early songs like "My Name Is" also articulated with a related political phenomenon of the 1990s: the so-called right-wing backlash (also referred to as the culture wars). In this regard there are some surprising parallels between Eminem's artistic strategy and the political maneuvering that accompanied the conservative movement of the 1990s. Thomas Frank describes the right-wing backlash as "a theory of how the political world works," which "also provides a ready-made identity" for its white conservative following, offering converts an "attractive and uniquely American understanding of authenticity and victimhood."[73] Franks argues that the Republican Party mobilized its base around issues such as abortion, gay marriage, and prayer in schools by casting themselves as the ultimate victims of a vast liberal conspiracy. The politics of the conservative backlash fostered feelings of marginalization and marshaled a righteous indignation against what they termed the "liberal elite." In other words, just as the white rapper mobilized class-based tropes to flip the script and cast himself as the ultimate hip hop underdog, white politicians and grass-roots activists were rearticulating their political identities by reimagining a white, male, and Christian populism that was embattled and under assault.

Some journalists even conflated the right-wing backlash with Eminem's popularity. After all, as his numerous critics pointed out, the frequent targets of Eminem's rhymes were women and homosexuals, two groups that were increasingly put on the defensive in the 1980s and 1990s. While Eminem's assault on "politically correct" values allowed his teenaged listeners to enact a rebellion against the world of their parents, some critics worried that it signaled that the conservative backlash had taken over popular culture. In a 2002 editorial for the *Village Voice*, for example, Richard Goldstein compared Eminem to shock jock Don Imus, characterizing their appeal as follows. "Imus and Eminem make it easier for fans to bear life in a multicultural society. Your boss may be a woman, your sergeant African-American, your teacher gay, but when you put the earphones on, you rule. . . . Eminem and Imus draw from the same well of resentment that has nourished the Angry White Male. These stars are part of the backlash, and their reach into the mainstream shows how far this attitude has advanced."[74]

Although Goldstein is correct in identifying a troubling streak of resentment and anger in Eminem's music, his equating Eminem with Don Imus, who was fired by CBS Radio after referring on the air to the Rutgers University women's basketball team as "nappy-headed hos," overlooks the way in which Eminem's work as a musician and his performance in *8 Mile* attempt a sincere reconciliation with blackness and black culture. Especially for people who care about rap music, the most compelling scenes in *8 Mile* are the various freestyle "battles." One such scene shows factory workers engaged in an impromptu cipher, a circle of rappers and onlookers taking turns trying to outdo one another. This battle becomes a brilliant reappropriation of their painfully short thirty-minute lunch break, illustrating the joy, jest, and pleasure in the most politically incorrect rapping. The rappers are practicing "signifying," which Henry Louis Gates, Jr., has described as the African American art of wordplay that creates difference through repetition, subverting dominant narratives by foregrounding the slipperiness of language.[75] The crux of such practices lies in the participants' demonstration of their own imaginative vocal capacities, not necessarily in the quality of information being transmitted.

Although we might lament the fact that it has taken numerous albums by Eminem and a movie about him as a white rapper for some to recognize the humor and creativity of African American cultural practices, *8 Mile* seems poised to counter such race-thinking. One of the most important, though implicit, suggestions made by the film is that to this generation, boundaries of culture are much more important than those of race. In one of the funniest and most memorable scenes, Rabbit (Eminem) and Future (Mekhi Phifer) do an impromptu rap revision of Lynyrd Skynyrd's "Sweet Home Alabama," heard playing from Rabbit's mother's trailer. The refrain "Sweet home Alabama" becomes "I live at home in a trailer," and by signifying on this rock and roll classic, Rabbit finds a way both to deal with the desperation of his situation and to illustrate that although he is white, his point of identification lies with Future and their mostly black crew.

The permeability of racial boundaries and subtlety of interracial bonds in *8 Mile* remain refreshing and positive, and they suggest why so many fans, African American or otherwise, have embraced Eminem as an artist and icon. Writing for the *New Yorker*, David Denby asserts that in *8 Mile*, "Race is an issue, but it's not the most important issue. The universal appreciation of talent matters more. . . . Fair is fair: the man [Eminem] can do it."[76] Indeed, very few journalists and rap musicians chose to condemn Eminem's popularity, despite the fact that his sudden rise to fame and financial success raised the specter of previous white artists who profited from their proximity to musical blackness, such as Elvis Presley, Benny Goodman, and Paul Whiteman. In fact, most critics who approached the subject defended Eminem against such charges, citing his genuine talent and the respect he had earned from his African American peers.[77] In this way, they advanced a meritocratic ethos that differed from neoliberal claims of color-blindness and reverse discrimination. It is possible, for example, to acknowledge the history of racism and to argue that more work needs to be done to fulfill the American promise of liberty and justice for all, while also recognizing hip hop and rap music as a forum where we might rehearse life in a world where the content of one's microphone skills truly does matter more than the color of one's skin.

Some have even argued that Eminem's ascendancy advances progressive political tendencies. Hip hop writer and pundit Bakari Kitwana, for example, claims that Eminem's popularity signaled a radical departure in the way young white Americans view race. Although a few critics did denounce Eminem's success as a white conspiracy to steal rap music from blacks and exploit its potential for profit, Kitwana suggests that this line of thinking reflects an outdated view of race relations. Such "old racial politics," he says, is mired in essentialism and debates about cultural ownership. From the perspective of the "new racial politics," Eminem's popularity points toward an unprecedented shared space for black, white, Latino, and Asian youth living in a multicultural nation.[78] The ability of a white boy to tell his story, to advance a working-class white identity and earn the respect of his African American peers, demonstrates the progressive nature of hip hop culture.[79] This interpretation is strengthened by Eminem's support of African American artists in his crew, especially D12.[80] In other words, when he had the opportunity to give other MCs a push, Eminem notably chose to support black rappers, not white ones. Thus, the widespread popularity of rap music points toward new political coalitions that might unite young activists across racial lines. One could argue that the historic election of U.S. president Barack Obama, which relied heavily on his ability to mobilize young white voters, justifies some of this optimism.

Kitwana recognizes hip hop and rap music as a site where culture has the potential to rearticulate race, to remake whiteness as something previously unimagined. Although Eminem participates in the lineage of Paul Whiteman *et alia*, benefiting from whiteness in terms of market access, he does produce a new construction of white identity that attempts a redistribution of symbolic power with notions of blackness. Appealing to his experiences as a drug user, trailer park resident, and high school drop out, Eminem negotiates a new kind of whiteness that is far from dominant. In his work, whiteness is never the norm, never the invisible universal standard by which all others are judged deviant. His whiteness is of another sort. It is itself marginalized, frustrated, angry, and at times even abject. In the context of rap music, a genre that has often been subject to attack by those unhappy with its portrayal of what they believe to be damaging forms of black deviance, Eminem's performance of whiteness suggests the possibility of sameness for (heterosexual male) white rap fans, not simply a voyeuristic adventure in which blackness offers excitement while whiteness remains the safe harbor of privilege and normality.

For some, this performance of whiteness was an extension of the right-wing backlash culture, proof that a new social meanness and neoconservatism intent on rolling back liberal policies had infected youth-oriented popular culture. For others, he was a positive symbol of a new era in race relations, signaling a promising shared space between white and black youth that rendered old paradigms of race obsolete. He even served as an inspiration to some facing unfavorable odds, an example of overcoming challenges through hard work and determination. For still others, Eminem was anything but new—simply an updated version of the archetypical white boy performing black culture for profit. What is significant about these opposing views is that they simultaneously occupied a historical moment in U.S. society when whiteness as a social category was undergoing profound change. By parodying his racial identity through an ironic use of hip hop conventions, Eminem rearticulated whiteness in rap music *in relation to* musical blackness, revealing one of the ways in which whiteness could adapt to changing societal conditions. Carl Hancock Rux gets it just right when he explains that Eminem "has not *arrived* at black culture. . . . He has *arrived* at white culture with an authentic performance of whiteness, influenced by a historical concept of blackness."[81]

Indeed, Eminem's performance of whiteness in rap music provides a mirror in which numerous tensions and political projects come into focus, a picture of U.S. race relations in which whiteness becomes just another way of being colored.

Conclusion

Sounding Race in the Twenty-First Century

Although unified by a common set of Afro-diasporic tendencies, rap music's projections of race are neither monolithic nor static. In other words, one could say that rap is "culturally black" but that the meaning and significance of blackness (or any other racial identity projected by the genre) often varies widely from artist to artist and from song to song. The diverse constructions of racial identity explored in this book's previous chapters depend on specific artistic decisions, including those related to how producers make beats. Ironically, by the end of the twentieth century, the same approach to working with breaks that enabled rap musicians to produce powerful soundings of blackness—from the militant nationalism of Public Enemy to the gangsta cool of Dr. Dre—also allowed whiteness to become audible. Eminem's preemptive strike on racial authenticity and his subsequent popularity suggested one possibility for outliers wishing to create space for themselves in the genre. By lampooning various white stereotypes through his lyrics, imagery, and beats, Eminem anticipated possible criticism that he did not belong in rap. Rather than attempt to conform to generic norms, Eminem and his team of producers subverted them to emphasize the white rapper's distance from stereotypical projections of blackness.

The success of Eminem's *The Slim Shady LP* (1999) and *The Marshall Mathers LP* (2000) did not prove, as some observers suggest, that Eminem simply transcended race. Had race not been a factor in Eminem's success, he should have been able to achieve commercial success with songs that avoided calling attention to his racial identity, such as those found on his independently released album, *Infinite* (1996).[1] However, as we observed in the previous chapter, Eminem did not find widespread popularity until after he began highlighting his racial identity through lyrics, sound, and imagery.

By rebelling from conventional portrayals of rap identity, Eminem rearticulated whiteness in relation to blackness, transforming his outsider status into an advantage. Following Eminem, other artists have also sought to sound race in ways that depart from common (and problematic) representations of black masculinity. Chinese American rapper Jin, for example, first flirted with fame in 2002, adopting a strategy similar to that of Eminem's "My Name Is." As he tried to create space for himself in the genre, however, he confronted challenges specific to his identity as an Asian American. As in the case of Eminem, Jin's experiences negotiating race *vis-à-vis* blackness help illuminate the contours of rap's racial matrix.

Born in Miami, Florida, to Cantonese-speaking parents, Jin gained notoriety via an appearance on cable television station BET's *106 & Park* program, which features a weekly "Freestyle Friday" contest pitting two MCs against each other before a live audience and a panel of judges. If a contestant manages to win seven weekly battles in a row, he (the contestants on the show have been almost exclusively male) earns a place in the show's Hall of Fame. Jin managed to do just that, despite the fact that most of his opponents were African American men who attacked him with racial epithets and rhymed couplets that questioned his authenticity. Jin's second opponent, Sterlin, for example, opened with a line admonishing the show's organizers for matching him against "Bruce Lee's grandson."[2] Further into his improvised verse, Sterlin expanded on the martial arts stereotype, claiming:

> When I'm on the mic, I spit fire
> He just kick and be like, "hai-ya!"

Imagining Jin as a kung fu artist, one of the stereotypical roles reserved for Asian and Asian American actors in U.S. popular culture, Sterlin implies that Jin doesn't belong in rap. Yet, rather than attempt to change the subject and distract the audience and judges from his identity, Jin was able to flip this racial script. In the same battle with Sterlin, he opened with a rhyme that simultaneously acknowledged his race and negated each insult that had been thrown in his direction:

> You wanna say I'm Chinese? Son, here's a reminder
> Check your Tims [Timberland shoes]; they probably say "Made in China"

In these two opening lines, Jin more or less sealed his victory. He owned up to being Chinese and simultaneously critiqued his opponent for relying on race in his attack. Calling attention to Sterlin's footwear, Jin demonstrated his ability to improvise—a key element of MC battles—and reminded his audience of the ubiquity of Chinese-made products. Invoking the familiar phrase stamped onto a plethora of everyday goods, Jin crea-tively reimagined "Made in China" as a symbol of rap domination. By using his wits, Jin defused Sterlin's series of racist jokes and brought the audience and panel of judges over to his side. Like Eminem's character Rabbit in the climactic battle scene of the film *8 Mile*, Jin took ownership of his racial identity in order to disarm foes and would-be critics alike.

Jin's embrace of his outsider status was balanced by a forceful counterat-tack that made his audience and the judges aware of his familiarity with street slang and other hip hop tropes. Using the word "Tims" for Timberland shoes, claiming that he saw one opponent "dancing for spare change on forty-deuce [42nd Street]," and telling another that after losing to Jin, he'd find himself "at the bodega asking for swiss cheese," Jin displayed an easy familiarity with the culture and geography of urban New York.[3] Such ref-erences were especially important in establishing his credentials in these battles because of the distance between Asian American and African American stereotypes in popular culture. Popular representations of black masculinity are associated with stereotypes of athleticism, sexuality, and physical aggression that stand in polar opposition to stereotypes of the Asian American male as awkward, asexual, and passive. For these reasons, sociologist and music critic Oliver Wang argues that Asian American rap-pers operate from a disadvantaged position within the genre.[4] To overcome this challenge, Jin did more than own up to his racial identity; he struck back to prove his "hardness," demonstrating his mastery of masculine tropes of domination and sexual aggression. In his battle against a woefully outmatched contestant named Lucky Luciano whose rhymes sounded writ-ten (i.e., not improvised), Jin concluded his verse with a couplet that pro-vocatively mixed gender, sexuality, and race. Illustrating once again how gender and sexuality mediate racial authenticity across the color line,[5] Jin's barb transformed typical Chinese food items into phallic symbols of sexual domination:

> Ask your girlfriend; she was doing something at my house
> As a matter of fact, she had my eggroll and dumplings in her mouth[6]

More than a defensive strategy, invoking race became a way for Jin to annihilate his opponents. The judges' and audiences' overwhelmingly posi-tive reaction to this aggressive lyrical strategy suggested the potential value of a rap star capable of capitalizing on his Asian-ness. Indeed after securing his place in the "Freestyle Friday" Hall of Fame, Jin announced that he was joining Ruff Ryders Entertainment, becoming the first Asian American rapper to sign a recording contract with a major label. In crafting the lead single for his debut album *The Rest Is History,* Jin and producer Wyclef Jean closely paralleled Dr. Dre's strategy for introducing Eminem to a mainstream audience.[7] The single "Learn Chinese," which was performed in English with a smattering of Cantonese lyrics, opens with Jin's voice defiantly proclaiming, "Yeah I'm Chinese. And what?" Challenging listeners to make an issue of his racial identity, something anyone who watched him on *106 & Park* would need to think carefully about doing, Jin goes on to proclaim: "The days of the pork fried rice and chicken wings coming to your house by me is over." Conjuring the stereotypical image of Chinese food delivery—the only face-to-face encounter some of his potential audience members might have with a Chinese person—Jin makes clear that he is out to overturn common expectation. In the music video for "Learn Chinese," Jin drives up to a single-family home and approaches the front door carrying a plastic bag presumably filled with Chinese takeout. Instead of delivering the food, however, he spits into the bag, dropping it on the porch before turning around and walking away. Like Eminem, Jin dresses up as a racial stereotype to acknowledge his identity and the challenge it poses from the start.

Although Jin faced a situation similar to white rapper Eminem *vis-à-vis* his distance from blackness, the particular history of Asian American exclusion and invisibility within U.S. popular culture limited his options in racially distinct ways.[8] Because whiteness has been at the center of American life for years, Eminem's flipping of rap's racial script repositioned him at the heart of popular culture. Where Eminem could signify on whiteness, which includes a rich variety of roles from late-night television show host to *The Brady Bunch,* Asian rappers have a more limited set of stereotypical and demeaning representations to choose from. Because Jin could not mock Chinese-ness without running the risk of further marginalizing himself, the single and music video for "Learn Chinese" sought to make him look more like conventional representations of blackness. At one point in the song, for example, Jin refers to himself as "the original chinky-eyed MC," adopting the racist epithet as a badge of pride in a way that parallels black MCs' use of "nigga" as a term of endearment.[9] As he did during his "Freestyle Friday" battles, Jin also demonstrates his hardness and proximity to conventional rap masculinity. Directing his second verse at an implied black audience (those who "roll dice in the 'hood"), Jin rhymes a challenge that dares listeners to "come to Chinatown" where they might "end up in the lost and found." The music video amplifies this message, casting Jin into a world of triad gangsters who operate in a dangerous and violent Chinatown. Rather than creating a true alternative to rap's 'hood-based authenticity, Jin merely gives it a Chinese makeover.[10] Evoking longstanding stereotypes of Chinatown as a place of mystery and peril, Jin invites would-be foes to come to Chinatown, where residents only speak Chinese and will be unable to serve as "eyewitnesses," presumably to the violence that befalls unwelcome visitors.

As if taking a cue from Dr. Dre's work on Eminem's "My Name Is," producer Wyclef Jean also sought to evoke a sense of sonic otherness in "Learn Chinese." The song's beat includes two prominent elements that signal Jin's racial difference. First, the backing track features a looped melody performed on a synthesizer with a twangy timbre approximating the *guzheng* (a stringed Chinese zither). The melody itself is an interpolation of "The Streets of Cairo," an Orientalist Tin Pan Alley song originally published in 1895. Sometimes referred to simply as "the snake charmer song," the melody remains well known in the U.S. as an exotic-sounding musical cliché. The other Chinese-sounding element in the song comes from an interpolation of Jamaican dancehall reggae star Yellowman's "Mr. Chin" (1981). This song tells the story of a Chinese Jamaican storeowner and his daughter, who Yellowman claims to have seduced. The chorus to "Mr. Chin" includes a pentatonic melody that (according to Yellowman) Mr. Chin and his daughter enjoy singing. Taking advantage of the aural similarities between "Chin" and "Jin," Wyclef Jean transformed Yellowman's somewhat mocking song about his Chinese Jamaican neighbors into a refrain that praises the sexiness and musical skill of "Mr. Jin." Even without knowledge of where these melodies come from, listeners familiar with U.S. popular culture can easily recognize that they are being used to evoke Jin's racial difference. Although there are certain ironies apparent to those aware of these origins, the primary significance of these melodies in "Learn Chinese" does not stem from their original meanings or contexts. Instead, as we have witnessed repeatedly in other cases throughout this book, the end result—in this case, the pentatonic, Asian-sounding "vibe" of the beat—is what helps make Jin's identity audible. Similarly to the way that the video portrays Jin dressed up as a triad gangster and a take-out food delivery boy, the backing track to "Learn Chinese" introduces a musical stereotype of Chinese-ness for Jin to explode with a virtuosic lyrical performance.

Unlike Eminem's "My Name Is," however, "Learn Chinese" did not lead to widespread commercial success or a large national following for Jin, and one could blame race for the discrepancy. As Eminem sought to establish himself as a credible rap star, his whiteness quickly went from liability to asset, a marketing advantage that the rapper has openly acknowledged in song lyrics and interviews. Given that the overwhelming majority of rap music buyers are white, Eminem's race became a selling point in ways that Jin's Chinese-ness never could.[11] As an Asian American MC, Jin found himself marginalized at the periphery of American race relations, positioned awkwardly between the dominant poles of White and Black.[12] Too racially other to attract a large white following, but not black enough to be regarded as an authentic rapper, Jin was unable, in "Learn Chinese," to transform his racial identity into a selling point.

Although it is impossible to pinpoint exactly why Jin, a lyricist who demonstrated prodigious skills in his "Freestyle Friday" appearances, failed as a recording artist, the musical strategies behind "Learn Chinese" prove that far from becoming irrelevant, race persists as a category of identity that rap musicians negotiate in presenting themselves to the public. Although some pundits and politicians ask us to believe in a "color-blind" or "post-racial" society, developments in rap music after 2000 suggest that we remain far from such a condition. In fact, for most of the 2000s Eminem remained *the* exception to mainstream rap's racially based standards of authenticity. This near-exclusive focus on artists conforming to particular modes of black representation has led scholars and activists to question whether rap still advances a progressive racial politics. Critiquing the "unholy trinity" of the black gangsta, pimp, and ho, Tricia Rose and others have roundly criticized the music industry's unwillingness to take a chance on anything but a narrow caricature of so-called black experience.[13] More attention to the formal dimensions of individual songs might help reveal noteworthy insights about the aesthetic dimensions of this body of "negative" representations.

As a concept that symbolizes social conflict by appealing to different skin colors and body types, race in rap music (as elsewhere) will continue to be meaningful as long as the experience of racial inequality remains a salient feature of U.S. life. Although observers do not always agree on exactly what music means, by sounding different identities rap songs create an index of the ongoing, unresolved problem of the color line. Does Eminem's popularity portend a bright future in which black and white youth will more often encounter one another as equals? Or does the white rapper's ascent signal a reassertion of white privilege based on a historic understanding of blackness? Although we ultimately need to look beyond the "music itself" to answer such questions, the discussions that people have about rap music are significantly shaped by the kinds of aesthetic decisions this book has explored. As each chapter has emphasized, a rap song's projection of identity depends on certain formal qualities. From Grandmaster Flash to Run-D.M.C., from Public Enemy to N.W.A., from Dr. Dre to

Eminem and beyond, the differences among rap's various projections of identity highlight the socially constructed nature of race, allowing us to observe how popular culture participates in racial formation.

The case studies I have presented do not add up to a comprehensive history of rap music. Rather, each chapter has focused on a popular song by a well-known artist in order to highlight the key roles that specific musical decisions play in defining what authenticity (or inauthenticity) can sound like in the genre at a given moment in time. Unlike studies that confine their scope to words and imagery, *Sounding Race* has attempted a more holistic approach sensitive to the way producers and fans experience rap music *as music*. By exploring the production of song-level meanings in rap, I have sought increased awareness of the aesthetic processes responsible for its production of racial identity. The isolation, manipulation, and looping of breakbeats is arguably the most important and influential musical innovation of the last few decades, and I believe that a break-centered approach to analyzing rap beats can serve future projects exploring the work of other artists who have exercised creative agency within (and against) the traditions and stylistic conventions of hip hop and rap music.

These and others examples of rap music in the first decades of the twenty-first century emphasize that the articulation of sounds, images, and ideas related to race have changed significantly over time. Musical meaning in rap is not frozen in the recordings themselves, but—as in all other music— depends on its surrounding context to become intelligible. Since its earliest years as a commercial genre, rap has been a site where various understandings of racial difference vie to be heard. Although practices of production and listening might change over time, understanding how rap becomes meaningful to listeners will require attention to music at the level of the song. Far from any single essentialized racial meaning, rap music reflects and helps construct the diversity of identities we encounter in this world; it is a sonic force helping us understand the meaning of our existence and our relationship to others. Exploring specific artistic decisions and paying attention to stylistic difference in the genre, we can continue to analyze and interpret how producers work with breaks to creatively recombine and reimagine ideas from the past in hitherto unrecognized ways.

Notes

INTRODUCTION

1. Guthrie P. Ramsey, Jr., *Race Music: Black Cultures from Be-Bop to Hip-Hop* (Berkeley: University of California Press, 2004), 177.

2. Rap began as a "singles" market (see chapter one), became more of an "album-oriented" genre in the late 1980s and 1990s, and in the era of digital downloads has returned in large part to "singles." Thus, the era of the cohesive album-as-musical-statement appears in retrospect as a blip in the overall history of hip hop music. However, by calling attention to the song as a basic unit of production and consumption, I do not wish to downplay the importance of rap albums in the past or the present moment; I seek only to emphasize that even the most elaborate concept album requires planning at the level of the song. Moreover, marketing for a new album often emphasizes the way that it includes tracks designed for specific target audiences: "for the ladies," "for the club," and so on. The Notorious B.I.G.'s 1994 album *Ready to Die* is a case in point, featuring songs addressing a heterosexual female audience, such as "Big Poppa," as well as tracks full of violent braggadocio, such as "Gimme the Loot," that appeal to adolescent male humor.

3. Janice C. Simpson, "Yo! Rap Gets on the Map: Led by Groups like Public Enemy, It Socks a Black Message to the Mainstream," *Time*, February 5, 1990, 60.

4. "Fight the Power" contains more than nineteen individual samples, more than some artists use in an entire album.

5. Robert Walser, "Rhythm, Rhyme, and Rhetoric in the Music of Public Enemy," *Ethnomusicology* 39, no. 2 (1995): 193–217.

6. Simpson, "Rap Gets on the Map," 60.

7. Peter Watrous, "Public Enemy Makes Waves and Compelling Music," *New York Times*, April 22, 1990.

8. Asked by *Guardian* film critic Jason Solomons if he knew that *Do The Right Thing* was an "incendiary film" when he made it, Spike Lee declined to answer and critiqued the question, explaining, "I really wouldn't use the word 'incendiary' because right away you'd think something was burning. I knew the

film would provoke discussion and debate, but in no way shape or form would black people come out of the theaters and start to riot. That was just ridiculous." Jason Solomons, Andy Gallagher, and Henry Barnes, "Spike Lee: 'Anyone Who Thinks We Move in a Post-Racial Society Is Someone Who's Been Smoking Crack,'" *Guardian.com*, October 6, 2009, www.theguardian.com/film/video/2009/oct/05/spike-lee-do-the-right-thing.

9. Mark Jenkins, "House of Hip-Hop: Boys Gotta Bad Rap," *Washington Post*, July 22, 1988, N19.

10. Stephen Holden, "Pop View: Pop's Angry Voices Sound the Alarm," *New York Times*, May 21, 1989, section 2, p. 1.

11. The story of Public Enemy's internal group dynamics and mainstream media reception, including charges of anti-Semitism, is told in great depth in Jeff Chang's *Can't Stop, Won't Stop: A History of the Hip-Hop Generation* (New York: St. Martin's Press, 2005), 232–96.

12. Ramsey, *Race Music*, 175.

13. Solomons, Gallagher, and Barnes, "Spike Lee."

14. Ramsey, *Race Music*, 180.

15. From Lee's journal, January 18, 1988: "The song Radio Raheem plays on his boom box has to be by Public Enemy, my favorite politically conscious rappers. Their new jam 'Bring the Noise' is vicious. I gotta get them to do this like Brutus." Spike Lee with Lisa Jones, *Do the Right Thing* (New York: Fireside, 1989), 59.

16. Adam Krims, *Rap Music and the Poetics of Identity* (Cambridge: Cambridge University Press, 2000).

17. Joseph Schloss, *Making Beats: The Art of Sample-Based Hip-Hop*, 2nd ed. (Middleton, CT: Wesleyan University Press, 2004), 9–10. Schloss's decision not to emphasize the ethnic and racial identities of his informants is part of a larger statement about the racial politics of hip hop studies. He seeks to shift the critical gaze away from race, not to promote a naive universalism but to shed light on aspects of the music (and the people who produce it) that become invisible when scholars assume that racial politics explains everything about hip hop.

18. Schloss, *Making Beats*, 10.

19. On the history of how Filipino American DJ communities first formed and thrived, see Oliver Wang, *Legions of Boom: Filipino American Mobile DJ Crews in the San Francisco Bay Area* (Durham, NC: Duke University Press, 2015). For more information on famous Filipino American hip hop DJs, see Mark Katz, *Groove Music: The Art and Culture of the Hip-Hop DJ* (New York: Oxford University Press, 2012).

20. See *Planet B-Boy*, directed by Benson Lee (New York: Arts Alliance America, 2008), DVD.

21. In his ethnography of the San Francisco Bay Area's underground hip hop scene, Anthony Kwame Harrison finds that young people have constructed their own standards of belonging and authenticity that render rigid notions of race obsolete. By mastering hip hop's formal elements and knowledge of its history, young black, Asian, Latino, and white rappers find common ground and create new forms of community. Although Harrison is careful to point out

ways that race continues to be salient and problematic in the underground scene, hip hop—like jazz before it—has come to embody for many of its practitioners a meritocratic field where status is awarded by achievement alone. Anthony Kwame Harrison, *Hip Hop Underground: The Integrity and Ethics of Racial Identification* (Philadelphia: Temple University Press, 2009).

22. Richard A. Peterson, *Creating Country Music: Fabricating Authenticity* (Chicago: University of Chicago Press, 1997).

23. Michael Omi and Howard Winant, *Racial Formation in the United States: From the 1960s to the 1990s* (New York: Routledge, 1994), 55.

24. Omi and Winant define racial formation as the "sociohistorical process by which racial meanings are created, inhabited, transformed, and destroyed" (*Racial Formation*, 55).

25. Christopher A. Waterman, "Race Music: Bo Chatmon, 'Corrine Corrina,' and the Excluded Middle," in *Music and the Racial Imagination*, ed. Ronald Radano and Philip V. Bohlman (Chicago: University of Chicago Press, 2000), 167–205; Karl Hagstrom Miller, *Segregating Sound: Inventing Folk and Pop Music in the Age of Jim Crow* (Durham, NC: Duke University Press, 2010).

26. Frederick Douglass, *Narrative of the Life of Frederick Douglass, An American Slave* (Oxford: Oxford University Press, 1999 [1845]); W. E. B. Du Bois, *The Souls of Black Folk* (New York: Dover, 1994 [1903]).

27. Imamu Amiri Baraka, *Blues People: The Negro Experience in White America and the Music That Developed from It* (New York: Morrow Quill, 1963)

28. Imamu Amiri Baraka, *Black Music* (New York: Da Capo Press, 1998 [1968]).

29. Philip Weitzman, *Worlds Apart: Housing, Race, Ethnicity, and Income in New York City* (New York: Community Service Society of New York, 1989).

30. Michelle Alexander, *The New Jim Crow: Mass Incarceration in the Age of Colorblindness* (New York: New Press, 2012).

31. George Lipsitz, *The Possessive Investment in Whiteness: How White People Benefit from Identity Politics* (Philadelphia: Temple University Press, 1998), 5.

32. Like film and other mass-mediated constructions of race and class identity, rap music symbolizes social conflict and presents listeners with "indexical markers of enduring crises in the cultural imaginary." Roopali Mukherjee, *The Racial Order of Things* (Minneapolis: University of Minnesota Press, 2006), 2.

33. In his study of how blind people experience the "micro-level" politics of race, Osagie Obasogie confirms empirically that physical differences in skin color and body type are not in and of themselves responsible ("constitutive," in his words) for the reality of race. If race were exclusively, or even primarily, visual in nature we would expect blind people to have a diminished understanding of race. However, even people who have been blind from birth develop remarkably vivid conceptualizations of racial difference, which they use in their daily lives to interpret and guide interactions with others. Osagie K. Obasogie, "Do Blind People See Race? Social, Legal, and Theoretical Considerations," *Law & Society Review* 44, no. 3/4 (2010): 585–616.

34. Sighted people, for example, regularly assume the racial identity of callers on the telephone (Obasogie, "Do Blind People See Race?" 610).

35. Obasagie, "Do Blind People See Race?" 598.

36. Ingrid Monson, *Saying Something: Jazz Improvisation and Interaction* (Chicago: University of Chicago Press, 1996), 131.

37. Keith Negus, *Popular Music in Theory: An Introduction* (Middleton, CT: Wesleyan University Press, 1996), 133.

38. Negus, *Popular Music in Theory,* 133.

39. As a way of calling attention to this mobilization of musical sounds and racial meanings, Radano and Bohlman describe race in music as a "soundtext": an image constituted within and projected onto the social through sound. Their neologism speaks to the *articulation*—the joining together—of sounds and the racialized discourse describing them. Philip Bohlman and Ronald Radano, "Introduction," in *Music and the Racial Imagination,* ed. Philip Bohlman and Ronald Radano (Chicago: University of Chicago Press, 2001), 5.

40. Kelefa Sanneh, "Jay-Z's 'Decoded' and the Language of Hip-Hop," *The New Yorker,* December 6, 2010.

41. In literary studies, see Adam Bradley, *Book of Rhymes: The Poetics of Hip-Hop* (New York: Basic Civitas, 2009); in music theory, see Kyle Adams, "Aspects of the Music/Text Relationship in Rap," *Music Theory Online* 14, no. 2 (May 2008).

42. "Flow" is a colloquial term that refers to an MC's distinctive combination of rhyme scheme and rhythmic delivery.

43. Bradley, *Book of Rhymes,* 3–48.

44. Robert Christgau, "Consumer Guide Reviews: *It Takes a Nation of Millions to Hold Us Back,*" www.robertchristgau.com/get_artist.php?name=Public+Enemy.

45. I am particularly grateful for Joseph Schloss's and Mark Katz's respective works on sample-based production and hip hop DJing.

46. Schloss cautions academic critics to tread lightly when applying methods of analysis developed in other contexts to the study of hip hop and rap music. He cites the mistakes made by some scholars committed to a postmodern interpretive model (i.e., hearing sampling as primarily about ironic recontextualization), arguing that they have misapplied the concept of "parody" to sample-based hip hop in assuming that producers intend the breaks that they sample to be recognized and interpreted as a commentary upon their original sources (*Making Beats,* 148).

47. Schloss, *Making Beats,* 147.

48. Tricia Rose, *The Hip Hop Wars: What We Talk About When We Talk About Hip Hop and Why It Matters* (New York: Basic Civitas, 2008), 13.

49. *Sounding Race* is indebted to the late music theorist Adam Krims, author of the first book devoted to analyzing rap music. Calling for a "musical poetics" of rap capable of accounting for its diverse identities, Krims concentrates on three general parameters: topic, musical style, and flow. Building a

genre system for rap music circa 1994, Krims explains how these formal qualities help to position a song and its artist relative to others. Identifying and describing a set of generic categories, such as "mack rap," "party rap," and "gangsta rap," Krims (*Rap Music*) argues that the differences between these various genres are marked not only by the topics that MCs rap about but also by the flow and musical styles that they employ. In other words, a song's aesthetic features are not neutral or arbitrary; they "transcode" social and musical meanings that mark songs and artists in culturally meaningful ways.

50. Although his work is highly inventive and insightful, Krims's choice to name his own genre categories and terminology (e.g., the "hip-hop sublime") to describe musical affect raises concerns about the usefulness of discussing rap's aesthetics in terms that most fans and producers might fail to recognize. In a similar vein, Krims's original approach to transcription isolates individual lines and harmonies he hears in the track—such as a looped saxophone melody or guitar riff—ignoring the break-centered musical procedures behind the creation of such sounds.

51. George Lipsitz, *Time Passages: Collective Memory and American Popular Culture* (Minneapolis: University of Minnesota Press, 1990), xii.

CHAPTER 1

1. Grandmaster Flash, as quoted in Nelson George, "Hip-Hop's Founding Fathers Speak the Truth," *The Source*, November, 1993, 44–50.

2. Chuck D, as quoted in Jeff Chang, *Can't Stop Won't Stop: A History of the Hip-Hop Generation* (New York: Civitas Books, 2005), 130.

3. Richard Taninbaum, interview with author.

4. Robert Ford, Jr., "Jive Talking N.Y. DJs Rapping Away in Black Discos," *Billboard*, May 5, 1979, 3.

5. Nelson George, "Rapping Records Flooding Stores in N.Y. Market," *Billboard*, December 22, 1979, 37, 53.

6. Steve Gordon and the Kosher Five, "Take My Rap . . . Please," Reflection Records MOM 667, 1979.

7. L'Ectrique, "Struck By Boogie Lightning," Reflection Records CBL 128, 1979.

8. Steve Gordon, interview with author.

9. According to Steve Gordon (interview with the author), the photograph was staged in the lobby of a hotel in White Plains, New York, but the group sought to evoke the atmosphere of a Jewish resort in the Catskills.

10. Richard Taninbaum, interview with author.

11. Ron Hunt/Ronnie G. and the S.M. Crew, "Spiderap" b/w "A Corona Jam," Reflection Records PT-7000, 1979; Lady T/M.C. Tee, "Lady D" b/w "Nu Sounds," Reflection Records PT-7001, 1979.

12. Although it did not garner widespread attention, The Fatback Band can boast the first recording featuring rapped vocals: "King Tim III (Personality Jock)" b/w "Love in Perfect Harmony," Polydor Records 2095214, 1979.

13. On Saturday, October 6, 1979, Eddie Cheeba took to the stage at the Armory in Jamaica, Queens, with an all-star line-up of New York City's black dance-club performers. Along with DJ Hollywood and Grandmaster Flash, both of whom also appeared on stage that evening, Cheeba was one of a handful of the city's best known and most in-demand rapping DJs. A surviving audio recording from that evening's performance reveals that, in the middle of his set, Cheeba suspended his routine to make an important announcement to his audience: "Now you might have heard on [radio station] WBLS tomorrow night we gonna take the sugar out the hill at Harlem World. Sugar Hill and Eddie Cheeba tomorrow night. But first we have some unfinished business to take care of right here in Jamaica [Queens]. First of all, we're gonna run down a few of the things that we know we made famous." Engaging in a bit of not-so-subtle wordplay, Cheeba declares himself one of the true innovators of rap music and announces an upcoming battle with the Sugarhill Gang, who had released "Rapper's Delight" less than a month earlier. Cheeba's defiant response at the Armory captured the sentiments of many more established New York artists. Despite having spent the previous years cultivating his reputation as a live performer, he could do little more than watch as Sugar Hill Records reaped the financial benefits of the seeds he and others had sown. Mark Skillz, "Master of Ceremonies: Introducing the Original Crowd Rocker Eddie Cheeba," *Wax Poetics*, no. 24 (August 2007), 74.

14. Joseph Schloss, *Making Beats: The Art of Sample-Based Hip-Hop* (Middletown, CT: Wesleyan University Press, 2004), 33.

15. Dan Charnas, *The Big Payback: The History of the Business of Hip-Hop* (New York: New American Library, 2010), 37–40.

16. Chang, *Can't Stop, Won't Stop*, 132.

17. Chang, *Can't Stop, Won't Stop*, 132.

18. Breakbeats are often defined as sections on recordings that feature drums or other percussion instruments—for example, moments when all instruments, except for drums and percussion, drop out of the mix. Listening to classic breakbeat recordings, however, it becomes apparent that the breaks often included non-percussion instrumentation. Joseph Schloss offers a more sensitive conception of the break as "the interruption of an integrated groove," a moment when certain parts of an established polyrhythmic arrangement are dramatically stripped away. See Joseph Schloss, *Foundation: B-Boys, B-Girls and Hip-Hop Culture in New York* (New York: Oxford University Press, 2008), 21.

19. Robert Ford, Jr., "B-Beats Bombarding Bronx: Mobile DJ Starts Something with Oldie R&B Disks," *Billboard*, July 1, 1978, 65.

20. Kool Herc demonstrates his "merry-go-round" using exactly this sequence of recordings in part 1 of the documentary *The Hip-Hop Years: Close to the Edge* (1999).

21. Will Hermes, "All Rise for the National Anthem of Hip Hop," *New York Times*, October 29, 2006, http://nytimes.com/2006/10/29/arts/music/29herm.html.

22. Schloss, *Foundation*, 17–39.

23. The story of "Apache," once described by Kool Herc as "the national anthem of hip hop," is one of the most fascinating illustrations of this point. "Apache" was recorded by Michael Viner's Incredible Bongo Band, a group that consisted of anonymous studio musicians passing through MGM Studios in Los Angeles. The Bongo Band never toured or played together at live shows, and their recordings remained virtually unknown and unremarked-upon until Bronx DJs and b-boys began turning to them for their infectious mix of funk drumming and Latin percussion (Hermes, "All Rise.")

24. Downstairs Records was one of the most famous shops oriented toward the discovery and sale of breakbeat records. Grandmaster Flash describes finding this record store, in the subway arcade at 42nd Street and 6th Avenue, as the "Gold Rush of 1975." Grandmaster Flash with David Ritz, *The Adventures of Grandmaster Flash: My Life, My Beats* (New York: Random House, 2008), 67.

25. Flash, *My Life, My Beats*, 53.

26. Mark Katz, *Groove Music: The Art and Culture of the Hip-Hop DJ* (New York: Oxford University Press, 2012), 56.

27. Matthew Honan, "Unlikely Places Where *Wired* Pioneers Had Their *Eureka!* Moments," *Wired*, March 24, 2008. http://archive.wired.com/culture/lifestyle/multimedia/2008/03/ff_eureka?slide=6&slideView=4.

28. Grandmaster Flash and the Furious Five consisted of Flash, Kid Creole, Cowboy, Rahiem, Melle Mel, and Mr. Ness/Scorpio. Before arriving at this name and solidifying their lineup, the group also performed as Grandmaster Flash and the 3 MCs and Grandmaster Flash and the Furious Four.

29. Flash recalls one of his favorite climactic records being the Incredible Bongo Band's "Apache" (*My Beats, My Life,* 109).

30. Bob James's "Take Me To the Mardi Gras" (1975), for example, was and continues to be an essential component in the hip-hop DJ's arsenal, but only for its opening measures (i.e., less than thirty seconds of music), which feature a syncopated mix of funk drumming and *agogo* bells.

31. Such formal changes align hip hop music with other black cultural practices, but they do not guarantee specific racial meanings (Schloss, *Making Beats,* 138).

32. "Grandmaster Flash & The Furious 4 MC's - Live At Audubon Ballroom," *Hip Hop On Wax, 1979–1999* [weblog], October 14, 2006. http://hiphoponwax.blogspot.com/2006/10/grandmaster-flash-furious-4-mcs-live.html.

33. Joseph Schloss makes an analogous point about musical notation and sample-based beats (*Making Beats,* 14).

34. The part of Flash's performance discussed here occurs at approximately six minutes into the recording.

35. Grandmaster Flash, as quoted in George, "Hip-Hop's Founding Fathers," 44–50.

36. Grandmixer D.ST, as quoted in Katz, *Groove Music,* 21.

37. Flash, *My Life, My Beats,* 109.

38. David Menconi, "The Riff That Lifted Rap," *NewsObserver.com*, March 14, 2010. www.newsobserver.com/2010/03/14/385149/the-riff-that-lifted-rap.html.

39. Oliver Wang, as quoted in Menconi, "The Riff."

40. Skillz, "Master of," 74.

41. Chang, *Can't Stop, Won't Stop*, 127.

42. After "Rapper's Delight," the spontaneity and creativity hip hop DJs demonstrated by looping and cutting a variety of breaks together became mostly an underground phenomenon. Exceptions to this rule include Grandmaster Flash's pioneering "Adventures on the Wheels of Steel" (1981), as well as the numerous "DJ tracks" on early rap albums in the early and mid-1980s. By the early 1990s, DJ-centered events and competitions, such as the DMC World DJ Championships, helped reinvigorate this aspect of hip hop culture, bringing the art to a younger, wider audience (Katz, *Groove Music*, 100–152).

43. Grandmaster Flash, *My Life*, 87–90.

44. Katz, *Groove Music*, 35.

45. What did differentiate early rap recordings from what DJs were doing at uptown clubs was the narrowness of the latter's musical selections. As hip hop impresario Michael Holman, who attended both downtown discos and uptown dance clubs explains (interview with the author), junior high kids in the Bronx "didn't really have the wherewithal to go to these clubs; they were too young. They didn't have the gear. They didn't have the money. . . . [Bambaataa, Kool Herc, and Flash] were creating parties for kids that *couldn't* go downtown to the discos. So this idea that hip hop was some sort of adversarial reaction to disco is ridiculous. The early hip hop parties were basically bringing disco to the neighborhood, to kids that really couldn't go to experience it. . . . What was different from the downtown discos was, DJs like [Bambaataa] were determined to play James Brown and other funk and soul tracks as well, that were so big a few years before, which they were not playing in downtown discos. They only played [recently released] disco [records] in discos!"

46. Rickey Vincent, as quoted in Murray Forman, *The 'Hood Comes First: Race, Space, and Place in Hip Hop and Rap Music* (Middletown, CT: Wesleyan University Press, 2000), 80.

47. Charnas, *The Big Payback*, 65–92.

48. Charnas, *The Big Payback*, 32–33.

49. Taninbaum, interview with author.

50. Forman, *The 'Hood Comes First*, 80–81.

51. The Younger Generation were actually Grandmaster Flash's rappers, the Furious Five, going under another name in order to work with producer Terry Lewis.

52. Cheryl Keyes, "At the Crossroads: Rap Music and Its African Nexus," *Ethnomusicology* 40, no. 2 (1996): 223–48.

53. Katz, *Groove Music*, 32–35.

54. At the center of the backlash was a young, white radio DJ named Steve Dahl. In 1978, at the height of disco fever, Dahl had been fired from radio

station WDAI after it converted from a rock to a disco format. Early in 1979, he was hired by WLUP, one of WDAI's rivals, and he used the radio platform to heap scorn on his former employer and disco music in general. At twenty-four years of age, the brash Chicago disc jockey became one of the engineers behind the carnivalesque spectacle known as Disco Demolition Night, which lit the fuse, both figuratively and literally, of the anti-disco explosion. On July 12, 1979, fans were offered reduced admission to the White Sox double-header against the Detroit Tigers if they donated a disco record to be destroyed. During the intermission between games, a giant wooden container of vinyl LPs that had been brought by fans was brought out into center field and detonated. After the explosion, hundreds of fans rushed onto the field and chaos ensued. Eventually, riot police were called in to disperse the crowd; the second game of the double-header had to be cancelled.

55. Elements common to so-called disco music—four-on-the-floor bass drum, sixteenth-note hi-hat patterns, and so on—continued to animate popular dance music in the 1980s, long after disco was supposed to have died.

56. Jeffrey Kallberg, "The Rhetoric of Genre: Chopin's Nocturne in G Minor," *19th-Century Music* 11, no. 3 (1988): 238–61.

57. Alice Echols, *Hot Stuff: Disco and the Remaking of American Culture* (New York: W. W. Norton, 2010).

58. Ford, "Jive Talking," 3.

59. George, "Hip-Hop's Founding Fathers," 44–50.

60. George, "Hip-Hop's Founding Fathers," 44–50.

61. Although it would be naive to reduce the genre's demise to a single factor, the backlash against disco reveals how musical genres articulate powerfully with socially constructed categories of identity, such as race, gender, class, and sexuality. Some of disco's loudest and harshest critics were white, heterosexual males who identified with rock music, and their barbs aimed at disco (e.g., "disco sucks") often revealed homophobic, misogynistic, and racist attitudes. Although Dahl himself denies charges of bias in his campaign against disco, his fans and other anti-disco crusaders regularly laced their rants with derogatory terms for racial and sexual minorities. Echols contextualizes the anti-disco movement in the late 1970s, a time when a number of taken-for-granted certainties seemed to be under assault. The recession, oil and hostage crises, and loss in Vietnam were some of the political and economic signs that the United States was no longer living up to its image as a global superpower. For white males, these changes were accompanied by an increasingly visible and militant feminism, gay rights, and civil rights culture. It is little surprise that disco, a gender-bending genre prominently featuring women and minorities, became a punching bag for a generation's anger and frustrations. As Echols puts it in *Hot Stuff*, "Discophobes might not be able to 'bomb bomb bomb Iran,' as Vince Vance and the Valiants urged in 1979, but they could demolish disco, the music of outsiders—racial minorities and gays."

62. Charnas, *The Big Payback*, 59.

63. Echols, *Hot Stuff*.

64. Paul Green, "New Chic Game Plan: No Disco," *Billboard,* December 15, 1979, 23.

65. "Talent in Action," *Billboard,* 22 December 1979, 6–50.

66. Green, "New Chic Game Plan," 23.

67. As scholar Imani Perry puts it in *Prophets of the Hood: Politics and Poetics in Hip Hop* (Durham, NC: Duke University Press, 2004, p. 6), "The juke joint has gone public."

68. George, "Rapping Records," 37.

69. John Rockwell, "The 'Rapping' Style in Pop," *New York Times,* October 12, 1980, D30; Robert Palmer, "Pop: The Sugar Hill Gang," *New York Times,* March 13, 1981, C23.

70. Rockwell, "The 'Rapping' Style in Pop;" Robert Palmer, "Pop: The Sugar Hill Gang."

71. Robert Palmer, "The Year of the Rolling Stones," *New York Times,* December 27, 1981, section 2, p. 23; Leah Y. Latimer, "Recording the Rap: Jive Talk at the Top of the Charts," *Washington Post,* August 31, 1980, G1; Rockwell, "The 'Rapping' Style."

72. Palmer, "Rolling Stones"; Rockwell, "The 'Rapping' Style."

73. A telling example of rap's liminal nature at this time is Spoonin Gee's 12-inch single "Spoonin Rap" (Sound of New York, USA QC 708, 1979), which was released soon after "Rapper's Delight" in 1979. The recording features one continuous track, but the label lists the different topics Spoonin Gee covers in order—"A Drive Down the Street," "I Was Spanking and Freaking," "I Don't Drink Smoke Or Gamble Neither," "I'm the Cold Crushing Lover"—as if it were a comedy album!

74. Tricia Rose, *Black Noise: Rap Music and Black Culture in Contemporary America* (Hanover, NH: Wesleyan University Press, 1994), 47.

75. When *The Source* magazine asked Grandmaster Flash in 1993 about the transition from live performance to recording songs, he replied, "I'd have to say, I wasn't ready. I was content with what I was doing. . . . I would have personally liked to stay away from records a little longer." Citing his love for the different aspects of live performance, from setting up his sound system to mixing dozens of records, Flash explained that one really has to observe a DJ over the course of hours to appreciate the skill it takes to move a crowd (George, "Hip-Hop's Founding Fathers," 44–50).

76. The next big hit after "Rapper's Delight" was, in fact, Kurtis Blow's single "The Breaks" (Mercury Records MDS 410, 1980).

CHAPTER 2

1. Hank Shocklee, as quoted in Jeff Chang, *Can't Stop, Won't Stop* (New York: Basic Civitas, 2005), 260.

2. Jon Pareles, "Public Enemy: Rap with a Fist in the Air," *New York Times,* July 24, 1988, H25.

3. Charise Cheney, *Brothers Gonna Work It Out: Sexual Politics in the Golden Age of Rap Nationalism* (New York: New York University Press, 2005), 72–73.

4. Pareles criticizes Chuck D for promising profundity and political analysis but delivering only empty slogans and familiar boasting.

5. Ronald Radano and Phillip Bohlman, "Introduction," in *Music and the Racial Imagination,* ed. Ronald Radano and Phillip Bohlman (Chicago: University of Chicago Press, 2000), 5.

6. Radano and Bohlman, "Introduction," 5.

7. Bomb Squad members included brothers Hank Shocklee and Keith Shocklee, Chuck D, Eric "Vietnam" Sadler, Gary G-Wiz, and Kerwin "Sleek" Young.

8. Scholars from many disciplines have written about Public Enemy. Here is an incomplete sample. Jeff Chang, *Can't Stop, Won't Stop: A History of the Hip-Hop Generation* (New York: St. Martin's Press, 2005); Dan Charnas, *The Big Payback: The History of the Business of Hip-Hop* (New York: New American Library, 2010); Charise Cheney, *Brothers Gonna Work It Out: Sexual Politics in the Golden Age of Rap Nationalism* (New York: New York University Press, 2005); Jeffrey L. Decker, "The State of Rap: Time and Place in Hip-Hop Nationalism," *Social Text* 34 (1993): 53–84; Kembrew McLeod and Peter DiCola, *Creative License: The Law and Culture of Digital Sampling* (Durham, NC: Duke University Press, 2011); Guthrie Ramsey, Jr., *Race Music: Black Cultures from Be-Bop to Hip-Hop* (Berkeley: University of California Press, 2004); Tricia Rose, *Black Noise: Rap Music and Black Culture in Contemporary America* (Middletown, CT: Wesleyan University Press, 1994); Robert Walser, "Rhythm, Rhyme, and Rhetoric in the Music of Public Enemy," *Ethnomusicology* 39, no. 2 (1995): 193–217.

9. Michael Omi and Howard Winant, *Racial Formation in the U.S.: From the 1960s to the 1990s* (New York: Routledge, 1994), 55.

10. Mark Dery, "Public Enemy: Confrontation," *Keyboard,* September 1990, 83.

11. Rose, *Black Noise,* 53.

12. Joseph Schloss, *Making Beats: The Art of Sample-Based Hip-Hop* (Middletown, CT: Wesleyan University Press, 2004), 36–43; see also Mark Katz, "Sampling before Sampling: The Link between DJ and Producer," *Samples* 9 (2010): 1–11.

13. Spectrum City, "Lies" b/w "Check Out the Radio," Vanguard SPV 76, 1984.

14. Hank Shocklee, who served as Spectrum City's DJ, emphasizes that turntable techniques remained an important touchstone for Public Enemy well into the sample-based era; even when using samplers and drum machines in the studio, the group continued to rely on turntables for scratching and cutting in snippets of sound (Katz, "Sampling before Sampling," 7–8).

15. Roy Spencer (DJ Moneyshot), "Public Enemy: It Takes a Nation of Millions to Hold Us Back," *Future Music,* no. 269 (August 2013).

16. Murray Forman, *The 'Hood Comes First: Race, Space, and Place in Hip Hop and Rap Music* (Middletown, CT: Wesleyan University Press, 2000), 79–81.

17. Rose, *Black Noise*, 75.

18. At the time of Rose's writing, rap music occupied a more precarious and marginal position in American life than it does today, and *Black Noise* defends and celebrates rap *as music*, illuminating the logic informing what many refused to recognize as a legitimate form of artistry. In other words, proving rap's cultural coherence was absolutely central to Rose's argument that the music was, in fact, music, not the work of unskilled, illiterate thieves.

19. Tricia Rose, *The Hip Hop Wars: What We Talk About When We Talk About Hip Hop and Why It Matters* (New York: Basic Books, 2008).

20. McLeod and DiCola, *Creative License*, 19–35.

21. Her observations that rap musicians hate "digital drums" (73) and that samplers are the "quintessential rap production tool" (78), for example, seem to reflect the practices and aesthetic preferences of Public Enemy and other late 1980s and early 1990s artists active in the period leading up to *Black Noise*'s publication.

22. Walser, "Rhythm, Rhyme, and Rhetoric," 197.

23. Schloss, *Making Beats*, 14.

24. The J.B.'s, "Hot Pants Road," People Records PE 607, 1972.

25. Forman, *The 'Hood Comes First*, 79–81.

26. Grandmaster Flash, *The Adventures of Grandmaster Flash: My Life, My Beats* (New York: Random House, 2008), 157.

27. Nelson George, Sally Banes, Susan Flinker, and Patty Romanowski, *Fresh: Hip Hop Don't Stop* (New York: Random House, 1985), 18.

28. In her essay exploring rap nationalism, Cheney singles out "The Message" as the beginning of politically engaged rap (*Brothers Gonna Work It Out*, 8–9). See also Chang, *Can't Stop, Won't Stop*, 177–179.

29. Forman, *The 'Hood Comes First*, 91–95

30. Forman, *The 'Hood Comes First*, 89.

31. Forman, *The 'Hood Comes First*, 87.

32. Songs like David Lampell's "I Ran Iran" (1979) and Brother D's "How We Gonna Make the Black Nation Rise?" (1980) had political themes, but they were set to familiar disco funk beats and did not attract attention as protest songs (see Chang, *Can't Stop, Won't Stop*, 179).

33. Ironically, the huge success of "The Message" marked the beginning of the end for Grandmaster Flash and the Furious Five. By encouraging Melle Mel to record the song without Flash's consent and without participation from him and the other members, Robinson had driven a wedge into group that would eventually lead to a painful breakup and protracted legal battle (Grandmaster Flash, *My Life*, 156–65).

34. Kid Creole, as quoted in Jim Fricke and Charlie Ahearn, *Yes, Yes Y'All: The EMP Oral History of Hip Hop* (New York: Da Capo Press, 2002), 210.

35. Chang, *Can't Stop, Won't Stop*, 179.

36. Adam Bradley and Andrew DuBois, eds., *The Anthology of Rap* (New Haven: Yale University Press, 2010), 13.

37. Robert Palmer, "'The Message' Is That 'Rap' Is Now King in Rock Clubs," *New York Times*, September 3, 1982, C4.

38. Geoffrey Himes, "Urban Anthems of Rap Music," *Washington Post*, December 30, 1982, D4.

39. Geoffrey Himes, "Urban Anthems."

40. John Rockwell, "Rap: The Furious Five," *New York Times*, September 12, 1982, section 1, part 2, p. 84.

41. Robert Fink, "The Story of ORCH5, or, the Classical Ghost in the Hip-Hop Machine," *Popular Music* 24, no. 3 (2005): 339–56.

42. The sounds from these drum machines were so distinctive and ubiquitous, in fact, that to this day people still refer to them by name (e.g. "an 808 kick"), and they have been included—again, by name—in pretty much all modern music production software. In other words, even when working at a digital audio workstation such as a laptop computer, music producers enjoy having access to the sounds of these earlier technologies.

43. Daniel Sofer, *DMX Owner's Manual*, 3rd ed. (Los Angeles: Oberheim Electronics, 1982), 15.

44. Tom Silverman, as quoted in Mark Dery, "Rap: Rock Is Dead," *Keyboard*, November 1988.

45. John Leland, "Singles," *Spin* 2, no. 7 (October 1986): 43.

46. Charnas, *The Big Payback*, 96–99.

47. Forman (*The 'Hood Comes First*, 125) notes that by 1984 rap was beginning to be discussed as "street music" in the trade press, a designation that was not made during the days of disco rap.

48. Gary Jardim, "John Who?" *Village Voice*, June 21, 1983.

49. Charnas, *The Big Payback*, 89–94.

50. Run-D.M.C., *Raising Hell*, Profile Records PRO-1217, 1986.

51. The "Walk This Way" break had been used by hip-hop DJs in live performance for many years. In fact, D.M.C. fondly remembers the moment when the group's DJ, Jam Master Jay, explained to Aerosmith's members how he used to use their record: "When Steven Tyler came into the studio, Jay was cutting up [Aerosmith's original recording of] 'Walk This Way' and he said, 'here's what we used to do with your record.' And Steve said, 'Yo, when are you gonna hear *me*?' And Jay looked up and said, 'We never get to hear you. After this guitar riff, it's back to the beginning.' And Steve thought that was so amusing. Those guys were real cool." Brian Coleman, *Check the Technique: Liner Notes for Hip-Hop Junkies* (New York: Villard, 2007), 401.

52. Perhaps seeking to downplay the implication that the crossover success of "Walk This Way" represented a watering-down of hip-hop culture, multiple authors have emphasized the song's origins in live DJ performance (Rose, *Black Noise*, 77; Katz, "Sampling," 1; Forman, *The 'Hood Comes First*, 150).

53. Music critic Robert Palmer noted the aesthetic fusion, explaining that "Walk This Way" takes Aerosmith's vocals and electric guitar and "grafts"

them onto rap's "typically minimal drum-machine rhythms" ("Rap Music, Despite Adult Fire, Broadens Its Teen-Age Base," *New York Times*, September 21, 1986, section 2, p. 23).

54. Will Fulton, interview with author, October 23, 2011.

55. One of the best demonstrations of this technique can be heard in "Peter Piper," another single from *Raising Hell*. In it, Jay uses different parts of Bob James's "Take Me To the Mardi Gras" to augment the DMX track with funky bells and electric piano riffs.

56. The Knack, "My Sharona," Capitol Records 4731, 1979. On top of that, Run-D.M.C. chant their lyrics to the same rhythm as the chorus of Toni Basil's song "Mickey" (Radialchoice TIC 4, 1981).

57. Bob James, *Two*, CTI Records CTI-6057, 1975.

58. Beastie Boys, *Licensed to Ill*, Def Jam/Columbia BFC-40238, 1986.

59. David Chapelle, John Maher, and Questlove, "White People Dancing," *Chapelle Show*, Season 2, Episode 3, February 4, 2004.

60. Rick Rubin, as quoted in Mark Dery, "Rap."

61. Bill Adler, as quoted in Mark Dery, "Rap."

62. J. D. Considine, "Rap & Hip-Hop: Rising Tide," *Washington Post*, August 29, 1986, 29.

63. Robert Palmer, "Rap Music." Palmer was quick to recognize and accept Run-D.M.C.'s (and their publicists') messaging. Early in 1985, he made the group's *King of Rock* album the center of his argument in favor of rap as more than a passing fad. Quoting Bill Adler, he compared rap's current state of affairs to R&B just prior to its mass popularization as rock and roll ("Street-Smart Rapping Is Innovative Art Form," *New York Times*, February 4, 1985, C13).

64. Jess Cagle and John Callan, "All Hell Breaks Loose at a Run-D.M.C. 'Raising Hell' Rap Concert in California," *People* 26, no. 9 (September 1, 1986).

65. George Ramos, "'Rap' Musicians' Concert Is Canceled at Palladium after Long Beach Fights," *Los Angeles Times*, August 19, 1986.

66. Rose, *Black Noise*, 132.

67. Richard Harrington, "Run-DMC and the Rap Flap: For a Hot Trio, Violence and Criticism on the Concert Trail," *Washington Post*, August 29, 1986, C1.

68. For a laundry list of such claims by industry insiders, see Mark Dery, "Rap."

69. "Sound Bite," *SPIN Magazine* 8, no. 6 (September 1992): 42.

70. Malcolm X, *Grass Roots Speech: Detroit, Michigan, November 1963*, Paul Winley Records L.P. 134, 1979.

71. In sample-based hip hop, *chopping* refers to the process of dividing a digital sample into any number of smaller parts and rearranging them to create a new pattern.

72. Quoted in Rose, *Black Noise*, 79.

73. Marley Marl dates his innovation to 1981 or 1982, but few, if any, sampling devices capable of this process were available at the time. It is more likely that Marl first experimented with sampled drum breaks in or around 1984

when the first devices with adequate memory and function, such as E-mu Emulator II and the Ensonique Mirage, began hitting the market. See Rose, Black Noise, 79.

74. Oliver Wang, "Beat Making," in Grove Dictionary of American Music, ed. Charles Hiroshi Garrett (New York: Oxford University Press, 2013).

75. Funkadelic, Connections & Disconnections, LAX Records JW-37087, 1981; Bobby Byrd, "I Know You Got Soul," King Records 45–6378, 1971.

76. "You'll Like It Too" was adopted immediately by hip-hop DJs upon its release in 1981. A 1981 bootleg tape of the Cold Crush Brothers battling the Fantastic Romantic 5 live at the club Harlem World features them rapping over a DJ quick-mixing this break.

77. Schloss, Making Beats, 137.

78. Schloss, Making Beats, 137.

79. Charnas, The Big Payback, 181.

80. Various online sources, including Wikipedia, misidentify the squealing instrument that opens the "The Grunt" as a trumpet. It is in fact a tenor saxophone, played by Robert McCullough. McCullough was hired to replace Maceo Parker in 1970 after Parker and Brown had a falling out over Brown's leadership policies. As Eric Leeds, the brother of Brown's tour manager Allen Leeds, remembers (personal communication), McCullough could not deliver a sax solo in Parker's virtuosic style, but he did have a knack for squawking on his horn. His squeaking glissandos can also be heard on James Brown's "Super Bad."

81. James Brown, "Funky Drummer, Pt. 1," King Records 45–6290, 1970; The J.B.'s, "The Grunt, Pt. 1," Mojo 2027–002, 1971; Chubb Rock, "Rock 'n' Roll Dude," Select Records FMS 62281, 1987.

82. Mark Dery, "Public Enemy: Confrontation," Keyboard, September 1990.

83. Katz, "Sampling before Sampling," 8.

84. For longer samples, like the drum break from "You'll Like It Too," producers had a few options: "shorten" the sample by recording it at a higher speed than 33rpm and then slow it back down during playback; or break the sample into smaller units that could be triggered in sequence to reconstruct the entire break, a feature that would become known as "chopping"; or revert back to analogue technologies, such as turntables and tape loops, to cut and paste desired samples into the mix.

85. Red Bull Music Academy Lecture, "Hank Shocklee: A Journey into Noise with Public Enemy's Chief Producer," Seattle, 2005. www.redbullmusicacademy.com/lectures/hank-shocklee--art-brut.

86. Schloss, Making Beats, 36.

87. Cheney, Brothers Gonna Work It Out, 67.

88. The Honey Drippers, "Impeach the President," Alaga Records AL-1017, 1973.

89. Quoted in John Leland, "Armageddon in Effect," in And It Don't Stop: The Best American Hip-Hop Journalism of the Last 25 Years, ed. Raquel Cepeda (New York: Faber and Faber, 2004), 69.

90. Chang, *Can't Stop, Won't Stop*, 264–70.

91. Stephen Holden, "Pop View: Pop's Angry Voices Sound the Alarm," *New York Times*, May 21, 1989, section 2, p. 1.

92. Omi and Winant, *Racial Formation*, 163.

93. K. Fitzpatrick, "More Hip Hop," *Courier-Mail*, January 21, 1988.

94. Quoted in DJ Moneyshot, "Solid Steel and the Hour of Chaos," *Solid Steel Radio Show*, February 28, 2013. https://soundcloud.com/ninja-tune/solid-steel-radio-show-2-8-1.

95. Although I do not suggest that these were the exact terms in which Public Enemy conceived of their sound, it is likely that the group encountered such theories about African American music through coursework at Adelphi University, where they were enrolled in jazz musician and lecturer Andrei Strobert's class "Black Music and Musicians" (Chang, *Can't Stop, Won't Stop*, 239–41).

96. Olly Wilson, "The Significance of the Relationship between Afro-American Music and West African Music," *Black Perspective in Music* 2, no. 1 (1974): 20.

97. Wilson, "Afro-American Music," 15.

98. Amiri Baraka, *Black Music* (New York: Da Capo Press, 1968), 180–212.

99. Bohemian rap groups, such as Digable Planets and A Tribe Called Quest, self-consciously sampled breaks evoking the instrumental timbres of jazz music, positioning their respective groups as cooler and more sophisticated than their peers. Justin A. Williams, "The Construction of Jazz Rap as High Art in Hip-Hop Music," *Journal of Musicology* 27, no. 4 (Fall 2010): 435–459.

100. For some listeners, 1988 represents hip-hop music's greatest year, in part thanks to the flowering of artistic diversity enabled by the sample-based approach to beat making; see Loren Kajikawa, "'Bringin' '88 Back': Historicizing Rap Music's Greatest Year," in *The Cambridge Companion to Hip-Hop*, ed. Justin A. Williams (Cambridge: Cambridge University Press, 2015).

CHAPTER 3

1. Robert Warshow, "The Gangster as Tragic Hero," in *Gangster Film Reader*, ed. Alain Silver and James Ursini (New York: Limelight Editions, 2007), 13.

2. Opening lyrics of the song "Straight Outta Compton," on *Straight Outta Compton* (Ruthless Records CDL-57102, 1988).

3. Robin D. G. Kelley, *Race Rebels: Culture, Politics, and the Black Working Class* (New York: Free Press, 1994), 202–03.

4. Kelley, *Race Rebels*, 187.

5. Kelley, *Race Rebels*, 228, 185–86.

6. Exhorting scholars to pay greater attention to the differences within rap as a genre, Adam Krims once observed that "the kind of inner city represented, and the relation between that location and the agency of those found there, has changed remarkably since rap was first marketed commercially." Adam Krims, *Music and Urban Geography* (New York: Routledge, 2007), 17.

7. Recent research on Los Angeles has explored how Southern California's urban geography is thoroughly racialized, as well as how everyday experiences of race and racism in the city are spatialized. Eric Avila, *Popular Culture in the Age of White Flight: Fear and Fantasy in Suburban Los Angeles* (Berkeley: University of California Press, 2004); João Costa Vargas, *Catching Hell in the City of Angels* (Minneapolis: University of Minnesota Press, 2006).

8. Murray Forman, *The 'Hood Comes First: Race, Space, and Place in Rap and Hip-Hop* (Middleton, CT: Wesleyan University Press, 2002), xvii.

9. Richard Harrington, "1989 Picks: A Six-Pack," *Washington Post*, December 29, 1989, N19.

10. I recall a specific example of this disjuncture from my childhood in Los Angeles. Shortly after the release of N.W.A.'s *Straight Outta Compton*, a friend of mine hosted visiting relatives from Boston, Massachusetts. Having grown up near Boston's Roxbury neighborhood, one of the city's black ghettos, they insisted on a driving tour of the infamous city of Compton, which they had heard so much about. They were astonished by what they saw: a relatively tranquil, suburban neighborhood completely at odds with the place they had imagined after listening to N.W.A.'s music. In retrospect, I wonder if their surprise stemmed from a particular East Coast image of ghettos as having a high population density (i.e. tenements and fifteen-story housing projects) commensurate with their location in the inner city. In other words, the idea of a more spread-out ghetto composed of single-family homes with lawns was totally outside their experience. It is possible that N.W.A.'s use of Public Enemy's dense, sample-based production style, associated with East Coast hip hop, added to their confusion.

11. Edward Soja, *Postmodern Geographies: The Reassertion of Space in Critical Social Theory* (London: Verso, 1989), 191.

12. Lawrence Kramer, *Music As Cultural Practice, 1800–1900* (Berkeley: University of California Press, 1993), 12.

13. Soja, *Postmodern Geographies*, 192.

14. Soja, *Postmodern Geographies*, 208–15.

15. Soja, *Postmodern Geographies*, 191.

16. Soja, *Postmodern Geographies*, 193–95.

17. Avila, *Popular Culture*, 215.

18. Avila, *Popular Culture*, 219.

19. Scott L. Bottles, *Los Angeles and the Automobile: The Making of a Modern City* (Berkeley: University of California Press, 1987), 1–21.

20. Avila, *Popular Culture*, 241.

21. Kelley, *Race Rebels*, 194–195; Eithne Quinn, *Nuthin' But a "G" Thang: The Culture and Commerce of Gangsta Rap* (New York: Columbia University Press, 2005), 41–43.

22. Michelle Alexander, *The New Jim Crow: Mass Incarceration in the Age of Colorblindness* (New York: New Press, 2010), 51–56.

23. Martin Cizmar, "What Ever Happened to N.W.A.'s Posse? The Eazy-E True Hollywood (or True Compton) Stories behind the Legendary L.A. Hip-Hop Cover," *LA Weekly*, May 6, 2010.

24. Jerry Heller, *Ruthless: A Memoir* (New York: Simon Spotlight Entertainment, 2006), 103.

25. Gabriela Jiménéz, "Something 2 Dance 2: Electro Hop in 1980s Los Angeles and Its Afrofuturist Link," *Black Music Research Journal* 31, no. 1 (2011): 131–44.

26. Heller, *Ruthless*, 56.

27. "We [Public Enemy] were in Vegas and they [N.W.A.] were on tour with us, and I had just got the vinyl in. That's what this is all about. Because Run-DMC and LL Cool J gave me energy. And if our energy happened to be transferred to N.W.A., then that's what this whole thing is for." Chuck D, as quoted in Brian Coleman, *Check the Technique: Liner Notes for Hip-Hop Junkies* (New York: Villard Books, 2007), 354.

28. In fact, when Ice Cube left N.W.A. in 1989, he hoped that Dre would continue to make beats for his solo project. When this proved impossible because of Dre's contractual obligations to N.W.A., Ice Cube began collaborating with Public Enemy's Bomb Squad, which served as the production unit for his album *AmeriKKKa's Most Wanted* (1990).

29. Although N.W.A. were less direct about their politics than Public Enemy, critics often described both groups as "militant" and "incendiary," noting that N.W.A. also offered a powerful critique of the white power structure (Richard Harrington, "The Rap Jive from MTV," *Washington Post*, May 24, 1989, D7).

30. The Winstons, "Amen Brother," Negrum NG 509, 1969. The so-called "Amen break" served as the foundation for dozens of songs in the UK's "jungle" genre (also known as drum and bass); see Simon Reynolds, *Generation Ecstasy: Into the World of Techno and Rave Culture* (New York: Routledge, 1998), 252.

31. Chad Kiser, "Stan the Guitar Man," *DUBCNN: West Coast News Network* www.dubcnn.com/interviews/stantheguitarman.

32. Even when using live musicians to replay or interpolate samples, producers still have to pay publishing rights ("songwriter's copyright").

33. Davy DMX, "One for the Treble," Tuff City/CBS Associated Records 4Z9 04955, 1984; Ronnie Hudson and the Street People, "West Coast Poplock," Birdie Records 1002, 1982; Funkadelic, "You'll Like It Too," on *Connections and Disconnections*, LAX 37987, 1981.

34. Tricia Rose, *Black Noise: Rap Music and Black Culture in Contemporary America* (Middleton, CT: Wesleyan University Press, 1994), 39.

35. David Toop, "Conventional Black; Rock; Records," *The Times* [London], August 26, 1989.

36. Rupert Wainwright, dir., "Straight Outta Compton," *The N.W.A. Legacy Videos* (Priority Records, 2002).

37. Emboldened by the media hype and public handwringing over the crack cocaine "epidemic," police chief Daryl Gates announced "Operation Hammer" and the CRASH (Community Response against Street Hoodlums) division, whose names did not attempt to conceal the LAPD's aggressive and confrontational policing style.

38. Turning our attention to the upper portion of the frame, we notice a strategically placed coffee and donut, invoking the familiar stereotype of the fat, lazy cop. N.W.A. might have confirmed some people's worst stereotypes about black people through their adoption of gangsta personas, but they also used their position to fire back at their enemies.

39. Vargas, *Catching Hell*, 42.

40. David Mills, "Rap's Hostile Fringe: From N.W.A. and Others, 'Reality'-Based Violence," *Washington Post*, September 2, 1990, G1.

41. This time, the group flees from and eventually outsmarts a team of corrupt FBI agents. The decision to lampoon the FBI stemmed from a letter protesting N.W.A.'s single "Fuck the Police," on *Straight Outta Compton*, which was sent to Ruthless Records by Milt Ahlerich, then director of the bureau. Ruthless Records owner Jerry Heller was initially alarmed by its intimidating tone, but he soon realized what a great piece of publicity he had been handed. The story of the letter circulated quickly and actually contributed to the group's album sales and notoriety (Heller, *Ruthless*, 141–42).

42. This putdown is a reference to the two main characters (played by Ricardo Montalbán and Hervé Villechaize) in *Fantasy Island*, which ran from 1978 to 1984. Villechaize was a dwarf, so presumably the insult was directed at Eazy-E, who at 5'5" was much shorter than the other members of N.W.A.

43. Jeff Chang, *Can't Stop, Won't Stop: A History of the Hip-Hop Generation* (New York: Picador, 2005), 419–20.

44. N.W.A., "Straight Outta Compton," on *Straight Outta Compton* (Priority Records 57102, 1988).

45. Dr. Dre, "Let Me Ride," on *The Chronic* (Interscope Records P257128, 1992).

46. Vargas, *Catching Hell*, 57.

47. Dr. Dre's meticulous approach to sound in his beat making reflects the influence of customized-car audiophile culture; see Justin Williams, *Rhymin' and Stealin': Music Borrowing in Hip Hop* (Ann Arbor: University of Michigan Press, 2013), 73–102.

48. Other tracks on *The Chronic* differ from this archetypical G-funk aesthetic. In fact, some of the most explicitly violent songs on the album feature loops one measure in length. "The Day the Niggaz Took Over," for example, features a minor-key bass ostinato that lends the tracks a menacing sense of conflict and impending doom, and leads me to wonder if conventional descriptions of G-funk might be based solely on Dr. Dre's production for a few of the album's tracks.

49. Forman, *The 'Hood Comes First*, 279.

50. Josh Tyrangiel, "All-Time 100 Albums," *Time*, January 22, 2010. http://entertainment.time.com/2006/11/02/the-all-time-100-albums/slide/the-chronic/.

51. The footage sampled is from a video of the 1977 Houston concert; see George Clinton and Parliament-Funkadelic, *The Mothership Connection*, Pioneer Entertainment PA-11664, 1998.

52. Parliament-Funkadelic did not play Los Angeles until the peak of their popularity in 1977. But the group must have been well known from recordings, because the two concerts they performed—complete with Mothership landings—took place at the Forum and the Coliseum, two of the city's largest venues.

53. Rickey Vincent, *Funk: The Music, the People, and the Rhythm of the One* (New York: St. Martin's Griffin, 1996), 256.

54. Mark Dery, "Black to the Future: Interviews with Samuel R. Delany, Greg Tate, and Tricia Rose," in *Flame Wars: The Discourse of Cyberculture* (Durham, NC: Duke University Press, 1993), 736.

55. Felicia Miyakawa, *Five Percenter Rap: God Hop's Music, Message, and Black Muslim Mission* (Bloomington: Indiana University Press, 2005), 114.

56. Even though "Nuthin' But a 'G' Thang" does not rely on a hook sampled from Parliament, the 1964 Impala pictured in the song's video continues to serve as the gangsta's "sweet chariot," carrying Dre, Snoop, and the D.O.C. from barbeque to house party and home again.

57. Samuel Floyd, Jr., *The Power of Black Music: Interpreting Its History from Africa to the United States* (New York: Oxford University Press, 1995), 212–25.

58. In George Clinton's P-Funk lore, these roles are parodied by characters such as Dr. Funkenstein, Sir Nose Devoid of Funk, and Starchild, while humanity finds itself divided into a number of mock ethnic groups including the Thumpasaurus People and Cro-Nasal Sapiens.

59. Michael Lieb, *Children of Ezekiel: Aliens, UFOs, the Crisis of Race, and the Advent of End Time* (Durham, NC: Duke University Press, 1998), 144–49.

60. Lieb, *Children of Ezekiel*, 1–2.

61. Lieb, *Children of Ezekiel*, 147.

62. Robert Farris Thompson, "The Song That Named the Land," in *Black Art/Ancestral Legacy: The African Impulse in African-American Art*, ed. Robert V. Rozelle, Alvia Wardlaw, and Maureen A. McKenna (Dallas: Dallas Museum of Art, 1989).

63. Thompson, "The Song That Named the Land," 98.

64. Thompson, "The Song That Named the Land," 98.

65. Jonah Weiner, "Lil Wayne and the Afronaut Invasion: Why Have So Many Black Musicians Been Obsessed With Outer Space?" *Slate.com*, June 20, 2008. www.slate.com/id/2193871/.

66. One might also want to point out that Clinton's Afro-futurism always drew heavily from the earthbound contexts of ghetto life. When Clinton descends from the Mothership as Dr. Funkenstein, his shaky walk and polyester suit signify on the smooth comportment and loud dress of a big-city pimp.

67. Paul Gilory, *Darker Than Blue: On the Moral Economies of Black Atlantic Culture* (Cambridge, MA: Harvard University Press, 2010), 20.

68. Gilroy, *Darker Than Blue*, 22.

69. 50 Cent, *Get Rich or Die Tryin'*, Aftermath/Interscope, 2003.

70. Quinn, *Nuthin' But a "G" Thang*, 143.

71. Quinn, *Nuthin' But a "G" Thang*, 143–45.

72. David Harvey, *A Brief History of Neoliberalism* (New York: Oxford University Press 2005), 2.

73. Harvey, *Neoliberalism*, 3.

74. Quinn, *Nuthin' But a "G" Thang*, 169.

75. Quinn, *Nuthin' But a "G" Thang*, 169.

76. Quinn, *Nuthin' But a "G" Thang*, 172.

77. Quinn, *Nuthin' But a "G" Thang*, 144.

78. Quinn, *Nuthin' But a "G" Thang*, xx.

79. "Rappers or Republicans," *The Daily Show with Jon Stewart*, July 28, 2008. http://thedailyshow.cc.com/videos/68ozaa/rappers-or-republicans.

80. In their song and music video "What They Do" (MCA Records DGC12–22227, 1996), underground hip hop group the Roots parodied gangsta rap's materialistic individualism.

81. Kelley, *Race Rebels*, 224.

82. Kelley, *Race Rebels*, 224.

83. Robert Christgau, "Dr. Dre," *Consumer Guide Reviews*. www.robertchristgau.com/get_artist.php?name=Dr.+Dre.

84. TMS, "Record Report: Albums," *The Source*, February 1993, 55.

85. The location of Dr. Dre's home is also a telling indication of his reorientation. Having moved out of the inner city, Dre chose a suburb in the San Fernando Valley that was central to the asymmetrical growth and patterns of white flight that Edward Soja discusses in his writings about Los Angeles (*Postmodern Geographies*, 233).

86. "Dr. Dre and Snoop Doggy Dogg: Pool Party," *Yo! MTV Raps*, 1993. https://www.youtube.com/watch?v=mNitNLAjn-4.

87. Krims, *Music and Urban Geography*, 119.

CHAPTER 4

1. Ronald Radano, *Lying Up a Nation: Race and Black Music* (Chicago: Chicago University Press, 2003), 22.

2. Shawnee Smith, "Rap Rips Up the Charts," *Billboard*, December 5, 1998, 27–28.

3. Smith, "Rap Rips Up the Charts."

4. Murray Forman, *The 'Hood Comes First: Race, Space, and Place in Hip-Hop and Rap* (Middletown, CT: Wesleyan University Press, 2002).

5. Smith, "Rap Rips Up the Charts."

6. Cameron McCarthy, "Living with Anxiety: Race and the Renarration of Public Life," in *White Reign: Deploying Whiteness in America*, ed. Joe L. Kincheloe and Shirley R. Steinberg (New York: St. Martin's Press, 1998), 329–30.

7. Woody Doane, "Rethinking Whiteness Studies," in *White Out: The Continuing Significance of Racism*, ed. Ashley Doane and Eduardo Bonilla-Silva (New York: Routledge, 2003), 5.

8. Eminem, *Infinite*, bootleg, 1996; Eminem, "My Name Is," Interscope Records 97470, 1999.

9. Eminem, *The Slim Shady LP*, Interscope Records 90287, 1999; Eminem, *The Marshall Mathers LP*, Interscope Records 490629, 2000.

10. Anthony Bozza, *Whatever You Say I Am: The Life and Times of Marshall Mathers* (New York: Crown, 2003), 15–16.

11. Mickey Hess, *Is Hip Hop Dead? The Past, Present, and Future of America's Most Wanted Music* (Westport, CT: Praeger, 2007), 115.

12. Hess, *Is Hip Hop Dead?*, 115.

13. Robert Marriott, "Allah's on Me," *XXL* 1, no. 1 (1997): 64–70.

14. Adam Krims, *Rap Music and the Poetics of Identity* (Cambridge: Cambridge University Press, 2000), 75.

15. Mark Anthony Neal, " . . . A Way Out of No Way: Jazz, Hip Hop, and Black Social Improvisation," in *The Other Side of Nowhere: Jazz, Improvisation, and Communities in Dialogue*, ed. Daniel Fischlin and Ajay Helble (Middletown, CT: Wesleyan University Press, 2004), 211.

16. The practice of setting a consistent, exact subdivision of the beat is what hip hop producers refer to as "quantizing." See Joseph Schloss, *Making Beats: The Art of Sample-Based Hip Hop* (Middletown, CT: Wesleyan University Press, 2003), 141.

17. Although in retrospect it seems clear that so many songs from this era share the same rhythmic feel, more research could help to explain how and why this particular convention became established. Did the sampling equipment producers were using suddenly include an option for sixteenth-note triplets? Was there a particular song or producer that inspired the shift? Did producers view this practice as defining a style (e.g., East Coast hip hop), or was it seen less as a limitation and more as an attempt to expand on what previous technologies had offered?

18. Bozza, *Whatever You Say I Am*, 5.

19. Vanilla Ice, *To the Extreme*, SBK Records 95325, 1991.

20. 3rd Bass, "Pop Goes the Weasel," Def Jam Recordings 44–73702, 1991.

21. Hess, *Is Hip Hop Dead?*, 118–20.

22. Quoted in Brian McCollum, "Best Bet," *Vancouver Sun*, May 6, 1999, C31.

23. Larry Starr and Christopher Waterman, *American Popular Music: From Minstrelsy to MP3* (Oxford: Oxford University Press, 2007), 195–96.

24. Eminem, "Without Me," on *The Eminem Show* (Shady/Aftermath 493 290-2, 2002).

25. Hess, *Is Hip Hop Dead?*, 124–25.

26. Eminem, quoted in Richard Lowe and Dana Heinz Perry, dir., "Part Five: My Name Is . . ." on *And You Don't Stop: Hip-Hop*. VH1, 2004.

27. Bozza, *Whatever You Say I Am*, 25.

28. Eminem's Detroit associates, Mark and Jeff Bass, were responsible for the majority of the music on *The Slip Shady LP*. Journalists did their part in aiding Eminem's publicity, emphasizing time and again Dr. Dre's role as the

white MC's producer, a stamp of approval that was critical to Eminem's positive reception.

29. Snoop Doggy Dogg was actually introduced to many rap listeners on the single "Deep Cover," recorded for the 1992 film of the same name. As the lead single to his solo album (*Doggystyle*, Death Row 63002, 1993), however, "Who Am I (What's My Name?)" played an important roll in broadening the rapper's fan base.

30. Edward G. Armstrong, "Eminem's Construction of Authenticity," *Popular Music and Society* 27, no. 3 (2004): 343. S. Craig Watkins puts it more succinctly, claiming that "the manner in which Eminem makes his race an issue also makes it a non-issue." S. Craig Watkins, *Hip Hop Matters: Politics, Popular Culture, and the Struggle for the Soul of a Movement* (Boston: Beacon Press, 2005), 107.

31. Linda Hutcheon, *A Theory of Parody: The Teachings of Twentieth-Century Art Forms,* (Chicago: University of Illinois Press, 1985), xii.

32. De La Soul, *Buhloone Mind State,* Tommy Boy 81063, 1993; the Roots, *Iladelph Halflife,* Geffen 24972, 1996.

33. Dr. Dre, *The Chronic,* Death Row 63000, 1992; N.W.A., "Straight Outta Compton," on *N.W.A. Legacy: The Video Collection.* DVD. EMI Video 77958, 2002.

34. The Beastie Boys, *License to Ill,* Def Jam 527351, 1986.

35. Quoted in Hess, *Is Hip Hop Dead?,* 116.

36. The radio edit of the song opens, "Hi kids! Do you like Primus?"—a reference to yet another "white" rock group.

37. Jon Pareles, "Pop Review: A Rapper More Gauche Than Gangsta," *New York Times,* April 17, 1999, B18.

38. Samuel A. Floyd, Jr., *The Power of Black Music: Interpreting Its History from Africa to the United States* (New York: Oxford University Press, 1995), 151.

39. Quoted in "Part Five: My Name Is . . ."

40. It may be more than mere coincidence that Eminem's music video invokes the television sitcom *Leave It to Beaver,* whose title character was played by child actor Jerry Mathers (Eminem's birth name is Marshall Mathers).

41. Dr. Dre and Philip G. Atwell, dir., *Eminem: E.* DVD. Universal Music and Video Distribution, 2000.

42. Labi Siffre, *Remember My Song,* Phantom 820427, 2006 [1975].

43. Schloss offers Prince Paul's sampling of the Daryl Hall and John Oates tune "I Can't Go for That (No Can Do)," which formed the beat for De La Soul's 1989 "Say No Go," as an example. One academic critic wrote that Prince Paul intended to poke fun at the "blue-eyed soul" duo. When Schloss presented Prince Paul with this interpretation, however, Paul was surprised and quick to clarify how much he sincerely enjoyed the original tune.

44. Krims, *Rap Music and the Poetics of Identity,* 43.

45. For more about the generic conventions of funk music, particularly the issue of an implied subdivision of the beat, also referred to as the rhythmic "density gradient," see Anne Danielsen, *Presence and Pleasure: The Funk*

Grooves of James Brown and Parliament (Middletown, CT: Wesleyan University Press, 2006), 44, 74–75.

46. Eminem's "My Name Is" was not the only track from the 1990s that sampled this same Labi Siffre song. In most cases, the producers of these songs took their samples from the first part of "I've Got The . . . ," which features a funky string-and-guitar riff and an array of off-beat accents resembling more conventional funk grooves. Jay-Z's "Streets Is Watching" (on *In My Lifetime, Vol. 1*, Def Jam 536392, 1997) and Def Squad's "Countdown" (on *El Niño*, Def Jam 558383, 1998) both take pieces of this syncopated string-and-guitar riff and interpolate them into an eight-count drum track.

47. Jon Pareles, "More Gauche Than Gangsta."

48. For an exploration of digital sampling's evolution *vis-à-vis* hip hop's aesthetics and cultural politics, see Dale Chapman, "That Ill, Tight Sound: Telepresence and Biopolitics in Post-Timbaland Rap Production," *Journal of the Society for American Music* 2, no. 2 (2008): 155–77.

49. Dr. Dre, *2001*, Aftermath Records 490486, 1999.

50. Forman, *The 'Hood Comes First*, xviii.

51. Although I don't have space to explore Eminem's voice in detail, I want to point out that the nasality of Eminem's delivery is contrived, not an essential attribute of his racial identity. At times, he plays up the "whiteness" of his voice, as in "My Name Is" and "The Real Slim Shady." In other songs, such as "Kill You" and "The Way I Am," he uses a raspier, throaty voice.

52. Hobey Echlin, "Where Hip Hop Lives: Sure, He's a Cute White Kid, but Detroit Rapper Eminem is Not the Official Candy of the New Millennium," *Detroit Metro Times*, February 17, 1999.

53. Contemporary reviewers picked up on this thread. "The most refreshing thing about 'The Slim Shady LP' is Eminem's (aka Marshall Mathers) self-deprecating humor. Sure, he can be cocky, but he knows how people see him and he doesn't mind confronting it. He also doesn't mind using his lack of self-esteem as a setup for a joke" (Christopher Gray, "Eminem Lets Humor Shine Through," *Portland Press Herald*, March 28, 1999, 5E).

54. Sway Calloway, "Eminem: The Gift and the Curse," MTV.com. www.mtv.com/bands/e/eminem/news_feature_052902/.

55. Barbara Ching, *Wrong's What I Do Best: Hard Country Music and Contemporary Culture* (New York: Oxford University Press, 2003).

56. McCollum, "Best Bet."

57. Hess, *Is Hip Hop Dead?*, 124–25; Armstrong, "Eminem's Construction of Authenticity," 343.

58. One of his rhyming couplets threatens to slit his critics' throats "worse than Ron Goldman" (one of the victims in the O. J. Simpson murder trial).

59. Eminem, *The Marshall Mathers LP*, Interscope Records 490629, 2000.

60. Armstrong, "Eminem's Construction of Whiteness," 334–35.

61. Robin D. G. Kelley, "Kickin' Reality, Kickin' Ballistics: 'Gangsta Rap' and Post-Industrial Los Angeles," in *Race Rebels: Culture, Politics, and the Black Working Class* (New York: Free Press, 1994).

62. Sean S. Cunningham, dir., *Friday the 13th*, DVD, Paramount Home Entertainment 124902, 2007 [1980]; Alfred Hitchcock, dir., *Psycho*, DVD, Universal Studios Home Video 61100450, 2008 [1960].

63. Ingrid Monson, "The Problem with White Hipness: Race, Gender, and Cultural Conceptions in Jazz Historical Discourse," *Journal of the American Musicological Society* 48, no. 3 (1995): 416.

64. Ray Pratt, *Rhythm and Resistance: Explorations in the Political Uses of Popular Music* (Westport, CT: Praeger, 1990), 36. See also George Lipsitz, *Dangerous Crossroads: Popular Music, Postmodernism, and the Poetics of Place* (London: Verso, 1997); Christopher Small, "Why Doesn't the Whole World Love Chamber Music?" *American Music* 19, no. 3 (2001): 340–59.

65. Henry A. Giroux, "Racial Politics and the Pedagogy of Whiteness," in *Whiteness: A Critical Reader*, ed. Mike Hill (New York: New York University Press, 1997), 295.

66. Writing for the *Seattle Weekly* in 1999 just after *The Slim Shady LP*'s release, Joseph Schloss zeroed in on the importance of class identity to Eminem's popularity. "What really distinguishes Eminem from other light-skinned MCs is that he doesn't think it's cooler to be black. He just hates being white. . . . In Eminem's world, whiteness doesn't represent power or privilege, but working-class anxiety" ("The Joke's on Us: The Outrageous Humor—and the Sheer Outrage—of Eminem," *Seattle Weekly*, April 14, 1999, www.seattleweekly.com/1999–04–14/music/the-joke-s-on-us/).

67. "The state shall not discriminate against, or grant preferential treatment to, any individual or group on the basis of race, sex, color, ethnicity, or national origin in the operation of public employment, public education, or public contracting" (Proposition 209: Text of Proposed Law, http://vote96.sos.ca.gov/Vote96/html/BP/209text.htm).

68. "Rebuttal to Argument Against Proposition 209," *Proposition 209 Ballot Pamphlet*. http://vote96.sos.ca.gov/BP/209norbt.htm.

69. In a 2014 split decision, the Supreme Court of the United States upheld Michigan's ban on affirmative action (Adam Liptak, "Justices Back Ban on Race as Factor in College Entry," *New York Times*, April 24, 2014, A1).

70. R.J. Smith, "Crossover Dreams: Class Trumps Race in Eminem's *8 Mile*," *Village Voice*, November 5, 2002. www.villagevoice.com/2002–11–05/news/crossover-dream/.

71. Curtis Hanson, dir., *8 Mile*, Universal Studios Home Video 61021981, 2002.

72. The website hosting this post has since disappeared from the internet; it was originally cited in a review of *8 Mile* that I published in 2002. Loren Kajikawa, "*8 Mile*: Rap, Rabbit, Rap," *ECHO: A Music-Centered Journal* 4, no. 2 (Fall 2002). http://archive.today/fhWe.

73. Thomas Frank, *What's the Matter with Kansas: How Conservatives Won the Heart of America* (New York: Henry Holt, 2004), 157–58.

74. Richard Goldstein, "Celebrity Bigots: John Rocker, Dr. Laura, Eminem, Don Imus . . . Why Is Hate So Hot?" *Village Voice*, July 11, 2000. www.villagevoice.com/2000–07–11/news/celebrity-bigots/.

75. Henry Louis Gates, Jr. *The Signifying Monkey: A Theory of African-American Literary Criticism* (New York: Oxford University Press, 1988), 21.

76. David Denby, "Breaking Through: *8 Mile* and *Frida,*" *The New Yorker,* November 11, 2002, 196.

77. Joseph Schloss suggested to me that for many journalists and supporters of hip hop music, defending Eminem was not necessarily about respecting him as a person as much as it was about defending a principle: that respect in hip hop should be conferred based on skill and artistry, rather than extramusical factors such as race or biography.

78. Bakari Kitwana, *Why White Kids Love Hip Hop: Wankstas, Wiggers, Wannabes, and the New Reality of Race in America* (New York: Civitas Books, 2005), 159–60.

79. Kitwana, *Why White Kids Love Hip Hop,* 154–60.

80. Eminem served as executive producer for his crew's mainstream debut album (D12, *Devils Night,* Interscope Records 069490897–2, 2001).

81. Carl Hancock Rux, "Eminem: The New White Negro," in *Everything but the Burden: What White People Are Taking from Black Culture,* ed. Greg Tate (New York: Broadway Books, 2003), 37.

CONCLUSION

1. Although *Sounding Race* has focused on successful, commercial rap songs, hip hop music's vast underground network of artists have produced recordings that also merit close reading. Rejecting "corporate rap" as exploitative and shallow, underground artists often espouse an ideology of artistic meritocracy where authenticity is determined by one's skills, not one's conformity to certain standards of black masculinity. Songs by underground artists such as People Under the Stairs, Living Legends, and Jurassic 5 often thematize artistic skill itself, promoting a kind of art-for-art's-sake ethos that celebrates dope beats and rhymes as ends in and of themselves. Attempting to avoid the gimmicks and clichés that make race audible in Eminem or Jin's music, such artists often advance a color-blind ideal that strives toward racially neutral authenticity.

2. Jin vs. Sterlin, "106 & Park's Freestyle Friday," *BET,* 2002.

3. Jin vs. Lucky Luciano, "106 & Park's Freestyle Friday," *BET,* 2002.

4. Oliver Wang, "Rapping and Repping Asian: Race, Authenticity and the Asian American MC," in *Alien Encounters: Popular Culture in Asian America,* ed. Mimi Thi Nguyen and Thuy Linh Nguyen Tu (Durham, NC: Duke University Press, 2007), 40–41.

5. Ingrid Monson, "The Problem with White Hipness: Race, Gender, and Cultural Conceptions in Jazz Historical Discourse," *Journal of the American Musicological Society* 48, no. 3 (1995): 416.

6. Jin vs. Lucky Luciano.

7. Jin, *The Rest Is History,* Ruff Ryders 7243 5 84087 2, 2004.

8. On the history and cultural politics of Asian American exclusion and invisibility, see Lisa Lowe, *Immigrant Acts: On Asian American Cultural Politics* (Durham, NC: Duke University Press, 1996).

9. There are additional levels to Jin's inversion of the phrase "chinky-eyed," which in African-American slang is sometimes used to describe the droopy-eyed appearance of a person high on marijuana. For example, see rapper Ludacris's verse in the song "Holidae In," in which he confesses, "My eyes chinky, I'm with Chingy at the Holiday Inn" (Chingy, *Jackpot,* Capitol Records 7243 5 81827 2 9, 2003). In similar fashion, "chinky-eyed" can be used to refer to non-Asians (or people of mixed Asian heritage) with almond-shaped eyes. So what Jin is actually saying in "Learn Chinese" is, "OK, if you like rappers with 'chinky' eyes, *I am actually Chinese.* It doesn't get any more 'chinky' than that."

10. Wang, "Rapping and Repping Asian," 56.

11. Wang, "Rapping and Repping Asian," 57.

12. Gary Okihiro, *Margins and Mainstreams: Asians in American History and Culture* (Seattle: University of Washington Press, 1994).

13. Tricia Rose, *The Hip Hop Wars: What We Talk About When We Talk About Hip Hop and Why It Matters* (New York: Basic Civitas, 2008).

Discography

Basil, Toni. "Mickey." Radialchoice TIC 4, 1981.

The Beastie Boys. *Licensed to Ill*. Def Jam/Columbia BFC-40238, 1986.

Blow, Kurtis. "The Breaks." Mercury Records MDS 410, 1980.

Brown, James. "Funky Drummer, Pt. 1." King Records 45–6290, 1970.

Byrd, Bobby. "I Know You Got Soul." King Records 45–6378, 1971.

Chingy. *Jackpot*. Capitol Records 7243 5 81827 2 9, 2003.

Chubb Rock. "Rock 'n' Roll Dude." Select Records FMS 62281, 1987.

Clinton, George, and Parliament-Funkadelic. *The Mothership Connection*. Pioneer Entertainment PA-11664, 1998.

D12. *Devils Night*. Shady/Interscope Records 069490897–2, 2001.

Davy DMX. "One For the Treble." Tuff City/CBS Associated Records 4Z9 04955, 1984.

Def Squad. *El Niño*. Def Jam 558383, 1998.

De La Soul. *Buhloone Mind State*. Tommy Boy 81063, 1993.

Dr. Dre. *2001*. Aftermath Records 490486, 1999.

———. *The Chronic*. Interscope Records P257128, 1992.

L'Ectrique. "Struck By Boogie Lightning." Reflection Records CBL 128, 1979.

Eminem. *The Eminem Show*. 2002 by Shady/Aftermath 493 290–2, 2002.

———. *Infinite*. Bootleg, 1996.

———. *The Marshall Mathers LP*. Interscope Records 490629, 2000.

———. "My Name Is." Interscope Records 97470, 1999.

———. *The Slim Shady LP*. Interscope Records 90287, 1999.

The Fatback Band. "King Tim III (Personality Jock)" b/w "Love in Perfect Harmony." Polydor Records 2095214, 1979.

50 Cent. *Get Rich or Die Tryin'*. Aftermath/Interscope 0694935442, 2003.

Funkadelic. *Connections and Disconnections*. LAX 37987, 1981.

Gordon, Steve, and the Kosher Five. "Take My Rap ... Please." Reflection Records MOM 667, 1979.

Grandmaster Flash and the Furious Five. "The Message." Sugar Hill Records SH 584, 1982.

The Honey Drippers. "Impeach the President." Alaga Records AL-1017, 1973.

Hudson, Ronnie, and the Street People. "West Coast Poplock." Birdie Records 1002, 1982.

Hunt, Ron/Ronnie G. and the S. M. Crew. "Spiderap" b/w "A Corona Jam." Reflection Records PT-7000, 1979.

James, Bob. *Two.* CTI Records CTI-6057, 1975.

Jay-Z. *In My Lifetime, Vol. 1.* Def Jam 536392, 1997.

The J.B.'s. "The Grunt, Pt. 1." Mojo 2027–002, 1971.

———. "Hot Pants Road." People Records PE 607, 1972.

The Knack. "My Sharona." Capitol Records 4731, 1979.

Lady T/M.C. Tee. "Lady D" b/w "Nu Sounds." Reflection Records PT-7001, 1979.

Malcolm X. *Grass Roots Speech: Detroit, Michigan, November 1963.* Paul Winley Records L.P. 134, 1979.

N.W.A. *Straight Outta Compton.* Ruthless Records CDL-57102, 1988.

The Roots. *Iladelph Halflife.* Geffen 24972, 1996.

———. "What They Do." MCA Records DGC12–22227, 1996.

Run-D.M.C. *Raising Hell.* Profile Records PRO-1217, 1986.

Siffre, Labi. *Remember My Song.* Phantom 820427, 1975/2006.

Snoop Doggy Dogg. *Doggystyle.* Death Row 63002, 1993.

Spectrum City. "Lies" b/w "Check Out the Radio." Vanguard SPV 76, 1984.

Spoonin Gee. "Spoonin Rap." Sound of New York QC 708, 1979.

3rd Bass. "Pop Goes the Weasel." Def Jam Recordings 44–73702, 1991.

Vanilla Ice. *To the Extreme.* SBK Records 95325, 1991.

The Winstons. "Amen Brother." Negrum NG 509, 1969.

Filmography

And You Don't Stop: Hip-Hop. Directed by Richard Lowe and Dana Heinz Perry. VH1, 2004.

The Best of Chappelle Show: Season 2, Volume 2 [2004.] Directed by Neal Brennan. New York: Comedy Central, 2005. DVD.

The Daily Show with Jon Stewart. "Rappers or Republicans." July 29, 2008. http://thedailyshow.cc.com/videos/68ozaa/rappers-or-republicans.

"Dr. Dre and Snoop Doggy Dogg: Pool Party." *Yo! MTV Raps*. Directed by Fab Five Freddy. 1993. https://www.youtube.com/watch?v=mNitNLAjn-4.

8 Mile. Directed by Curtis Hanson. Los Angeles: Universal Studios Home Video, 2002. DVD.

Eminem: E. Directed by Dr. Dre and Philip G. Atwell. Los Angeles: Universal Music and Video Distribution, 2000. DVD.

Friday the 13th. Directed by Sean S. Cunningham. 1980. Los Angeles: Paramount Home Entertainment, 2007. DVD.

The Hip-Hop Years: Close to the Edge. Directed by David Upshal. London: Channel 4, 1999.

The N.W.A. Legacy Videos. Directed by Rupert Wainwright. Los Angeles: Priority Records, 2002. DVD.

106 & Park. "Freestyle Friday: Jin vs. Lucky Luciano." *BET*, 2002. https://www.youtube.com/watch?v=CzzDi2OsTSw.

———. "Freestyle Friday: Jin vs. Sterlin." *BET*, 2002. https://www.youtube.com/watch?v=xN-8ySP8-A0.

Planet B-Boy. Directed by Benson Lee. New York: Arts Alliance America, 2008. DVD.

Psycho. Directed by Alfred Hitchcock. 1960. Los Angeles: Universal Studios Home Video, 2008. DVD.

Bibliography

Adams, Kyle. "Aspects of the Music/Text Relationship in Rap." *Music Theory Online* 14, no. 2 (May 2008). www.mtosmt.org/issues/mto.08.14.2 /mto.08.14.2.adams.html.

Alexander, Michelle. *The New Jim Crow: Mass Incarceration in the Age of Colorblindness.* New York: New Press, 2012.

Armstrong, Edward G. "Eminem's Construction of Authenticity." *Popular Music and Society* 27, no. 3 (2004): 335–55.

Avila, Eric. *Popular Culture in the Age of White Flight: Fear and Fantasy in Suburban Los Angeles.* Berkeley: University of California Press, 2004.

Baraka, Imamu Amiri. *Black Music.* 1968. Reprint, New York: Da Capo Press, 1998.

———. *Blues People: The Negro Experience in White America and the Music that Developed From It.* New York: Morrow Quill, 1963.

Bohlman, Philip, and Ronald Radano. "Introduction." In *Music and the Racial Imagination,* edited by Philip Bohlman and Ronald Radano, 1–56. Chicago: University of Chicago Press, 2001.

Bottles, Scott L. *Los Angeles and the Automobile: The Making of a Modern City.* Berkeley: University of California Press, 1987.

Bozza, Anthony. *Whatever You Say I Am: The Life and Times of Marshall Mathers.* New York: Crown, 2003.

Bradley, Adam. *Book of Rhymes: The Poetics of Hip-Hop.* New York: Basic Civitas, 2009.

Bradley, Adam, and Andrew Dubois. "The Old School." In *The Anthology of Rap,* edited by Adam Bradley and Andrew Dubois, 1–14. New Haven: Yale University Press, 2010.

Cagle, Jess, and John Callan. "All Hell Breaks Loose at a Run-D.M.C. 'Raising Hell' Rap Concert in California." *People,* September 1, 1986.

Calloway, Sway. "Eminem: The Gift and The Curse." *MTV.com,* 2007. www.mtv.com/bands/e/eminem/news_feature_052902/.

Caramanica, Jon. "100 Best Albums." *Time,* 2006. www.time.com/time/2006 /100albums/0,27693,The_Chronic,00.html.

Chang, Jeff. *Can't Stop, Won't Stop: A History of the Hip-Hop Generation*. New York: St. Martins Press, 2005.

Chapman, Dale. "That Ill, Tight Sound: Telepresence and Biopolitics in Post-Timbaland Rap Production." *Journal of the Society for American Music* 2, no. 2 (2008): 155–77.

Charnas, Dan. *The Big Payback: The History of the Business of Hip-Hop*. New York: New American Library, 2010.

Cheney, Charise. *Brothers Gonna Work It Out: Sexual Politics in the Golden Age of Rap Nationalism*. New York: New York University Press, 2005.

Ching, Barbara. *Wrong's What I Do Best: Hard Country Music and Contemporary Culture*. New York: Oxford University Press, 2003.

Christgau, Robert. "Dr. Dre." *Consumer Guide Reviews*. www.robertchristgau.com/get_artist.php?name=Dr.+Dre.

Cizmar, Martin. "What Ever Happened to N.W.A.'s Posse? The Eazy-E True Hollywood (or True Compton) Stories behind the Legendary L.A. Hip-Hop Cover." *LA Weekly*, May 6, 2010. www.laweekly.com/2010–05–06/music/whatever-happened-to-n-w-a-s-posse/.

Coleman, Brian. *Check the Technique: Liner Notes for Hip-Hop Junkies*. New York: Villard, 2007.

Considine, J. D. "Rap & Hip-Hop: Rising Tide." *Washington Post*, August 29, 1986, 29.

Costa, João Vargas. *Catching Hell in the City of Angels*. Minneapolis: University of Minnesota Press, 2006.

Danielsen, Anne. *Presence and Pleasure: The Funk Grooves of James Brown and Parliament*. Middletown, CT: Wesleyan University Press, 2006.

Decker, Jeffrey L. "The State of Rap: Time and Place in Hip-Hop Nationalism." *Social Text* 34 (1993): 53–84.

Denby, David. "Breaking Through: *8 Mile* and *Frida*." *New Yorker*, November 11, 2002, 196–97.

Dery, Mark. *Flame Wars: The Discourse of Cyberculture*. Durham, NC: Duke University Press, 1993.

———. "Public Enemy: Confrontation." *Keyboard*, September 1990, 83.

———. "Rap: Rock Is Dead." *Keyboard*, November 1988.

Doane, Woody. "Rethinking Whiteness Studies." In *White Out: The Continuing Significance of Racism*, edited by Ashley Doane and Eduardo Bonilla-Silva, 3–20. New York: Routledge, 2003.

Douglass, Frederick. *Narrative of the Life of Frederick Douglass, An American Slave*. 1854. Reprint, Oxford: Oxford University Press, 1999.

Du Bois, W. E. B. *The Souls of Black Folk*. 1903. Reprint, New York: Dover, 1994.

Echlin, Hobey. "Where Hip Hop Lives: Sure, He's a Cute White Kid, but Detroit Rapper Eminem is Not the Official Candy of the New Millennium." *Detroit Metro Times*, February 17, 1999.

Echols, Alice. *Hot Stuff: Disco and the Remaking of American Culture*. New York: W. W. Norton, 2010.

Fink, Robert. "The Story of ORCH5, or, the Classical Ghost in the Hip-Hop Machine." *Popular Music* 24, no. 3 (2005): 339–56.

Fitzpatrick, K. "More Hip Hop." *Courier-Mail,* January 21, 1988.

Flash, Grandmaster, with David Ritz. *The Adventures of Grandmaster Flash: My Life, My Beats.* New York: Random House, 2008.

Floyd, Samuel, Jr. *The Power of Black Music: Interpreting Its History from Africa to the United States.* New York: Oxford University Press, 1995.

Ford, Robert, Jr. "B-Beats Bombarding Bronx: Mobile DJ Starts Something with Oldie R&B Disks." *Billboard,* July 1, 1978, 65.

———. "Jive Talking N.Y. DJs Rapping Away in Black Discos." *Billboard,* May 5, 1979, 3.

Forman, Murray. *The 'Hood Comes First: Race, Space, and Place in Hip Hop and Rap Music.* Middletown, CT: Wesleyan University Press, 2000.

Frank, Thomas. *What's The Matter With Kansas: How Conservatives Won the Heart of America.* New York: Henry Holt, 2004.

Fricke, Jim, and Charlie Ahearn. *Yes, Yes Y'All: The EMP Oral History of Hip Hop.* New York: Da Capo Press, 2002.

George, Nelson. "Hip-Hop's Founding Fathers Speak the Truth." *The Source,* November 1993, 44–50.

———. "Rapping Records Flooding Stores in N.Y. Market." *Billboard,* December 22, 1979, 37.

George, Nelson, Sally Banes, Susan Flinker, and Patty Romanowski. *Fresh: Hip Hop Don't Stop.* New York: Random House, 1985.

Gilory, Paul. *Darker Than Blue: On the Moral Economies of Black Atlantic Culture.* Cambridge, MA: Harvard University Press, 2010.

Giroux, Henry A. "Racial Politics and the Pedagogy of Whiteness." In *Whiteness: A Critical Reader,* edited by Mike Hill, 294–315. New York: New York University Press, 1997.

Goldstein, Richard. "Celebrity Bigots: John Rocker, Dr. Laura, Eminem, Don Imus . . . Why Is Hate So Hot?" *Metro Times: Detroit's Weekly Alternative,* August 1, 2000.

"Grandmaster Flash and the 4 MCs: Live at the Audubon Ballroom." *Hip Hop on Wax, 1979–1999,* 2006. http://hiphoponwax.blogspot.com/2006/10/grandmaster-flash-furious-4-mcs-live.html.

Gray, Christopher. "Eminem Lets Humor Shine Through." *Portland Press Herald,* March 28, 1999, 5E.

Green, Paul. "New Chic Game Plan: No Disco." *Billboard,* December 15, 1979, 23.

"Hank Shocklee: A Journey into Noise with Public Enemy's Chief Producer." *Red Bull Music Academy Lecture,* 2005. www.redbullmusicacademy.com/lectures/hank-shocklee--art-brut.

Harrington, Richard. "1989 Picks: A Six-Pack." *Washington Post,* December 29, 1989, N19.

———. "The Rap Jive from MTV." *Washington Post,* May 24, 1989, D7.

———. "Run-DMC and the Rap Flap: For a Hot Trio, Violence and Criticism on the Concert Trail." *Washington Post,* August 29, 1986, C1.

Harrison, Anthony Kwame. *Hip Hop Underground: The Integrity and Ethics of Racial Identification.* Philadelphia: Temple University Press, 2009.

Harvey, David. *A Brief History of Neoliberalism.* New York: Oxford University Press, 2005.

Heller, Jerry. *Ruthless: A Memoir.* New York: Simon Spotlight Entertainment, 2006.

Hermes, Will. "All Rise for the National Anthem of Hip Hop." *New York Times,* October 29, 2006. http://nytimes.com/2006/10/29/arts/music/29herm .html.

Hess, Mickey. *Is Hip Hop Dead? The Past, Present, and Future of America's Most Wanted Music.* Westport, CT: Praeger, 2007.

Himes, Geoffrey. "Urban Anthems of Rap Music." *Washington Post,* December 30, 1982, D4.

Holden, Stephen. "Pop View: Pop's Angry Voices Sound the Alarm." *New York Times,* May 21, 1989, section 2, p. 1.

Honan, Matthew. "Unlikely Places Where *Wired* Pioneers Had Their *Eureka! Moments.*" *Wired,* March 24, 2008. http://wired.com/culture/lifestyle/mul-timedia/2008/03/ff_eureka?slide=6&slideView=8.

Hutcheon, Linda. *A Theory of Parody: The Teachings of Twentieth-Century Art Forms.* Chicago: University of Illinois Press, 1985.

Jardim, Gary. "John Who?" *Village Voice,* June 21, 1983.

Jenkins, Mark. "House of Hip-Hop: Boys Gotta Bad Rap." *Washington Post,* July 22, 1988, N19.

Jiménez, Gabriela. "Something 2 Dance 2: Electro Hop in 1980s Los Angeles and Its Afrofuturist Link." *Black Music Research Journal* 31, no. 1 (2011): 131–44.

Kajikawa, Loren. "*8 Mile*: Rap, Rabbit, Rap." *ECHO: A Music-Centered Journal* 4, no. 2 (2002). http://archive.today/fhWe.

———. "'Bringin' '88 Back': Historicizing Rap Music's Greatest Year." In *The Cambridge Companion to Hip-Hop,* edited by Justin A. Williams. Cambridge: Cambridge University Press, 2015.

Kallberg, Jeffrey. "The Rhetoric of Genre: Chopin's Nocturne in G Minor." *19th-Century Music* 11, no. 3 (1988): 238–61.

Katz, Mark. *Groove Music: The Art and Culture of the Hip-Hop DJ.* New York: Oxford University Press, 2012.

———. "Sampling before Sampling: The Link between DJ and Producer." *Samples* 9 (2010): 1–11.

Kelley, Robin D. G. *Race Rebels: Culture, Politics, and the Black Working Class.* New York: Free Press, 1994.

Keyes, Cheryl. "At the Crossroads: Rap Music and Its African Nexus." *Ethnomusicology* 40, no. 2 (1996): 223–48.

Kiser, Chad. "Stan 'The Guitar Man' Jones." *DUBCNN: West Coast News Network,* 2010. www.dubcnn.com/interviews/stantheguitarman/.

Kitwana, Bakari. *Why White Kids Love Hip Hop: Wankstas, Wiggers, Wannabes, and the New Reality of Race in America.* New York: Civitas Books, 2005.

Kramer, Lawrence. *Music as Cultural Practice, 1800–1900*. Berkeley: University of California Press, 1993.

Krims, Adam. *Music and Urban Geography*. New York: Routledge, 2007.

———. *Rap Music and the Poetics of Identity*. Cambridge: Cambridge University Press, 2000.

Latimer, Leah Y. "Recording the Rap: Jive Talk at the Top of the Charts." *Washington Post*, August 31, 1980, G1.

Lee, Spike, with Lisa Jones. *Do the Right Thing*. New York: Fireside, 1989.

Leland, John. "Armageddon in Effect." In *And It Don't Stop: The Best American Hip-Hop Journalism of the Last 25 Years*, edited by Raquel Cepeda, 67–85. New York: Faber and Faber, 2004.

———. "Singles." *Spin*, October 1986, 43.

Lieb, Michael. *Children of Ezekiel: Aliens, UFOs, the Crisis of Race, and the Advent of End Time*. Durham, NC: Duke University Press, 1998.

Lipsitz, George. *Dangerous Crossroads: Popular Music, Postmodernism, and the Poetics of Place*. London: Verso, 1997.

———. *The Possessive Investment in Whiteness: How White People Benefit from Identity Politics*. Philadelphia: Temple University Press, 1998.

———. *Time Passages: Collective Memory and American Popular Culture*. Minneapolis: University of Minnesota Press, 1990.

Liptak, Adam. "Justices Back Ban on Race as Factor in College Entry." *New York Times*, April 24, 2014, A1.

Lowe, Lisa. *Immigrant Acts: On Asian American Cultural Politics*. Durham, NC: Duke University Press, 1996.

Marriott, Robert. "Allah's on Me." *XXL* 1, no. 1 (1997): 64–70.

McCarthy, Cameron. "Living with Anxiety: Race and the Renarration of Public Life." In *White Reign: Deploying Whiteness in America*, edited by Joe L. Kincheloe and Shirley R. Steinberg, 329–42. New York: St. Martin's Press, 1998.

McCord, Mark. "Master of Ceremonies: Introducing the Original Crowd Rocker Eddie Cheeba," *Wax Poetics*, no. 24 (August 2007): xx.

McCollum, Brian. "Best Bet." *Vancouver Sun*, May 6, 1999, C31.

McLeod, Kembrew, and Peter DiCola, *Creative License: The Law and Culture of Digital Sampling*. Durham, NC: Duke University Press, 2011.

Menconi, David. "The Riff That Lifted Rap." *newsobserver.com*, 2010. www.newsobserver.com/2010/03/14/385149/the-riff-that-lifted-rap.html.

Miller, Karl Hagstrom. *Segregating Sound: Inventing Folk and Pop Music in the Age of Jim Crow*. Durham, NC: Duke University Press, 2010.

Mills, David. "Rap's Hostile Fringe: From N.W.A. and Others, 'Reality'-Based Violence." *Washington Post*, September 2, 1990, G1.

Miyakawa, Felicia. *Five Percenter Rap: God Hop's Music, Message, and Black Muslim Mission*. Bloomington: Indiana University Press, 2005.

Monson, Ingrid. "The Problem with White Hipness: Race, Gender, and Cultural Conceptions in Jazz Historical Discourse." *Journal of the American Musicological Society* 48, no. 3 (1995): 396–422.

———. *Saying Something: Jazz Improvisation and Interaction.* Chicago: University of Chicago Press, 1996.

Mukherjee, Roopali. *The Racial Order of Things.* Minneapolis: University of Minnesota Press, 2006.

Neal, Mark Anthony. " . . . A Way Out of No Way: Jazz, Hip hop, and Black Social Improvisation." In *The Other Side of Nowhere: Jazz, Improvisation, and Communities in Dialogue,* edited by Daniel Fischlin and Ajay Helble, 195–223. Middletown, CT: Wesleyan University Press, 2004.

Negus, Keith. *Popular Music in Theory: An Introduction.* Middleton, CT: Wesleyan University Press, 1996.

Obasogie, Osagie K. "Do Blind People See Race? Social, Legal, and Theoretical Considerations." *Law & Society Review* 44, no. 3/4 (2010): 585–616.

Okihiro, Gary. *Margins and Mainstreams: Asians in American History and Culture.* Seattle: University of Washington Press, 1994.

Omi, Michael, and Howard Winant. *Racial Formation in the United States: From the 1960s to the 1990s.* New York: Routledge, 1994.

Palmer, Robert. "'The Message' Is That 'Rap' Is Now King in Rock Clubs." *New York Times,* September 3, 1982, C4.

———. "Pop: The Sugar Hill Gang." *New York Times,* March 13, 1981, C23.

———. "Rap Music, Despite Adult Fire, Broadens Its Teen-Age Base." *New York Times,* September 21, 1986, section 2, p. 23.

———. "Street-Smart Rapping Is Innovative Art Form." *New York Times,* February 4, 1985, C13.

———. "The Year of the Rolling Stones." *New York Times,* December 27, 1981, section 2, p. 23.

Pareles, Jon. "Pop Review: A Rapper More Gauche Than Gangsta." *New York Times,* April 17, 1999, B18.

———. "Public Enemy: Rap with a Fist in the Air." *New York Times,* July 24, 1988, H25.

Perry, Imani. *Prophets of the Hood: Politics and Poetics in Hip Hop.* Durham, NC: Duke University Press, 2004.

Peterson, Richard A. *Creating Country Music: Fabricating Authenticity.* Chicago: University of Chicago Press, 1997.

Pratt, Ray. *Rhythm and Resistance: Explorations in the Political Uses of Popular Music.* Westport, CT: Praeger, 1990.

"Proposition 209: Text of Proposed Law." *Proposition 209 Ballot Pamphlet,* 1996. http://vote96.sos.ca.gov/Vote96/html/BP/209text.htm.

Quinn, Eithne. *Nuthin' But a "G" Thang: The Culture and Commerce of Gangsta Rap.* New York: Columbia University Press, 2005.

Radano, Ronald. *Lying Up a Nation: Race and Black Music.* Chicago: Chicago University Press, 2003.

Radano, Ronald, and Phillip Bohlman, "Introduction." In *Music and the Racial Imagination,* edited by Ronald Radano and Phillip Bohlman, 5. Chicago: University of Chicago Press, 2000.

Ramos, George. "'Rap' Musicians' Concert Is Canceled at Palladium after Long Beach Fights." *Los Angeles Times,* August 19, 1986.

Ramsey, Guthrie P., Jr. *Race Music: Black Cultures from Be-Bop to Hip-Hop.* Berkeley: University of California Press, 2004.

"Rebuttal to Argument against Proposition 209." *Proposition 209 Ballot Pamphlet,* 1996. http://vote96.sos.ca.gov/BP/209norbt.htm.

Reynolds, Simon. *Generation Ecstasy: Into the World of Techno and Rave Culture.* New York: Routledge, 1998.

Rockwell, John. "The 'Rapping' Style in Pop." *New York Times,* October 12, 1980, D30.

———. "Rap: The Furious Five." *New York Times,* September 12, 1982, section 1, p. 84.

Rose, Tricia. *Black Noise: Rap Music and Black Culture in Contemporary America.* Hanover, NH: Wesleyan University Press, 1994.

———. *The Hip Hop Wars: What We Talk About When We Talk About Hip Hop and Why It Matters.* New York: Basic Civitas, 2008.

Rux, Carl Hancock. "Eminem: The New White Negro." In *Everything but the Burden: What White People Are Taking from Black Culture,* edited by Greg Tate, 15–38. New York: Broadway Books, 2003.

Sanneh, Kelefa. "Word: Jay-Z's 'Decoded' and the Language of Hip-Hop." *New Yorker,* December 6, 2010.

Schloss, Joseph. *Foundation: B-Boys, B-Girls and Hip-Hop Culture in New York.* New York: Oxford University Press, 2008.

———. "The Joke's on Us: The Outrageous Humor—and the Sheer Outrage—of Eminem." *Seattle Weekly,* April 14, 1999. www.seattleweekly.com/1999-04-14/music/the-joke-s-on-us/.

———. *Making Beats: The Art of Sample-Based Hip-Hop.* 2nd ed. Middleton, CT: Wesleyan University Press, 2004.

Simpson, Janice C. "Yo! Rap Gets on the Map: Led by Groups Like Public Enemy, It Socks a Black Message to the Mainstream." *Time,* February 5, 1990, 60.

Skillz, Mark. "Master of Ceremonies: Introducing the Original Crowd Rocker Eddie Cheeba." *Wax Poetics* 24 (August 2007): 71–80.

Small, Christopher. "Why Doesn't the Whole World Love Chamber Music?" *American Music* 19, no. 3 (2001): 340–59.

Smith, R. J. "Crossover Dreams: Class Trumps Race in Eminem's *8 Mile.*" *Village Voice,* November 5, 2002.

Smith, Shawnee. "Rap Rips Up the Charts." *Billboard,* December 5, 1998, 27–28.

Sofer, Daniel. *DMX Owner's Manual.* 3rd ed. Los Angeles: Oberheim Electronics, 1982.

Soja, Edward. *Postmodern Geographies: The Reassertion of Space in Critical Social Theory.* London: Verso, 1989.

Solomons, Jason, Andy Gallagher, and Henry Barnes. "Spike Lee: 'Anyone Who Thinks We Move in a Post-Racial Society Is Someone Who's Been Smoking

Crack.'" *Guardian.com*, October 5, 2009. www.theguardian.com/film/video/2009/oct/05/spike-lee-do-the-right-thing.

"Sound Bite." *SPIN Magazine*, September 1992, 42.

Spencer, Roy (DJ Moneyshot). "Public Enemy: It Takes a Nation of Millions to Hold Us Back." *Future Music* 269 (August 2013).

———. "Solid Steel and the Hour of Chaos." *Solid Steel Radio Show*, 2013. https://soundcloud.com/ninja-tune/solid-steel-radio-show-2–8–1.

Starr, Larry, and Christopher Waterman. *American Popular Music: From Minstrelsy to MP3*. Oxford: Oxford University Press, 2007.

"Talent in Action." *Billboard*, December 1979, 6–50.

Thompson, Robert Farris. "The Song That Named the Land," in *Black Art/ Ancestral Legacy: The African Impulse in African-American Art*, edited by Robert V. Rozelle, Alvia Wardlaw, and Maureen A. McKenna. Dallas: Dallas Museum of Art, 1989.

TMS. "Record Report: Albums." *The Source*, February 1993, 55.

Toop, David. "Conventional Black: Rock; Records." *The Times* [London], August 26, 1989.

Vincent, Rickey. *Funk: The Music, the People, and the Rhythm of the One*. New York: St. Martin's Griffin, 1996.

Walser, Robert. "Rhythm, Rhyme, and Rhetoric in the Music of Public Enemy." *Ethnomusicology* 39, no. 2 (1995): 193–217.

Wang, Oliver. "Beat Making." In *Grove Dictionary of American Music*, edited by Charles Hiroshi Garrett, 397–401. New York: Oxford University Press, 2013.

———. *Legions of Boom: Filipino American Mobile DJ Crews in the San Francisco Bay Area*. Durham, NC: Duke University Press, 2015.

———. "Rapping and Repping Asian: Race, Authenticity and the Asian American MC." In *Alien Encounters: Popular Culture in Asian America*, edited by Mimi Thi Nguyen and Thuy Linh Nguyen Tu, 35–68. Durham, NC: Duke University Press, 2007.

Warshow, Robert. "The Gangster as Tragic Hero." In *Gangster Film Reader*, edited by Alain Silver and James Ursini, 11–16. New York: Limelight Editions, 2007.

Waterman, Christopher A. "Race Music: Bo Chatmon, 'Corrine Corrina,' and the Excluded Middle." In *Music and the Racial Imagination*, edited by Ronald Radano and Philip V. Bohlman, 167–205. Chicago: University of Chicago Press, 2000.

Watkins, S. Craig. *Hip Hop Matters: Politics, Popular Culture, and the Struggle for the Soul of a Movement*. Boston: Beacon Press, 2005.

Watrous, Peter. "Recordings: Public Enemy Makes Waves and Compelling Music." *New York Times*, April 22, 1990.

Weiner, Jonah. "Lil Wayne and the Afronaut Invasion: Why Have So Many Black Musicians Been Obsessed with Outer Space?" *Slate.com*, 2008. www.slate.com/id/2193871/.

Weitzman, Philip. *Worlds Apart: Housing, Race, Ethnicity, and Income in New York City*. New York: Community Service Society of New York, 1989.

Williams, Justin A. "The Construction of Jazz Rap as High Art in Hip-Hop Music." *Journal of Musicology* 27, no. 4 (2010): 435–59.

———. *Rhymin' and Stealin': Music Borrowing in Hip Hop*. Ann Arbor: University of Michigan Press, 2013.

Wilson, Olly. "The Significance of the Relationship between Afro-American Music and West African Music." *Black Perspective in Music* 2, no. 1 (1974): 3–22.

Index

Italic page numbers refer to illustrations.